Transforming Libraries, Building Communities

The Community-Centered Library

Julie Biando Edwards
Melissa S. Robinson
Kelley Rae Unger

THE SCARECROW PRESS, INC.
Lanham • Toronto • Plymouth, UK
2013

Published by Scarecrow Press, Inc.
A wholly owned subsidiary of
The Rowman & Littlefield Publishing Group, Inc.
4501 Forbes Boulevard, Suite 200, Lanham, Maryland 20706
www.rowman.com

10 Thornbury Road, Plymouth PL6 7PP, United Kingdom

British Library Cataloguing in Publication Information Available

Library of Congress Cataloging-in-Publication Data

Edwards, Julie Biando.
  Transforming libraries, building communities : the community-centered
library / Julie Biando Edwards, Melissa S. Robinson, Kelley Rae Unger.
     pages cm
  Includes bibliographical references and index.
  ISBN 978-0-8108-9181-4 (pbk.) — ISBN 978-0-8108-9182-1 (ebook)
  1. Libraries and community—United States. 2. Public libraries—Cultural
programs—United States. 3. Public services (Libraries)—United States.
I. Robinson, Melissa S., 1983– II. Unger, Kelley Rae, 1978– III. Title.
  Z716.4.E39 2013
  021.2—dc23   2013007581

For Martha, of course.

Contents

**PART III: INSPIRATION FOR
COMMUNITY-CENTERED LIBRARIES**

Foreword

The public library is in its third century as a community-funded public good. In 1876 W. C. Todd foretold the spread of the public library reading room as a means to extend civic involvement (Todd 1876). This was the beginning of the body of writing that views libraries as more than repositories of books in our democratic nation.

In *Transforming Libraries, Building Communities: The Community-Centered Library*, Julie Biando Edwards, Melissa S. Robinson, and Kelley Rae Unger demonstrate how public libraries can position themselves as active and vibrant centers of community life in the twenty-first century. This ambitious 2013 volume is the latest manifestation of our understanding of the evolution of the public library—a manifestation that flows from the findings of the mid-twentieth-century "Public Library Inquiry" (Leigh 1950). Throughout the twentieth century public library services for adults were characterized as part of the adult education movement and grew ever more inclusive.

By 1954 dozens of public library services for adults were identified by Helen Lyman Smith (Smith 1954). The concept of the library as an agency of culture began to be firmly established and the role of the library as "undergirding the democratic process" became more apparent (Preer 2001, 136).

As an effect of the Great Society the outreach role of the library in the community was a focus of library scholarship study in the 1960s and 1970s (Stevenson 1968; Warnke 1968; Weibel 1983). Librarians were active in the War on Poverty, establishing model programs and innovative services in storefronts, public housing, and neighborhood centers. The community-centered concept for public libraries was explored in *Emerging Patterns of Community Service* (Monroe and Heim 1979).

In a now elegiac reprisal of the 1954 Lyman report, Heim and Wallace (1990) explored the range of public library services in the 1980s study *Adult Services: An Enduring Focus for Public Libraries* on the cusp of the new Internet-based digital era. The essay "Adult Services as Reflective of the Changing Role of the Public Library" sees the catalyst role of the library in civic dialogue as part of a robust tradition (Heim 1986).

The American Library Association millennial presidents Sarah Ann Long (1999–2000) and Nancy C. Kranich (2000–2001) focused on community building and community engagement (Christensen and Levinson 2003, 2007). From 2000 to 2006 the Librarian at Every Table discussion list and website extended these ideas in a national dialogue. The focus was that librarians participating in comprehensive community initiatives would move to a goal of service integration.

In this third century of public library service Edwards, Robinson, and Unger seek to reposition libraries as active centers serving to build vibrant communities. They summarize the historical contributions of community-focused library services and provide a fresh, compelling series of analyses that firmly position public libraries as community centers. In *Transforming Libraries, Building Communities* dozens of model programs that reflect the idea of the abundant community are discussed. The book is an evaluation of twenty-first-century society and the values that define it (McKnight and Block 2010) with a library orientation that carries a mandate for convergence.

Using multiple compelling examples of real libraries in action as civic action centers, as centers for sustainability, and as cultural reflections of the community, *Transforming Libraries, Building Communities* shows how allocation of resources is an innovation to centralize the place of the library in the community.

Central concepts like networking for relevance are used to demonstrate that community members have a meaningful role in planning. The authors show in a persuasive manner that the best way to have a great library is to have staff spend time outside the library building making local connections that get people inside the library

The authors characterize the benefits of collaboration as helping to build human capital and social capital. They note that resilient community-centered librarians often find themselves in a position to create partnerships that extend their sphere of influence, recognizing that all are assets—individuals and partner agencies from city planners to union members.

Rich examples of public libraries throughout the nation creating centers of civic action and models of sustainable communities provide inspirational blueprints that can be accomplished through creativity and commitment. *Transforming Libraries, Building Communities* is an engaging book because we know these library workers. They are just like us. We can be just like them.

Libraries can operate as facilitators of the public sphere taking on big ideas like Banned Books Week or the September Project as a means of fostering civic dialogue. They can also address closer-to-home challenges such as homelessness, hunger, workforce development, and teen parenting education. This volume provides well-documented case studies of libraries taking on projects that contribute to a community-centered vision.

The roles libraries play in preserving local history and identity are described with energy and creativity by the authors. Viewing the library as a cultural reflection of the community is a different way to enhance the library's position as essential to a community's identity. Archives, projects like the Nashville Civil Rights Oral History Project, the Plainfield, New Jersey, StoryCorps on minority groups, or the Bayonne Veterans History Project place the library and its staff amid deeply revered community pasts.

Diversity—a topic that means people from diverse language groups, with different abilities, or with different sexualities—is treated with sensitivity and respect. The authors are clear that for libraries to be transformed into true community centers there must be concerted and sustained commitment to outreach and inclusion of all people in the communities served.

The focus on the arts is an extraordinarily strong feature of this book as it examines library programs that bringing musical missions to life, art galleries, exhibits, and cultural opportunities. Standout programs like those at San Diego Public Library, New Canaan Public Library, Pima County (AZ) Public Library's Focus on Art, Chelmsford (MA) Public Library's Cultural Road Show all show the exploration of ideas that characterize a library's commitment to lifelong learning.

Adult education and lifelong learning including community discussion groups have persisted as a key public library function (Coleman 2008). However, a twenty-first-century analysis has been needed.

Transforming Libraries, Building Communities provides the link between the peoples' university ideals of the past and the community-based library of the present. Youth services are viewed as part of this continuum with storytelling, homework programs, early literacy, library outreach bus, reading programs, multicultural internships, and teen programs—ideas that are given a contemporary look. In the chapters "Libraries as Universities" and "Libraries as Champions of Youth," the "Make It Happen" features that end the chapters provide bulleted key ideas that offer realistic options for action.

The first librarian director of the U.S. Institute of Museum and Library Services, Robert S. Martin, recognized the importance of librarians to the community as he launched the 21st Century Learner Conference at the beginning of this century in 2001 (Martin 2011). So do Julie Biando Edwards, Melissa S. Robinson, and Kelley Rae Unger. *Transforming Libraries, Building Communities: The Community-Centered Library* synthesizes the public library traditions of lifelong learning, extension of the public sphere, and civic engagement to locate the library at the center of the nation's many cities, towns, and rural localities. This book is a rich and thoughtful compilation of past achievements, contemporary successes, and future pathways that lodge the public library as a societal anchor and key to the engagement of people in the life of their communities.

Kathleen de la Peña McCook is Distinguished University Professor at the University of South Florida, School of Information, and author of *Introduction to Public Librarianship* (ALA editions, 2011).

BIBLIOGRAPHY

Christensen, Karen, and David Levinson. 2003. *Encyclopedia of Community: From the Village to the Virtual World.* Thousand Oaks, Calif.: Sage.
———. 2007. *Heart of the Community: The Libraries We Love: Treasured Libraries of the United States and Canada.* Great Barrington, Mass.: Berkshire.
Coleman, Brenda Weeks. 2008. "Keeping the Faith: The Public Library's Commitment to Adult Education, 1950–2006." PhD thesis, University of Southern Mississippi.
Heim, Kathleen M. 1986. "Adult Services as Reflective of the Changing Role of the Public Library." *Journal of the Reference and Adult Services Division* [*RQ*] 26: 180–87.

Heim, Kathleen M., and Danny P. Wallace. 1990. *Adult Services: An Enduring Focus for Public Libraries.* Chicago: American Library Association.

Leigh, Robert Devore. 1950. *The Public Library in the United States: The General Report of the Public Library Inquiry.* New York: Columbia University Press.

A Librarian at Every Table. 2001–2006. "Libraries Building Communities." Website and Discussion list. http://shell.cas.usf.edu/mccook/alaet/libraries.html.

Martin, Robert S. 2011. "21st Century Learner Conference, U.S. Institute of Museums and Library Services, November 7, 2001." In *Introduction to Public Librarianship,* edited by Kathleen de la Peña McCook, 469–73. Chicago: ALA Editions.

McKnight, John, and Peter Block. 2010. *The Abundant Community: Awakening the Power of Families and Neighborhoods.* San Francisco, Calif.: Berrett-Koehler.

Monroe, Margaret Ellen, and Kathleen M. Heim. 1979. *Emerging Patterns of Community Service.* Urbana: University of Illinois Graduate School of Library Science.

Preer, Jean L. 2001. "Exploring the American Idea at the New York Public Library." *American Studies* 42 (3): 135–54.

Smith, Helen Lyman. 1954. *Adult Education Activities in Public Libraries: A Report of the ALA Survey of Adult Education Activities in Public Libraries and State Library Extension Agencies of the United States.* Chicago: American Library Association.

Stevenson, Grace T., ed. 1968. "Group Services in Public Libraries." *Library Trends* 17 (1).

Todd, W. C. 1876. "Free Reading Rooms." In *Public Libraries in the United States of America: Their History, Condition, and Management,* 460–64. United States Bureau of Education. Washington: D.C. Govt. print off.

Warnke, Ruth. 1968. "Library Objectives and Community Needs." *Library Trends* 17 (1): 6–13.

Weibel, Kathleen. 1983. *The Evolution of Library Outreach 1960–75 and Its Effect on Reader Services: Some Considerations.* Champaign: University of Illinois Graduate School of Library and Information Science.

Acknowledgments

This book wouldn't have been possible without the support of many individuals. We would like to extend our thanks to *Public Libraries* for publishing the article that served as the basis for this book. Thank you to Martin Dillon and Scarecrow for shepherding the manuscript through the editing process. Thank you to Kathleen de la Peña McCook for authoring the foreword and for providing such excellent advice upon receiving the manuscript. And thank you to the Peabody Institute Library for unending inspiration for, and support of, this project.

Personal and professional thanks go to our colleagues at the Peabody Institute Library and the Mansfield Library. Special thanks to Martha Holden and to Gerri Guyote in Peabody, for leading the library in such a community-centered way and for teaching us, by example, how to be good librarians. Many of the projects described in this book would not have been possible without the help of Peabody's patient and team-oriented children's librarian, Carol Bender, so we offer thanks to her as well. Thanks also to the librarians and reference technicians at the Mansfield Library, especially Sue Samson, who showed great enthusiasm for this project, and Kim Granath, for understanding the need for time to write.

Julie would like to especially acknowledge her father, Stephen R. Biando, and her grandfather, Anthony C. Dalimonte, who both knew about this book and were proud of it, even if they didn't get to see the final product. She also extends thanks to her mother and friend, Linda Biando. And, always, thanks to Steve Edwards, who also thinks and writes about community—and who carried her through this year. He is an expert citation checker, critical and careful reader, and still the best person to talk with about anything under the sun.

Kelley would like to thank her parents, Judy and Paul Brown, for always knowing that books make the best gifts and for believing in her first. And, of course, she thanks her husband, Jon Unger, for teaching her that sometimes the steepest mountains bring us the greatest joy.

Melissa's thanks go out to her mother, friend, and biggest advocate, Evelyn Rauseo, who first inspired her love of librarians. Melissa also wishes to thank her father, Ken Rauseo, for his unwavering belief in her. And, special thanks always go to Erika Robinson for the love and friendship of a lifetime.

Finally, thank you to all of the librarians, directors, trustees, Friends, volunteers, and elected officials who work to make their libraries more community centered. You are doing good work—the work of the future.

Introduction

Although we didn't know it at the time, the idea for this book was born back in 2007. In that year, we presented on the topic of programming for public libraries at the Public Library Association National Conference in Minneapolis. Our presentation, "Running the One Woman Show: Successful Programming When You Have a Million Things to Do," drew on the great series of programs that we had developed at the Peabody (Massachusetts) Institute Library, where we were all working as public librarians. The Peabody Library had a reputation in the area for programming, and the three of us spent a significant amount of our time imagining, developing, planning, seeking funding for, and executing programs in all areas of the library. Kelley planned everything from art projects to petting zoos for children, Melissa planned everything from rock concerts to library lock-ins for teens, and Julie planned everything from calligraphy workshops to lectures and performances for adults. We each ran successful departments and there was a lot of cross-pollination and bouncing back and forth of ideas. With the strong support of our director, board of trustees, and Friends group, we were programming so often and so successfully that for a while it was hard to find a day when there was *not* something going on at the library.

Given that none of us were hired as programming librarians and given the fact that we were also responsible for collection development, reference, and all the other things that go on at a busy public library, we thought that other librarians would be interested in our strategies of balancing programming with everything else that librarians need to do. We put together a presentation and Julie took it to Minneapolis. We knew that librarians were interested in programming and hungry for inspiration and ideas, but we were surprised to see that our presentation drew over two hundred people! The presentation itself provided a great opportunity for us to highlight what worked for us and to also hear some of the amazing things that public librarians around the country were doing. We came away with reignited energy and a renewed sense of the creativity and dedication of public librarians.

At the time, we were focused on programming for the sake of programming. We knew that our programming numbers were as important as—if not more important than—our circulation numbers. We knew that programs kept our patrons interested in the library and us interested in and inspired by our jobs. We learned that the more we programmed, the more our reputation locally and regionally grew, and that this drew patrons, participants, and donors to the library. We also knew that we were having a lot of fun—and really, a big part of planning programs is that, despite the work it takes, it is just plainly and simply a blast. The Peabody Library was busy and bustling, we were always bursting with new ideas (not all of which worked, of course. We could probably fill another book with our programming failures!), and we were all involved with really satisfying and enriching work. None of us were thinking at that time about why we programmed, what it did for our community, or what it did for the idea of the library.

Fast-forward five years and we come to this book. In that time things have both changed and grown. Julie moved to Montana and now works as an academic librarian with an interest in libraries, community, and human rights. Kelley took over as the adult services librarian at Peabody and has continued to build upon and grow programming for adults, combining it with a skilled and deliberate approach to outreach and marketing. Melissa has continued to seek and secure tens of thousands of dollars in grant funds with which she also has grown and expanded her programs for teens, often building partnerships with other city agencies to create services that truly address community needs and expectations. And we've all begun to think a bit more about why we do what we do, and what it means for libraries and their communities. In 2011 we collaborated on an article for *Public Libraries* magazine. In that article, "Community Centered: 23 Reasons Why Your Library Is the Most Important Place in Town," we looked at some of the ways in which libraries meet community needs in interesting and innovative ways (Edwards, Rauseo, and Unger 2011). The article was well received and we loved working together again so much that we decided to expand our ideas into a book. Which leads us to these pages.

This book is born of experience and reflection. It isn't a book about programming, per se, although you will find a lot of useful tips, real-world examples, and inspiring ideas in these pages. It isn't a book about library theory, either, although you'll find that we spend more time reflecting on *why* we do what we do than some other books aimed at public librarians. We want to combine what we know about successful programming with what we believe programming can do for a library, and for a community. And we use the term *programming* fairly loosely, as you will see. We don't just mean organized book groups or concerts. We have come to understand that programming is much more than that. In these pages we'll talk about library websites and collections, library spaces and missions, and traditional library programs. Really, library *programming* is just one aspect of library *services*, and we'll be looking at the ways in which library services reach beyond simply providing access or entertainment to the ways in which they grow community. Our understanding about what a library does, and is, and means, has evolved over the years. Programming and planning library services for the sake of the work itself is great fun, of course. But we want to take a step back here and reflect a bit on what library services actually do for patrons, for communities, and for libraries. We've come to believe that one of the most important—perhaps *the* most important—things a library can do is create and build community.

This book has two main premises: that public libraries need to look beyond just providing access to information to focus on the ways in which library services create and expand community and that, in repositioning themselves as the centers of an active and vibrant community life, libraries will be in the best position to demonstrate their worth in a more compelling way. We're all familiar with the doomsday predictions about the future of the library in the digital age. And we're also familiar with the questions—sometimes genuinely curious, sometimes more hostile—about what value we add to public life, and about why public funds should go to libraries when "it's all on the Internet anyway." The problem is, there are enough people who believe that statement—and, though wildly overblown, it isn't without its own grain of truth—that as long as libraries are primarily defined as information access points we will have a very difficult time truly demonstrating our worth. Often, well-meaning librarians and patrons will counter that line of reasoning with the equally vague "But it's *not* all on the Internet!" Sometimes we will even provide concrete examples to back up this claim. But this isn't reframing the discussion; it's simply engaging in an argument which we probably can't ultimately win—not because our position is false, but because it isn't very compelling to people.

In light of this argument, repositioning the library accomplishes two things. First, it acknowledges that information is in abundance in contemporary life. And while accessing (and learning how to analyze, interpret, and use) that information will always be at the heart of what we do, it isn't the only thing we do. It may not be, in the future, even the most important thing that we do. In acknowledging the ways in which access to information has changed, we can admit that our role has also evolved and reframe the discussion so that it is not about what others think we can't do (remain relevant in the age of the Internet) but about what we actually *can* do (play an essential role in meeting community needs and building strong and vibrant local communities). And building community and meeting social needs, as we will argue in this book, is more than just something that we *can* do. Repositioning libraries as community-centered institutions, we believe, is a responsibility. Libraries bring people together. They create community, and they also create minicommunities—everything from book groups to writing circles to new citizen groups to linguistic or ethnic communities reflected in programming and in collections. These minicommunities help provide fellowship and foster relationships among the group members but also, because they exist in the public place that is the library, help the larger community recognize and learn about the minicommunities that create the larger community. This, we argue, is the work of libraries.

Secondly, in doing this work, in repositioning our place within our communities, we are able to reframe the debate about the worth of libraries. We can highlight the ways in which we add value, and turn the discussion away from those areas in which we can't compete to those areas in which we can excel. If we really claim our role as community-centered institutions, we can then work to convince others of the value we bring to our communities.

As we begin to think about the ways in which our libraries can and do add value to our communities, there is a strong tradition within the community development field from which we can draw. The goals and work of community development professionals will resonate with librarians. Gary Paul Green and Anna Haines (2012) define community development as "a planned effort to build assets that increase the capacity of residents to improve their quality of life" (xi). While we've never defined the mission of public libraries in this way, this is the work that we do. Our programs and services are all designed to build assets for our patrons in one way or another. In the following pages, we will discuss some of the types of assets that library services can build and how and why these are important to our communities. One of the strengths of the community development field is that people see creating strong communities and building assets for individuals as compelling, contemporary needs. Adopting some of the language and strategies of the community development field can help librarians reconceptualize the importance of their work, help us explain our value to the public, and help us identify new ways to add value to our communities. Redefining what we do will mean that we have a new basis from which to advocate for our profession, our staff, our buildings, and our budgets. Being community centered means also that the individuals who make up our communities will be more connected to the library, and will perhaps be more likely to advocate on our behalf as well. We can move into the future in a new way—revitalizing our communities and reimagining ourselves at the same time.

We should note that none of us are community development experts. Melissa's interest in community building stems from graduate work she did at the University of Massachusetts, Boston, in the Program for Women in Politics and Public Policy. For the most part, though, all three of us have developed a passion for this topic through simply reading the inspiring work of those in the community development field. We rely on their work throughout this book.

This book is divided into three parts. In part I we will take a big-picture look at the services and programs we highlight in later chapters. We'll focus on seven sets of services: libraries as civic action centers, libraries as centers for sustainability, libraries as cultural reflection of the community, libraries as community centers for diverse populations, libraries as centers for the arts, libraries as universities, and libraries as champions of youth and we will explore why these services are important for librarians to consider as they reposition their libraries in their communities. We'll argue in chapter 1 that these aspects of library services, far from being quaint, are actually as important as many of the digital and technological services that libraries provide.

Chapter 2 will introduce and define key concepts in community asset building and explore how library services help create, build, and strengthen not only individual library patrons, but also communities large and small. We will briefly go over what others have written about libraries and community building and then we will turn our attention to how the language, concepts, and methods of Asset-Based Community Development relate to and can be used by libraries. We maintain that in the digital age, people are still seeking—perhaps even more actively seeking—places where they can connect with each other and with their community on a local level. We'll go on to highlight how the library can mediate and accommodate this need.

We'll close part I by shifting the focus away from how a library can become a community-centered institution, and what that focus means for the community in question, to look at what being community centered means for the library itself. We believe that by building and creating community for patrons, public libraries have a chance to reposition themselves in their communities in a way that highlights their value. Libraries are institutions that do—and *should* do—much more than simply provide access to information. But, as long as they are seen as only places where people can access information, they run the risk of being seen as obsolete, or even potentially becoming obsolete. We will argue that libraries are far from obsolete because they are *not* just places to access information—they are places, perhaps some of the only places left, where people can build community in rich and nuanced ways. In repositioning themselves in the community, libraries have an opportunity to both define and leverage their value in new ways. It is this repositioning of libraries that will continue to ensure that they remain vibrant, flexible, and adaptable as they meet what may be unmet community needs.

Part II will bring us from concepts to strategies. The chapters in this section will focus less on the *why* of being community centered and more on *how* libraries can reposition themselves and respond to their communities. We dedicate a chapter to allocating resources, including not only budgetary resources but also personnel and physical resources. We'll also look at how library foundations and active, progressive, and specialized Friends groups can bring in resources that can be specifically dedicated to library services and programs. Chapters 5 and 6 will focus on how to think like a programmer, including how to tap into your personal and professional relationships in order to develop new and innovative services. In chapter 7, we will explore some of the ways in which librarians can collaborate with other social agencies and institutions, including those with whom libraries might not traditionally partner with. We'll look not only at those agencies that share a similar mission, but also spend some time on how to build relationships with those who desire the similar outcome of meeting a social need or addressing a local issue. Of course, services cost money, and we'll close out part II by focusing on where to find, how to write, and how to administer grants.

Part III will circle back to part I and include seven chapters, each containing several real-world examples from public libraries around the United States and the world. The examples will illustrate ways in which libraries successfully meet various community needs. We will look at the wide variety of ways in which libraries are community centered and will examine the importance of libraries engaging in the community's political life; fostering civil discourse; revitalizing struggling or depressed neighborhoods and downtowns; providing important business resources, especially for small local businesses; preserving historic artifacts, oral histories, digital history projects, and monographs relevant to the community; providing information, resources, and support for patrons with disabilities; providing access to nonmainstream points of view and giving voice to local artists; going beyond providing content to enabling patrons to create their own content; and partnering in youth development. These are just a few of the ways in which libraries are community centered, and we will highlight these and many more examples of libraries repositioning themselves in the community. The real-world examples form a purely subjective list of interesting models we've come across, and we encourage readers to scour the web for other examples of libraries doing amazing things in their buildings and in their towns. In the "Make It Happen" section of each chapter we'll provide tips for readers about how specific services could be adapted for their own libraries.

Whether you're a seasoned librarian looking to broaden and deepen your services, or whether you're fairly new to libraries and want to see what kinds of library services you can offer your community, we think that you'll find something useful in these pages. And this book isn't just for librarians—if you're a library director, a library board member, or an elected official responsible for setting municipal budgets, this book is written for you, too. Hopefully this book will help you rethink and reposition your library as a way of meeting community needs and staying relevant as a public institution. The arguments we present in part I and the tools we share in part II will be useful for helping you reframe your services and reposition your library. If you're looking to expand your library's offerings into more innovative programs and services, the examples and tips we provide in part III should help you adapt ideas to your library and your community. So, we encourage you to take this book and use it to reimagine what your library is and does. We also urge you to start conversations with your colleagues, your patrons, and your community leaders about how to best reposition your library in your community, so that instead of having to answer the question "Why should public funds go to support libraries?" we can reframe the debate and demonstrate the value of public libraries well into the ever-evolving digital age.

BIBLIOGRAPHY

Edwards, Julie Biando, Melissa S. Rauseo, and Kelley Rae Unger. 2011. "Community Centered: 23 Reasons Why Your Library Is the Most Important Place in Town." *Public Libraries* 50 (4): 42–47.

Green, Gary Paul, and Anna Haines. 2012. *Asset Building & Community Development*. Thousand Oaks, Calif.: Sage.

Part I

THE WHAT AND WHY OF
COMMUNITY-CENTERED LIBRARIES

CHAPTER 1

Community-Centered Library Services: Their Importance and Relevance

It is our intention that this book provide you with the tools and inspiration you need to put your community at the heart of your library services and programs. In this first part, though, we want to share with you the logic behind creating a community-centered library. As we said in the introduction, we will disengage from debates we can't win and focus instead on what librarians do well, and how they can do it even better. In chapter 3, we will look more closely at why libraries need to define themselves as something other than information access points, but this entire book is based on that concept—that information, while important, can't and shouldn't be the primary way in which libraries define themselves. We need to look beyond information and toward how people in our communities use the information, services, and programming that we provide. In doing so, we will revitalize our institutions and strengthen our communities.

We passionately believe that libraries build community, and know that we are not alone in this belief. Our faith in libraries' ability to strengthen communities puts us in the company of many insightful professionals in the library and community development fields. Inside libraries, Kathleen de la Peña McCook, Chrystie Hill, several past American Library Association presidents, the Urban Libraries Council, and many others have been working for years to convince those inside and outside our profession that libraries should embrace their role as partners in community development. Outside librarianship, we have allies in some of the leading minds in the community development field: Robert Putnam, John Kretzmann and John McKnight, Wayne Senville, and others. In chapter 2, we will explore briefly the connections that many of these individuals see between libraries and their communities, but for now it boils down to this: if we want to live in vibrant, engaged, and healthy cities and towns, public libraries need to play an integral role in community development and this role needs to be recognized, appreciated, and utilized by other municipal stakeholders. In this chapter, we will look at some of the characteristics of a community-centered library and then explore the library's role in community development through seven specific service areas where the library can, in a proactive and nuanced way, have the greatest positive impact on its community.

CHARACTERISTICS OF A COMMUNITY-CENTERED LIBRARY

Each library will be as different as the community it serves, but there are a few general characteristics we have identified that help define a community-centered library.

Look beyond Information and Technology

Providing access to information shouldn't necessarily be our sole priority. Although equitable access to information will always be a responsibility of libraries, we need to recognize that many people find value in libraries for other reasons entirely. Without abdicating our responsibility to equitable access, as well as freedom of inquiry and expression, branching out from this concept should be at the top of our minds as we look at how to stay relevant. Similarly, the Internet isn't the enemy. It's a tool, a reality, and an incredible asset to our institutions and our patrons. It isn't *us*, though. And it's not going to replace libraries as long as we can find new ways in which to demonstrate our value—which means recognizing the incredible benefits of the Internet while refusing to position ourselves against it.

Build Assets, Become an Asset

Libraries should exist to help people and communities meet their full potential. Of course, we've always done this, but as the world changes, we must stake out new methods of meeting our missions and develop a clear vision of how libraries fit into the world. To begin with, community-centered libraries need to figure out what assets currently exist in their communities and focus on connecting and strengthening them. Put simply, assets are the skills and talents of the residents, groups, and institutions in a community. As libraries strengthen the assets in their communities, they will transform our institutions into places with a new kind of value.

Reframe the Narrative

If libraries can inventory and articulate all the ways in which we build community assets, and then communicate that outward, we will shift the conversation about our relevance away from "Why should libraries exist?" to "How can our community afford to *not* have a library?" As the narrative shifts, we will find ourselves in a better position from which to advocate for funding.

Get Creative and Take Risks

Consider moving into areas of service, programming, and community involvement that aren't traditionally within the purview of libraries. We will discuss this in more detail throughout the book, but stretching your library's mission and vision beyond providing information means that you will find yourself taking action in your community in new, surprising, and sometimes controversial ways. It also means that your library will become central in building both individual and community assets in ways that you may never imagined.

Serve and Shape Your Community

If the community is at the center of the library's interest, the library will have to recognize, meet, and eventually work with community members to anticipate the needs of the community and design services and programs to address them. At the same time, the library should not be a passive player in the community, being acted upon by the community without influencing the community in any way. The library, as Julie has argued elsewhere (Edwards 2010), should actively shape the community, helping it realize its nuances and negotiate its identity in all of its complexity.

AREAS OF SERVICE

As libraries reposition themselves as community-centered institutions, there are several service areas where they can make real contributions to their patrons and communities. Scott (2011) interviewed twenty-five library and community development professionals and through these conversations identified five ways that libraries build community. These five themes mirror the service areas on which community-centered libraries need to focus. When libraries act as universities and take an active role in youth development, they "serve as a conduit to access information and to learn." When they fulfill their duty to be civic action centers, they "foster civic engagement." By serving as centers for diverse populations, they "create a bridge to resources and community involvement," and when they devote themselves to fostering true sustainability, they "encourage social inclusion and equity" and "promote economic vitality within the community" (197).

Libraries as Civic Action Centers

Public libraries are integral to both democratic societies and the idea of democracy. If democracy "presupposes an informed citizenry" as the American Library Association (ALA) asserts in its Core Values of Librarianship, then the public library, which provides open and equal access to materials on a variety of subjects from a variety of viewpoints, is essential for educating citizens on topics of interest and importance. California's state librarian emeritus Kevin Starr (2012) agrees, noting on the state library's website that "free public library service is the basis of our democracy and will keep us a free nation. Democratic values depend on the free flow of information and knowledge with each individual assured the right and the privilege and the ability to choose and to pursue any direction of thought, study, or action." Of course, an informed citizenry is more than just a collection of individuals who have access to information. We believe that democracy presupposes an informed and *engaged* citizenry. We believe, like others, that democracy is a verb, not just a noun, and to assume that access to information equals an informed citizenry misses a fundamental point of democracy. Community-centered public libraries do provide the information necessary for an informed citizenry, but they also provide a forum for people to put that information into practice though opportunities for civic engagement and civil discourse. In this way, community-centered public libraries not only support democracy as a noun—they support it as a verb, encouraging active engagement in civic life. ALA president Nancy Kranich said in an interview with the American Democracy Project that

> an informed public constitutes the very foundation of a democracy; after all, democracies are about discourse—discourse among the people. If a free society is to survive, it must ensure the preservation of its records and provide free and open access to this information to all its citizens. It must ensure that citizens have the skills necessary to participate in the democratic process. It must allow unfettered dialogue and guarantee freedom of expression. All of this is done in our libraries, the cornerstone of democracy in our communities. (Orphan 2011)

Outside of the United States and the ALA, the International Federation of Library Associations (IFLA) states up front in the Public Library Manifesto (2004) that

> freedom, prosperity and the development of society and of individuals are fundamental human values. They will only be attained through the ability of well-informed citizens to exercise their democratic rights and to play an active role in society. Constructive participation and the development of democracy depend on satisfactory education as well as on free and unlimited access to knowledge, thought, culture and information. The public library, the local gateway to knowledge, provides a basic condition for lifelong learning, independent decision-making and cultural development of the individual and social groups.

In an impassioned article in *Library Journal* written a year after the September 11 attacks, Michael Baldwin (2002) declares that Thomas Jefferson's statement that "no nation can remain both ignorant and free" should be the "mantra of all public libraries." He goes on to say that "the public library should be considered a primarily political institution, providing citizens with the information they need to fulfill their civic duties in our democracy" and then outlines the important ways in which public libraries can "remake our profession and institutions and in the process remake America," including:

1. Revising mission statements to prioritize the maintenance of democracy through the provision of civic information.

2. Dispensing with the concept of passively providing information and the errant "give them what they want" philosophy.
3. Educating and training librarians as civic information specialists who develop critical issues programs, actively disseminate issues-oriented information, and encourage responsible political activity in a nonpartisan manner.
4. Fomenting public interest in social/political issues. Creatively marketing your library as the civic information/action center.
5. Partnering with local and national organizations that promote democracy, ethical leadership, and civic responsibility. (52)

Like Baldwin, we believe that the role of the public library in preparing informed citizens who are willing and able to participate in democracy is more than just a value. We assert that public libraries have a responsibility to help create the active, informed citizenry on which democracy rests. Particularly in our own age of partisan fracturing and specialized media, the role of the library as a nonpartisan, credible, and diverse source of information, and as a center for community civic action, is more important than ever. As Kranich (2001) argues in *Libraries and Democracy*, "We now have access to more of the same ideas, with alternatives marginalized by such forces as corporate profiteering, political expediency, and the whimsy of the marketplace" (111). Librarians know that the homogenization of information is a threat to democracy. One of the professionals interviewed by Scott (2011), Jill Jean identified one of the responsibilities and benefits of thoughtful library programs: "Making people feel a little uncomfortable, by really allowing all aspects of an issue to be explored" (201).

Frances Moore Lappé (2007), best known for her book, *Diet for a Small Planet*, is among those who see the lack of civil discourse in our world as a troubling sign. After years of involvement in the global food movement, she has come to believe that in order to solve our most pressing global problems, we need to cultivate a "culture of democracy" (86). This dramatic cultural shift requires that we all learn "Ten Arts of Democracy": active listening, creative conflict, mediation, negotiation, political imagination, public dialogue, public judgment, celebration, evaluation and reflection, and mentoring (88). Libraries may very well be our communities' most promising civic spaces and, in chapter 9, we will show

how creative library programs and services are being designed to help foster these arts of democracy.

The vision of libraries as civic action centers is important, but not new to libraries. More than sixty years before Baldwin wrote his post-9/11 article, Archibald MacLeish (1940), the librarian of Congress, wrote an article in June 1940, drawing upon the events of his own time to articulate this responsibility:

> If librarians accept a responsibility for the survival of democracy in so far as they can assure that survival, if librarians accept a responsibility to make available to the people the precedents for decision and for action in order that the people may govern by them—then librarians cannot satisfy that responsibility merely by delivering books from public libraries as books are called for . . . they must do far more. They must themselves become active and not passive agents of the democratic process. (388)

Svenhild Aabø (2005), writing about the value of public libraries in the digital age, confirms the need for places of engagement and states that "democracy presupposes meeting places where we are confronted with other values and interests than our own and accept them as legitimate. We need a kind of meeting place where one can meet across different cultures, interests, generations and social belonging. The public library, which is frequented by all groups in the community, might have the potential . . . as such a place" (208). Libraries, with their community space and with a history of providing a wide variety of materials on a wide variety of subjects from a wide variety of perspectives, are uniquely suited for tackling problems of civil discourse. We would suggest, in fact, that public libraries might be one of the last places where people can find credible resources and engage in respectful discussions to challenge their own ideas and perceptions. If for no other reason than this, libraries are essential to promoting civil discourse, nurturing the skills of democracy, and encouraging people to communicate across boundaries in order to learn from each other and work toward building stronger communities.

Libraries as Centers for Sustainability

When we talk about sustainability, we often focus solely on the health of our environment. True sustainability, however, is multifaceted. As

Petra Hauke and Klaus Ulrich Werner (2012) write, "Being green is an element of being sustainable, but sustainability is actually a larger and more holistic concept than being green" (60). In recognition of this, there has been a global discussion of how to discuss and implement environmentally sustainable policies in a holistic manner that still values social and economic realities. Although there are critics of this idea, there is a general acknowledgment that truly sustainable development must be built upon sound economic, environmental, and equitable public policy (Urban Libraries Council 2010, 2).

Libraries are one of few public institutions currently well positioned to work with these three ingredients to build a path to sustainable communities. For this reason, the Urban Libraries Council hailed libraries as the perfect partners for local governments wishing to create sustainable futures for their communities. We discuss in chapter 10 the ways in which libraries contribute to their local economies through workforce development, small business support, and by going "green." According to the Urban Libraries Council, the conditions of "social equity" are met when "all residents have equal access to economic activity and are not exposed to environmental harm based on social class" (2). This component of social equity is a foundational value for a community-centered library and we consider it in depth in several places in this book, including the chapters on democracy, diversity, the arts, and youth services. Dedication to social equity in our communities is so pervasive in the work that libraries do that a discussion of it could not be contained within one chapter. Instead, we include it as an overarching theme in this book.

Libraries as Cultural Reflections of the Community

A 2010 survey conducted by the Knight Foundation set out to answer the question "What attaches people to their communities?" The foundation, "after interviewing close to 43,000 people in 26 communities over three years . . . found that three main qualities attach people to place: social offerings, such as entertainment venues and places to meet, openness (how welcoming a place is) and the area's aesthetics (its physical beauty and green spaces)" (Knight Foundation 2012). In an online article on "The Distinctive City" Edward T. McMahon (2012) expanded upon the Knight Foundation's findings to argue that "to foster distinctiveness, cities must plan for built environments and settlement patterns that are both uplifting and memorable and that foster a sense of belonging and stewardship by residents . . . distinctiveness involves streetscapes, architecture, and historic preservation but . . . also involves cultural events and facilities, restaurants and food, parks and open space and many other factors."

Though he doesn't specifically reference libraries, as both buildings and centers of community life they fit the descriptions of those architectural and cultural events spaces that can contribute to a distinct community. Well-thought-out and culturally reflective library buildings, and the events, programs, and services inside of them, are culturally significant and communicate to a community both the value of the library and its role within the community. But even beyond the building and its contents, the *idea* of the library communicates something powerful. Archibald MacLeish (1972) stated the case as elegantly as anyone, before or since. "What is more important in a library than anything else—than everything else," he writes, "is the fact that it exists" (359). The idea of the library is extraordinary. The idea made manifest—the fact that libraries *exist*—is foundationally important to what we are arguing in this book. As community-centered institutions, libraries both symbolize and actualize the aspirations of a community.

In her excellent book *Libricide*, on the destruction of books and libraries, Rebecca Knuth (2003) makes a series of strong arguments about why libraries as institutions are important reflections of the communities in which they are situated. "The contents of books and libraries," she writes, "reflect the social and cultural needs of their societies" (26). Tracing the history of libraries into the twentieth century, she writes that the library

> evolved into an institution that met critical societal needs. Among its many responsibilities were preserving the information that forms the basis for government, the economy, property rights, and national and ethnic identity; rationalizing and supporting social, political, and religious systems, creeds, world views, and ideologies; disseminating information and underpinning education, intellectual development, and social progress; and supporting advanced or "high" culture. (27)

Shifting her focus from libraries in general to public libraries specifically, she asserts that public libraries, which have become largely homogenized in contemporary times, still play an important role in their communities, even as they are a part of a larger system that preserves cultural heritage as a whole:

> While a public library mainly provides general materials for the ordinary person, it might also contain a unique collection of local and specialized materials that are of interest to the scholar, or it might provide computer access or instruction that allows patrons to tap into external databases. While libraries collectively shelter much of society's recorded memory, most libraries are quite idiosyncratic and hold bits and pieces of the whole heritage. (28)

It is these bits and pieces that make public libraries unique. The ways in which they respond to local community needs, through collections, programming, local preservation, or culturally responsive buildings matter in communities. These unique elements, belonging only to *this* library or only to *that* community, can be seen as part of what creates that sense of distinctiveness that McMahon talks about. It is this distinctiveness, these idiosyncrasies in our local institutions, that makes our libraries *our libraries*. At the same time, the fact that these institutions are libraries at all, and not other cultural institutions, is significant because "libraries simultaneously express local cultural values *and* represent the achievement of civilizations far beyond their own borders" (Knuth 2003, 30).

Chapter 11 will highlight how libraries reflect the cultures of their communities in ways that increase both individual and group assets. The libraries featured in that chapter are accomplishing exactly what Knuth highlights in her book—they reflect their specific communities even as they contribute to a globally connected knowledge base and collection of cultural heritage. We believe that this is an important part of the community-centered library—enhancing community assets while at the same time actively contributing to a broader network of libraries and cultural institutions. Building upon local idiosyncrasies makes the library an important local institution *and* an important part of a broader system. We believe that, while unique services and programs are important in actual, local, communities, it is also important to consider these elements as part of something much bigger—the library as an *idea*.

Libraries as Community Centers for Diverse Populations

As public librarians, we want to believe that our institutions serve everyone in our community, as they have a duty to do, but the truth remains that there are community members who simply do not feel welcome in the library. Community development librarians involved in the Working Together project in Canada received an unpleasant shock when they discovered that among those who are "socially excluded" due to race, language, immigration status, sexual orientation, disability status, or income level, "many people are critical and even angry at libraries because of their experiences. Many did not think of the library as a place for them. 'Their kind' was not welcome" (Working Together 2008, 5). Community-centered libraries need to be proactive in addressing these feelings of alienation.

To do this, librarians may need to reposition the way they see themselves and their role in the community. As libraries move from being primarily information access points to community asset builders, librarians need to recognize that their most important role may very well no longer be information expert. The toolkit created by Working Together to help libraries become "community led" points out that oftentimes what librarians need to be for their communities is *facilitators*. Librarians have long connected people to information in the form of books, films, websites, and other physical collections. Now, though, librarians must begin to connect people to community assets in various forms: institutions, informal groups, and other members of the community.

Public libraries can be lifelines for individuals who are unwelcome or excluded by others. Ghada Elturk (2003) describes the reality:

> When these communities (newcomers and minorities) come to the library, especially the public library, it is sometimes the only and last safe and welcoming place left in their lives. By the time they are at our doors they have already experienced discrimination at every stop on their way: the gas station, school, workplace, restaurant . . . the list goes on. (5)

That's if they come in our doors at all. Libraries are all too good at mounting barriers that keep some residents at bay. Requiring photo identification and proof of address to get a library card, writing policies that set inequitable standards about patron hygiene and behavior, charging overdue fines and restricting access as a result of these fines, and allowing staff prejudices to affect the service people receive in our institutions are some of the ways that we have failed to live up to our standards of equitable services. Debates about these issues raise important topics of fairness, but ultimately community-centered libraries need to make radical inclusion a cornerstone of their missions. If libraries are truly a place of last resort for some members of our communities, how tragic it is when we too let their potential remain untapped.

The good news is that even while many community members feel excluded from and angry with their libraries, Working Together (2008) discovered that "people want to see themselves represented in the library and to have an opportunity to participate" (8). This is a perfect opportunity then for librarians to practice being facilitators and connectors, rather than experts. Even as libraries help improve lives by strengthening assets for individuals from all walks of life, library staff should also remember that all community members are assets themselves and they have much they can add to the health and strength of the community and the library. The World Youth Congress (2005) that took place in Scotland in 2005 adopted the motto "Nothing for us without us" (6) to describe the commitment to including youth in planning projects aimed at them. We suggest that libraries adopt this mantra when it comes to serving the diverse populations that make up their communities.

A 1920 Carnegie study found that for the new-immigrant population of the day, "amongst all the institutions in American life, libraries had achieved the best results . . . [without] de-racializing, divesting, remodeling or otherwise 'Americanizing' immigrants; rather, libraries interested immigrants in American life by first interesting themselves in the life of the immigrant" (Maxwell 2006, 71). Coming from a more contemporary perspective, we realize that libraries have not and do not always play this idealized role in the community. Libraries have a varied and sometimes quite appalling history of racism, xenophobia, and homophobia. These are not always attitudes of the past, either. Still, we think that the vision of libraries "first interesting themselves in the life of the immigrant" is one worth striving for. As we will see in chapter 12, this is what a community-centered library does for all its residents: it learns about and interests itself in people's lives and then invites them to contribute to and take part in the life of the library and the community.

Libraries as Centers for the Arts

Green and Haines (2012) point out that "unfortunately, cultural resources are often viewed as something consumed by the rich and not related to middle-class and working class residents" (255). Museums and galleries may feel too rarified for some people, and may project an unfortunate air of exclusivity. Entrance fees may prove to be prohibitive for many, although many museums offer discounts, free days, or other promotions. Among public institutions, though, it is public libraries that hold tremendous potential for both bringing art to people and engaging people in creating art themselves. As Kretzmann and McKnight (1993) point out, "If we start with the idea that art and culture can be found not only in museums and similar institutions but also in the everyday lives of ordinary people, we are already closer to uncovering the true artistic and cultural resources that can be found in local communities" (95).

Art (and we mean art in the broadest sense of "the arts"—music, painting, drawing, dancing, photography, writing, and on and on) in libraries accomplishes two things. First, it allows all members of the community to engage with and appreciate art in the form of attending concerts, readings, and exhibits. By hosting such events, through programming that focuses on this kind of artistic and cultural enrichment, the library brings art to the community at large. Second, the library has the opportunity to continue this kind of enrichment by offering programs that encourage people to create their own art. In a public library patrons can learn to paint, draw, and write in new ways. They can learn a new instrument or, if the library space accommodates such a thing, practice their own instrument. This engagement with the arts on a personal level then connects beautifully back to arts programming, as patrons begin to create artistic content and master skills that they can share with others in local concerts, exhibits, or workshops. This twofold engagement with art in libraries—especially when local artists are encouraged to share their work and skills with the community as a whole—helps build both individual and community assets. After all, "people in communities have always come together to celebrate, to sing and dance and play music, to tell each other stories, to produce and share things of beauty. All of this activity is sometimes called 'culture' and it is the glue which holds people together and helps to form strong communities" (161).

Often, in the field of community development, the focus is on how arts improve the local economy. Art is, of course, an important way in which a community can support and grow other aspects of the economy but we believe that, while arts in the library can add value to the local economy, they are also inherently valuable in and of themselves, for the reasons mentioned by Kretzmann and McKnight above. We would further argue that because engagement with the arts is so enriching for individuals and communities on basic, human, levels that it is the inherent value of art with which libraries should be most concerned. Nurturing a community's creative life is good in and of itself, and the library can play an important role in bringing art appreciation and artistic expression into the lives of all patrons, as we will see in chapter 13.

Abby Scher (2007) brings up an important aspect of art in community life. She quotes a dancer and leader of an arts organization in Los Angeles who believes that "the arts open boundaries among cultures . . . we need to be able to create community between cultures—creating something new out of the ways that we are not the same"—a belief that Scher summarizes as "a sense of urgency in creating respectful and new communities across our differences" (5). This project—to create communities across difference—provides the opportunity for libraries to take a leading role in addressing the challenges of diversity listed above. Julie has argued, in fact, that one of the library's most essential roles in the community is to help it negotiate its various elements. Since no community is homogenous, and since all have subcommunities or communities within communities, libraries should "become active . . . in the creation of culture in the community, not in such a way as to force the homogenization of the community or the assimilation of parts of the community, but in such a way as to highlight the richness of the cultures in a community and to reaffirm that all of the cultures together combine to create an extraordinary whole" (Edwards 2010, 40). If arts, as Scher asserts, open boundaries between cultures, and if the role of the library is to create community, then it stands to reason that engaging people with arts in the library has profound potential.

Libraries as Universities

Since their founding, public libraries in the United States have had the education of individuals as one of their primary roles. In tracing the history of the first true public library in the United States, the Boston Public Library, Grace-Ellen McCrann (2005) notes that, in the mid- to late nineteenth century, "It is fairly clear that the view of a public library as an educational institution was common. In 1899 Josiah Quincy was quoted in the *Saturday Evening Post* saying 'Our library [the Boston

Public] is indeed an educational institution for adults, rather than a mere collection of books'" (227).

Quincy's view was shared by the man who did more than anyone else to establish public libraries in the English-speaking world. Andrew Carnegie spent nearly $40 million building 1,689 libraries in the United States between 1890 and 1919 (Maurizi 2001, 346). Carnegie's own upbringing, watching "his father convince his fellow weavers to pool a portion of their salaries to buy books" (347) and becoming "educated himself" off the private library of a local colonel (Lorenzen 1999, 76) inspired him to donate a significant portion of his vast wealth to the establishment of institutions that would benefit the educational aspirations of others. Lorenzen writes that

> Carnegie had two main reasons for donating money to the founding of libraries. First, he believed that libraries added to the meritocratic nature of America. Anyone with the right inclination and desire could educate himself. Second, Carnegie believed that immigrants like himself needed to acquire cultural knowledge of America, which the library allowed immigrants to do. Carnegie indicated that it was the first reason that was the most important to him. As a boy working a hard job with long hours, he had no access to education. (75)

Carnegie has been criticized for this second belief and, as McCrann (2005) points out, many people coupled their "high-mindedness" about the value of libraries with the belief that "education and libraries as agents for social guidance and control" (228) were a benefit to society. Nonetheless, the public library as a source of education for common people was built into its character from the start. As "few people were educated beyond the eighth-grade level . . . Andrew Carnegie's view of public libraries as universities for working men was not far-fetched" (Geppert Jacobs 2010, 143). George Peabody, the founder of our own Peabody Institute Library, also believed that education was a debt owed one generation to the next, and founded his eponymous institute explicitly for that reason.

In setting up these public libraries, Carnegie did more than tie the institutions to education—he tied them to communities. Any library interested in applying for a grant to found a Carnegie library

> had to put into place a taxation mechanism to annually guarantee an amount equal to 10 percent of the grant for a library's upkeep . . . if a community

wanted one of his grants, it would have to show a real commitment. It would have to show that it valued a library every bit as highly as any other community service and demonstrate it by reaching into its own pocketbook . . . he wanted to give towns the incentive to create institutions for their communities that would move the whole community ahead. (Maurizi 2001, 347–48)

Over a century later, public libraries are still moving their communities forward and serving as educational institutions. Working both in partnership with and beyond schools and colleges, public libraries today support both early literacy and lifelong learning. From children's story times through book groups, lecture series, and digital literacy classes, public libraries have continued to serve as the place where patrons can go to supplement or substitute formal education. They "are built on the foundational assumption that citizens have 'academic freedom.' Libraries, like higher education, seek to protect a learner's right to know" (Yancey 2005, 18).

Many of the areas of service we cover in this book intertwine, and libraries as universities are as much about education as they are about diversity, democracy, and equality of access. Kathleen Blake Yancey argues that "in the United States, libraries, like schools, have served as 'information equalizers.' Historically, if you were a person of color, a person without means, or a person new to the country, you went to the library to learn to read, to become socialized into a local version of American life, and to acquire the skills and knowledge required to become a citizen" (14). Librarians were, and indeed still are, partners in these educational pursuits because "they model research behavior and identify learning opportunities and materials that the patron doesn't know about" (15). Yancey notes that while "libraries complement the instruction delivered by schools" (17) they also "became identified as [sites] where lifelong literacy and learning would be supported" (14). She draws a direct link between libraries, education, and communities—noting that "libraries . . . make available many kinds of community, both scheduled and spontaneous" (19).

Community-centered public libraries in the twenty-first century still support this early ethic of lifelong learning and literacy. And, as the concept of literacy is expanded, and as the demands of citizenship grow, public libraries will continue to play an essential role in serving as universities of the people. We believe that action in this area, which libraries demonstrate in their communities in myriad ways, is a fundamental responsibility of librarianship—one that has informed our own professional ethics. The statements in the ALA Code of Ethics dealing with equity of access, user privacy, and fair representation regardless of personal belief grow from and inform the role of libraries as educational institutions. But even beyond professional codes, we believe that libraries have a responsibility to level the playing field in a democracy by providing both self-directed and library-initiated educational opportunities for all patrons.

Libraries as Champions of Youth

In their work with youth, libraries have tremendous opportunities to truly invest in the lives within their communities. The voices of youth are far too often silenced and their perspectives treated as inconsequential. Libraries are in a unique position to help reveal the rich potential youth have to improve our communities. To ensure that youth are not ignored or dismissed in a community means that community-centered librarians must advocate on their behalf. The list of areas where youth might need a librarian's advocacy is no doubt different from community to community, but there is a lot of common territory. Inside the library world, matters that affect youth will almost always include issues of access, intellectual freedom, the right to information, and the right to be respected members of the community. And other community issues—even those not directly connected to the library—are still a librarian's concern if they affect the community's youth. To be clear, we are saying that if community-centered librarians are going to be youth advocates, this often literally involves advocacy on behalf of youth. Advocating for the youth in our communities can take many forms. It may require librarians to write letters to the editor or speak at community forums or at city council or town meetings. This may be outside the comfort zone of many librarians, but it is a skill set that librarians today need to cultivate. In chapter 15 we will look at the benefits that cultivating this skill set has on a community's youth, and throughout this book we will point out other skills librarians need to have in order to create a community-centered library.

Another way libraries can become champions for our communities' youth is to make sure that youth are getting what they need for their healthy development. The Search Institute, an organization dedicated to identifying what children and teens need to succeed, has developed lists of assets that youth need for healthy development. These lists include assets like youth having "adult relationships," "family support," "caring neighborhoods," "safety," "creative activities," and "integrity." Librarians will be thrilled to know that "reading for pleasure" also makes the lists (The Search Institute 2009). Even a cursory glance at these assets will reveal how library programs and services support positive youth development.

Indeed, the Search Institute recognizes the importance of libraries in youth development. Their website proclaims, "Librarians are doing some of the most important work in positive youth development today." Creating and positioning library services for youth in terms of developmental assets is a solid way for libraries to demonstrate why their asset-strengthening youth services programs are vital offerings for the community. Indeed, libraries that have begun to present their services in this way are finding it extremely beneficial. In a report on the role that libraries play in the lives of teens, one librarian reported, "Knowing about youth developmental assets and putting our library programming into that framework has really lifted our position to another level with funders and our community. It's lifted our profession to another level" (Spielberger et al. 2004, 8).

Free public libraries are purported to be a "great equalizer" in our society. At a time of growing income inequality, this matters more than ever and it especially matters for youth. One category of the Search Institute's youth assets is "Commitment to Learning" (The Search Institute 2009). There is a natural link here to libraries, which have always been committed to helping youth learn. This commitment is particularly crucial for the low-income children and teens in our communities.

Experts in education are discovering that income inequality has startling negative effects on the educational opportunities available to youth from poorer families. While test scores cannot paint a complete picture of a child's learning, it is still telling that a study completed by the Russell Sage Foundation concluded that since 1978 the gap between the SAT math scores for low- and high-income students has grown by a third (Duncan and Murnane 2011, 2). These test scores too often mean that low-income youth do not complete as much schooling as their wealthier counterparts. By the 1990s, one in five American men actually had *less* education than his parents. The statistics for women are similar (3). With income inequality continuing to grow in the second decade of the twenty-first century, these patterns can only continue. The authors sum up what these numbers and facts mean:

Since education has been the dominant pathway to upward socio-economic mobility in the United States, the growing gap in educational attainment between children from rich and poor families is likely to result in increased income inequality in future generations and hinder the intergenerational socio-economic mobility that has been a source of pride for Americans. (3)

Libraries alone cannot reverse such a disturbing trend but, as we will argue throughout the book, community-centered libraries do not work alone. In conjunction with our municipal governments, community schools, day-care centers, museums, businesses, and residents, libraries can help support youth of all income brackets and create services that level the academic playing field. This, in fact, is a role that our communities see as a fitting one for our institutions. The Wallace Foundation Report, in language reminiscent of Carnegie's initial belief about the role of libraries, suggested that "libraries, publicly funded and present in most communities, are viewed as a promising resource for low-income youth who have less access than their more affluent peers to the educational and career development services they need to become productive adults" (Spielberger et al. 2004, 3). Again, part of the trouble is that librarians are not fully articulating the value and worth that libraries add to their communities with their educational services. Libraries need to claim their role as full educational partners, and communities need to follow through with appropriate funding and support to ensure that libraries can fulfill their potential.

The service areas discussed here will form the basis of the rest of the book. In part III we will look at specific ways in which individual libraries are taking local action in these areas. These service areas form the foundations for community building in our institutions, cities, and towns. If libraries can take an active interest in these areas, and provide services and programs that meet community needs in locally relevant and innovative ways, they will begin to be truly community centered.

BIBLIOGRAPHY

Aabø, Svenhild. 2005. "The Role and Value of Public Libraries in the Age of Digital Technologies." *Journal of Librarianship and Information Science* 37: 208–9.

Baldwin, Michael. 2002. "BackTalk: Can Libraries Save Democracy?" *Library Journal* 127 (17): 52.

"Core Values of Librarianship." 2012. American Library Association. Accessed December 13. http://www.ala.org/offices/oif/statementspols/corevalues statement/corevalues#democracy.

Duncan, Greg, and Richard Murnane. 2011. "Executive Summary: Whither Opportunity? Rising Inequality, Schools and Children's Life Chances." Russell Sage Foundation. https://www.russellsage.org/sites/all/files/Whither Opportunity_Executive Summary.pdf.

Edwards, Julie Biando. 2010. "Symbolic Possibilities." In *Beyond Article 19: Libraries and Social and Cultural Rights*, edited by Julie Biando Edwards and Stephan P. Edwards, 7–40. Duluth, Minn.: Library Juice Press.

Elturk, Ghada. 2003. "Diversity and Cultural Competency." *Colorado Libraries* 29 (4): 5–7.

Geppert Jacobs, Laureen M. 2010. "Carnegie Libraries: The Jumpstart to Public Libraries in Texas." *Texas Library Journal*, Winter: 142–45.

Green, Gary, and Anna Haines. 2012. *Asset Building and Community Development*. Thousand Oaks, Calif.: Sage.

Hauke, Petra, and Klaus Ulrich Werner. 2012. "The Second Hand Library Building: Sustainable Thinking through Recycling Old Buildings into New Libraries." *IFLA Journal* 38 (1): 60–67.

"IFLA/UNESCO Public Library Manifesto." 2004. International Federation of Library Associations IFLANET. Last modified November 3. http://archive.ifla.org/VII/s8/unesco/eng.htm.

Knight Foundation. 2012. "Soul of the Community." Knight Foundation. Accessed December 13. http://www.soulofthecommunity.org/.

Knuth, Rebecca. 2003. *Libricide: The Regime-Sponsored Destruction of Books and Libraries in the Twentieth Century*. Westport, Conn.: Praeger.

Kranich, Nancy. 2001. "*Libraries, the New Media and the Political Process.*" In *Libraries and Democracy*, edited by Nancy Kranich, 108–12. Chicago: ALA Editions.

Kretzmann, John P., and John L. McKnight. 1993. *Building Communities from Inside Out: A Path toward Finding and Mobilizing Communities' Assets*. Evanston, Ill.: Northwestern University Center for Urban Affairs and Policy Research.

Lappé, Frances Moore. 2007. *Getting a Grip: Clarity, Creativity and Courage in a World Gone Mad*. Cambridge, Mass.: Small Planet Media.

Lorenzen, Michael. 1999. "Deconstructing Carnegie Libraries: The Sociological Reasons behind Carnegie's Millions to Public Libraries." *Illinois Libraries* 81 (2): 75–78.

MacLeish, Archibald. 1940. "The Librarian and the Democratic Process." *ALA Bulletin* 34 (6): 385–88, 421–22.

————. 1972. "The Premise of Meaning." *American Scholar* 41 (3): 357–62.

Maurizi, Dennis. 2001. "Carnegie and His Legacy: The Little Libraries That Could." *Public Libraries* 40 (6): 346–48.

Maxwell, Nancy Kalikow. 2006. *Sacred Stacks: The Higher Purpose of Libraries and Librarianship.* Chicago: American Library Association.

McCrann, Grace-Ellen. 2005. "Contemporary Forces That Supported the Founding of the Boston Public Library." *Public Libraries* 44 (4): 223–28.

McMahon, Edward T. 2012. "The Distinctive City." Urbanland, April 4. http://urbanland.uli.org/Articles/2012/April/McMahonDistinctive.

Orphan, Cecelia M. 2011. "Interview with Nancy Kranich on Libraries and Democracy." American Democracy Project. Last modified January 4. http://adpaascu.wordpress.com/2011/01/04/interview-with-nancy-kranich-on-libraries-and-democracy/.

"Resources for Libraries." 2012. The Search Institute. Accessed December 13. http://www.search-institute.org/librarians-0.

Scher, Abby. 2007. "Can the Arts Change the World? The Transformative Power of Community Arts." *New Directions for Adult & Continuing Education*, no. 116: 3–11.

Scott, Rachel. 2011. "The Role of Public Libraries in Community Building." *Public Library Quarterly* 30 (3): 191–227.

The Search Institute. 2009. "Developmental Assets and Library Connections." Neal-Schuman. http://www.search-institute.org/system/files/librarians8x14.pdf.

Spielberger, Julie, Carol Horton, and Lisa Michels. 2004. "New on the Shelf: Teens in the Library." Chapin Hill Center for Children. http://www.libraryworks.com/INFOcus/0812/New-On-The-Shelf-Teens-in-the-Library.pdf.

Starr, Kevin. 2012. "Greetings from the State Librarian Emeritus, Dr. Kevin Starr." California State Library. Accessed December 13. http://www.library.ca.gov/about/starr/starr.html.

Urban Libraries Council. 2010. "Partners for the Future: Public Libraries & Local Governments Creating Sustainable Futures." Urban Libraries Council. http://www.urbanlibraries.org/filebin/pdfs/Sustainability_Report_2010.pdf.

Working Together. 2008. "Community-Led Libraries Toolkit." Working Together Project. http://www.librariesincommunities.ca/resources/Community-Led_Libraries_Toolkit.pdf.

World Youth Congress. 2005. "Nothing for Us without Us." World Youth Congress. http://www.youthfordevelopment.ch/files/docs/toolkit/actiontoolkit wyc2005.pdf.

Yancey, Kathleen Blake. 2005. "'The People's University': Our (New) Public Libraries as Sites of Lifelong Learning." *Change* 37 (2): 12–19.

CHAPTER 2

Community-Centered Libraries:
The Hearts of Revitalized Communities

Librarians who commit themselves to creating a community-centered library fall into the tradition of "civic librarianship" as defined by Ronald McCabe: "Civic librarianship is an effort to apply the community movement ideas and strategies to the public library" (McCabe 2001, 60). They are also taking to heart the declaration of former Chicago mayor Richard M. Daley, an ardent library supporter who told librarians in his city, "Unless you are out there changing neighborhoods, you are not completing the work you are to do" (Putnam and Feldstein 2003, 42). Changing neighborhoods is a great goal for a community-centered library. Daley did not specify how librarians should go about achieving this, but we think that the Asset-Based Community Development (ABCD) approach is perfect for libraries.

As an alternative to problem-focused, expert-driven attempts to build community, John P. Kretzmann and John L. McKnight (1993) pioneered the ABCD approach. Staff at the Halifax (Nova Scotia) Public Library, which has embraced ABCD, note that the drawbacks of traditional community development methods include "wasting energy on identifying deficiencies, creating fragmented responses to needs [and] creating a sense of dependency—where people are viewed as consumers of services" (Williment and Jones-Grant 2012, 2). In contrast, the ABCD model starts at the grassroots level, building its foundation on the assets, or skills and talents of local residents, associations, and organizations. Kretzmann and McKnight (1993) firmly believe that revitalization must come from inside a community: "The key to neighborhood regeneration, then, is to locate all of the available local assets, to begin connecting them with one another in ways that multiply their power and effectiveness, and to begin harnessing those local institutions that are not yet available for local development purposes" (5–6). This internally driven approach to creating vibrant, livable, and healthy communities is a natural fit for community-centered libraries precisely because they are rooted in their communities and are experienced in connecting resources for the good of their communities.

Kretzmann and McKnight recognize that libraries are valuable partners in the ABCD process. They encourage community builders to see that "libraries can play an essential role in the process of community-building and should be seen as vital assets that exist at the very heart of community life" (191). We'll talk more about libraries identifying the assets they bring to the community development table in chapter 7, but as a starting point, Kretzmann and McKnight suggest that all libraries' assets include personnel, space and facilities, materials and equipment, expertise and economic power (in the form of purchasing power, as a creator of jobs, and with their grant writing knowledge) (192–93).

Just as important as libraries' internal assets are the ways that they, as institutions, strengthen the skills and talents of their local residents. It is this type of asset building that we are primarily concerned with in this book. Libraries build assets for individuals and in the process strengthen their entire community. Building on the work of Kretzmann and McKnight, Gary Paul Green and Anna Haines (2012) list of seven types of assets: social, human, cultural, financial, political, environmental, and physical. Individual and group assets combine to form the larger community's assets or its "community capital." Green and Haines use the term *capital* along with assets for a deliberate reason. They believe "investments in these resources yield greater returns in the quality of community life" (xiii). Public libraries build all seven types of community capital, and we'll define and briefly discuss the library's role in each type here. In the coming chapters, we will point out many examples of community-centered libraries that have created services that build assets in their neighborhoods.

SOCIAL CAPITAL

We're beginning our discussion of community assets with social capital because as Green and Haines put it, "Social capital is at the center of asset building for all the forms of community capital. . . . It is an essential feature of community action" (xiv). As a concept, social capital, or networks and relationships of trust and reciprocity, gained notoriety through the work of political scientist Robert Putnam. Putnam's book *Bowling Alone* (2000) describes how technology and changes in society have led to decreasing levels of social capital in the United States. In his followup book (with Lewis Feldstein), *Better Together*, Putnam (2003) profiles the work that is being done at the community level by churches, neighborhood groups, schools, and yes, *libraries*, to reconnect people to each other, their neighbors, and their communities. In fact, Putnam devotes one full chapter to the social capital building work of the Chicago public libraries. Putnam, like Kretzmann and McKnight, sees the potential of public libraries as partners in reconnecting communities. Since Putnam's pioneering works on social capital, others have explored its connection to libraries. For example, Catherine Johnson (2012) found that the interactions between library staff and patrons can build social capital (52).

Strengthening social capital within communities is not just a feel-good exercise. High levels of social capital have tangible benefits for individuals and for cities and towns. Putnam (2000) identifies social capital as having a positive effect on people's health and happiness, levels of education, and the overall well-being of children. At the community level, social capital is a necessary ingredient to build stronger communities. As Green and Haines (2012) point out, it allows community members to "draw on the social resources in their community and increase the likelihood that the community will be able to address adequately collective concerns in their community" (152). Places with higher levels of social capital see greater rates of political participation, and their residents have a higher level of trust in their governments. The community development world is full of stories of neighborhoods, towns, and cities that have pulled themselves back from terrible circumstances, and social capital often plays a game-changing role in these transformations.

To establish exactly how a community-centered library can help strengthen social capital, it is helpful to distinguish between the two types of social capital, bonding and bridging. Both are important in community life and libraries can foster both. Bonding social capital creates stronger ties between people who are similar to each other. Public libraries play an important role in connecting community members with similar interests in crucial face-to-face settings (144). These are often the minicommunities of interest we mentioned earlier. Historical fiction book discussion groups, teen magna clubs, story times for children with autism, and other library services that bring together groups with similar interests or demographics build bonding social capital. This type of asset can help people create social networks they can depend on for mutual aid and help them unite behind their similarities to work for changes within their community.

While social capital can, and has, helped communities and individuals in myriad ways, it's important to acknowledge that there can be a downside to social capital. Tight-knit, homogeneous communities, while high in bonding social capital, can be exclusionary, discriminatory, or worse. In the 1980s French sociologist Pierre Bourdieu argued that social capital is a means by which the economic elites maintain and guard their wealth (Gauntlett 2011, 132). Obviously, this is the very antithesis of what a community-centered library seeks to accomplish. As David Gauntlett (2011) argues, however, social capital, "suggest[s] a path towards a better society, which we should not dismiss just because there are—as always—possible antisocial applications of the idea" (130).

Public libraries can act as agents to mitigate some of these negative possibilities by fostering *bridging* social capital, which builds connections between individuals who are fundamentally different from each other (Green and Haines 2012, 144). In today's increasingly diverse communities, bridging social capital is essential. It is what libraries build when they make their services, collections, and programs accessible to and representative of the rich diversity of their communities. Human Library programs, for example, foster bridging social capital by breaking down stereotypes through face-to-face conversation. As the Urban Libraries Council (2005) points out, libraries are "uniquely positioned to 'bridge'—build networks that bring together different types of people who may not share experiences with each other otherwise" (5).

All the library services that are highlighted in this book have the potential to increase social capital. As we discuss in chapter 7, community-centered libraries do their work in collaboration with other community players (groups and individuals). This approach immediately paves the way for stronger social ties. These ties only strengthen when libraries bring members of the community together in person, whether it's to attend arts programming (chapter 13), create their own music videos or inventions (chapter 14), improve their children's early literacy skills (chapter 15) or start a new "green" business (chapter 10).

HUMAN CAPITAL

Human and cultural capital are perhaps the two types of community assets most associated with libraries. Green and Haines (2012) define human capital as "general education background, labor market experience, artistic development and appreciation, health and other skills and experiences" (117). They focus specifically on human capital in the form of workforce development. We address how libraries strengthen their local workforces in chapter 10, but there is not one chapter in part III of this book that does not illustrate how libraries build human capital. When libraries serve as "the people's universities" they strengthen educational background. When they embrace the role of centers for the arts they help develop artistic skills and appreciation. Their nutrition programs for teens, their community garden projects, and their meditation workshops enable their residents to live healthier lives. When they serve as community centers for diverse populations and act as youth development advocates, they ensure that the human capital of all community members is being leveraged and strengthened. There is literally no end to the skills people can learn (and teach) and the experiences they can cocreate within a community-centered library.

CULTURAL CAPITAL

We define the cultural life of communities very broadly to encompass both "high" cultural fine arts, music, and so forth, and also popular culture, the traditions of the minority communities within our larger communities, and "historical buildings, archaeological sites, museums, farmers' markets and ethnic festivals" (Green and Haines 2012, 255). The importance of a community's cultural assets cannot be overemphasized. Kretzmann and McKnight (1993) see them as the "glue" that holds communities together (161) and Green and Haines (2012) say that cultural resources "in many ways define and bring identity to a community" (255). Tom Borrup's (2011) *The Creative Community Builder's Handbook* revolves around the premise that arts and culture strengthen local assets and that cultural organizations are some of the strongest community builders. His book is both a strong defense of the importance of building cultural capital and a helpful guide as to how to get started in asset building. Perplexingly, he fails to acknowledge libraries among the cultural organizations who do valuable community development work. Still, his passionate advocacy for arts and culture is compelling:

> Some of the most successful strategies for establishing understanding and connection are through the medium of cultural and artistic activities. Experiencing and appreciating the expressions of another's culture, and being able to communicate on a deeper level, is the most profound way to understand and participate in substantive dialogue. (10)

Libraries are priceless cultural capital in and of themselves, but they are also important places for the very culture of a community to be created. Cultural creation spaces are necessary for vibrant, relevant communities. In chapters 13 and 14, we discuss how libraries are facilitating the creation of the arts through classes, workshops, and digital media and fabrication labs. What these libraries are doing is strengthening the cultural capital of their communities by bringing creators of art and culture together in ways that connect them to each other and to their community. This includes the art and culture of minority groups that are traditionally trivialized or ignored. The power of this type of capital lies in the fact that while strengthening it, libraries are also strengthening human capital through the creation of artistic skills in individuals, financial capital by supporting creative economy businesses, and political capital through the unique ability of the arts to engage residents in civic life.

FINANCIAL CAPITAL

This asset is the most traditional form of "capital." In community development, it refers to people's ability to access monetary credit to do things like buy houses and start businesses. Financial capital is probably the asset that your community is least likely to associate with public libraries. Since libraries aren't banks, mortgage companies, or local credit unions, many individuals and community stakeholders may assume libraries don't play a role in strengthening financial capital for their communities. If so, they are underestimating creative librarians! Green and Haines (2012) point out that "poor and minority communities generally lack access to financial capital" (189) and, even within wealthier communities, there will be segments of the population that have trouble accessing credit. In their role of societal equalizers, libraries can help. The first step to remedying this is to make sure that all members of our communities are financially literate. This is where library workshops on financial topics come in. In chapter 12, we highlight libraries that extend the reach of these workshops to non–English speakers and new immigrants. The significant help that libraries can provide to existing small business and aspiring entrepreneurs is another major contribution they make to communities' financial capital. For examples of some innovative partnerships libraries have developed to support their communities' businesses, take a look at chapter 10. Throughout this book, the examples of ways libraries strengthen financial capital can be a reminder to librarians, residents, and decision makers that there isn't one area of community life to which libraries can't contribute.

POLITICAL CAPITAL

Political capital is both the level of resident participation in civic life and their "access to decision making" (Green and Haines 2012, 239). This asset is even more tightly entwined with social capital than the other forms of community capital. Higher levels of social capital lead to higher rates of political participation and create ties to other individuals who can together effectively agitate for change within their communities. As we discussed in the last chapter, the skills necessary to be an active and effective participant in our democracy need to be learned. Libraries strengthen political capital for the people of their communities by providing opportunities to practice Frances Moore Lappé's Arts of Democracy. Yet again, libraries can play a role as a community equalizer for disenfranchised individuals and groups. This idea is especially evident in our chapters on library services to diverse populations (chapter 12) and to youth (chapter 15). At the same time that they are strengthening political capital, libraries are also acting as local institutions to help address social problems within their communities. In chapter 9, we will show in detail how community-centered libraries are becoming civic centers and developing creative partnerships to spur collective action around pressing local needs.

ENVIRONMENTAL CAPITAL

Environmental capital is a community's natural resources. The importance of a community's environmental capital cannot be underestimated. Green and Haines assert, "Because natural resources may produce a variety of values, it is important to consider the best use of the resources for the long-term viability of a community" (213). We couldn't agree more. Well-managed natural resources add a great deal of value to our communities in the form of clean air and water, beautiful natural places, and healthy residents. It's inspiring to see how libraries have taken a leadership role in protecting and strengthening environmental capital. We most directly address this role in chapter 10 when we discuss the important work that libraries are doing by "greening" their buildings and spaces, and through programs and services that support environmental literacy for children, teens, and adults.

PHYSICAL CAPITAL

This type of community capital is, quite simply, the buildings and infrastructure that make up a place (Green and Haines 2012, 159). This includes library buildings, and also housing, roads, and vacant land. Libraries contribute to the physical capital of their cities and towns in a number of ways. In chapter 11 we will discuss how library buildings are culturally significant for their communities, and in chapter 10 we give you examples of libraries that are strengthening both physical and environmental capital through green building practices. The creation and maintenance of their buildings is the most direct impact that libraries have on their physical capital, but it is not the only one. Also in chapter 11, we discuss libraries that have developed tool libraries. Providing the tools that community members can use to maintain, or even build, their homes and other structures is a way that libraries can contribute to the physical capital of their hometowns. A library project that we discuss in chapter 9, designed to help library patrons facing foreclosure, is yet another way a creative community-centered library has tried to ensure the integrity of its physical capital. Later in this chapter, we'll investigate how libraries can make a strong investment in their communities by transforming their buildings and spaces into vibrant asset-building places.

ASSET MAPPING

Now that you know about these types of community capital, how do you identify the existing assets within your city or town so that you can connect them with each other to strengthen your library, patrons, and community? One tool of the trade employed by ABCD practitioners is asset mapping. This literally involves creating a schematic of the skills and talents of individuals, groups, and institutions. The Halifax Public Library used asset mapping as a service planning method to improve their services to new immigrants. The first step in asset mapping is to identify appropriate organizations and individuals within the community. After that, librarians need to get out of their buildings and "ask questions, listen and learn from members of the community" (Williment and Jones-Grant 2012, 5). By asking residents and organizational representatives a set of predefined questions librarians can begin to learn how those within the community define their assets and needs. After these conversations, Halifax created an internal database to keep track of the resources they identified. Each one-on-one chat completed during asset mapping also helps refine the questions staff should ask other people and groups.

Many of the skills needed to create an asset map involve making connections with potential partners, which we address in chapter 7. Even though it is rewarding, asset mapping is not always an easy process. It is important to remember that even the most experienced librarians are not experts in all of their community's needs. ABCD requires that "library staff acknowledge that community members are the experts at identifying their own needs" (3). As the Halifax Library started the process of talking to community members about their strengths and assets, they found it "a bit humbling because we became aware of how our preconceptions of community assets and needs did not align with what we heard from the community" (8). Of course, this is precisely the value of asset mapping.

Communities are far too large to map all of their assets in one attempt. Halifax focused their first asset map on the immigrant community, so they spoke only to service providers who work with immigrants and with individual immigrants themselves. Their advice for libraries that want to undertake asset mapping is to be specific about what their asset map covers and to be strategic about who is interviewed and what questions are asked (6).

One final note on asset mapping: the Halifax Library warns librarians, "If a library system is not willing to adjust services based on community feedback, asset mapping can set false expectations for the community" (9). This is a good general piece of advice. If your library is not committed to becoming community centered (yet), proceed with care so you don't set up your community for disappointment and make future efforts more difficult. When you are committed to community-centered programs and services, however, asset mapping is a planning tool that libraries should seriously consider. Staff at the Halifax Library conclude that it can result in "community based mobilization, empowerment and sustainability" (2). It is also rewarding. Borrup (2011) says of the process: "Identifying the historic and contemporary assets of your community is truly a creative exercise. The goal is to uncover or create an identity built upon the best of the past with a vision for what's to come" (168).

PLACE MATTERS

Part of being a community-centered library is getting out of your building and into the community. At the same time, library buildings are critical community places and their very physical presence is vital to communities. The Project for Public Spaces (PPS; 2012a, 2012b), which is committed to creating great public places that can nurture vibrant community life, suggests on their website a way that libraries can move forward through "placemaking." Placemaking uses an ABCD type approach to "capitalize on a local community's assets, inspiration, and potential, ultimately creating good public spaces that promote people's health, happiness, and well being." When a library becomes a truly great public place it can achieve marvelous things. PPS extols the virtues of forward-thinking libraries that "now see success being linked to their role as public places and destinations" (Nikitin and Johnson 2012).

Public places matter for a number of reasons. One is that they build critical social capital. By creating a welcoming environment that fosters meaningful gatherings, they can help mitigate the isolating effects of technology. As Robert Putnam (2000) points out, many of today's technological advances pull people away from each other. We all spend more and more time interacting with screens and less with our friends, neighbors, and families. While Gauntlett and others point out that some technology (mainly Web 2.0 platforms) can help nurture social bonds, the creation of social capital that can build healthier, happier communities requires people to spend time together *in person*. Face-to-face interaction is necessary to the well-being of people and communities. As a result, Green and Haines (2012) assert, "There is clearly a need to build new opportunities for social interaction that will generate trust and reciprocity among residents" (146). Libraries can fill this need by transforming themselves into "places where people gather and where information comes alive through teaching and personal interaction" (Nikitin and Johnson 2012). We believe that this path is the most meaningful way forward for community-centered libraries.

To make their spaces desirable destinations for community members, libraries should consider the advice of the PPS. Their "Eleven Principles for Creating Great Community Places" include online guidelines for libraries to consider when they design their buildings. Libraries should acknowledge the community's expertise in its own desires and needs, look for partners, have a vision, start with small and inexpensive change, ignore naysayers, and recognize that the process of creating a community gathering spot is never finished.

Interestingly, one of the principles of PPS is that "money is not the issue." We can agree with this only up to a point. This principle should not be an excuse for communities to shirk their responsibility to fully fund their libraries. Community-centered libraries need, first and foremost, staff and then also space and money for their innovative programs. Where the PPS principle can help is to encourage libraries to take the important, small first steps even if their funding levels are not yet where they ought to be. Later chapters in this book will give librarians the tools to find outside grant funding, leverage the talents of community members, and eventually advocate for the funding they need to bring their vision for the library and the community to life.

Libraries that focus on becoming what PPS deems a "Community Front Porch" (Nikitin and Johnson 2012) can have a transformative impact on their cities and towns. Due to seismic shifts in the economy in recent decades, many communities have depressed city centers and neighborhoods that have been essentially abandoned. Around the country, however, revitalization efforts are under way and there are many of examples of libraries that have been at the center of successful campaigns to breathe new life into their communities. The Urban Libraries Council (2010) succinctly sums up the value libraries bring to revitalization efforts: "[Libraries'] ability to attract people and their reputation as safe and stable community assets make them attractive additions to both downtown and neighborhood economic development efforts" (16).

Wayne Senville from the *Planning Commissioners Journal* took a trip to "Circle the USA" and find libraries doing important revitalization work. He points to libraries in Denver; Salt Lake City; Hudson, Ohio; Seattle; Putney, Vermont; Moab, Utah; Saint Paul, Minnesota; Brattleboro, Vermont: and other cities and towns as examples of communities that have leveraged the powerful asset-building power of libraries. He concludes, "When libraries are located in downtown, village, or neighborhood centers, there's . . . a special synergy at work" (Senville 2009, 18). This synergy can exist in any community that invests in and does the work to create a community-centered library.

Kankakee, Illinois, is a story of a library successfully leading the revitalization of a downtown community. When a new director, Cynthia Fuerst, took over the library in 1995, she came into an economically depressed neighborhood. Her immediate efforts to position the library as a force of good in the area earned the notice of city officials. Fuerst's belief that a new central library could kick-start urban renewal spurred her to apply for grants and assess the community's needs and budget capacity. The mayor of Kankakee eventually offered the library the chance to make a major influence on the downtown by spearheading a project to convert a vacant seven-story building to a multiuse space that would house a new, expanded library (Hamilton-Pennell 2008, 6). Since the rapid renovation of the library, it has been credited with starting the process of bringing life back to downtown. Fuerst says, "Several new businesses have popped up since our arrival—two new banks, a coffee shop, an insurance company and more" (quoted in Hill 2009, 117). A *New York Times* Op-Ed piece by Luis Alberto (2006) concluded that "Kankakee is pulling itself back from the brink, and it all started with the library" (118).

Your library does not necessarily need a big, modern new building before you can contribute to the revitalization of your surroundings. In fact, in Pittsburgh, the "library without walls" doesn't have a traditional building at all. Instead, they have created a branch at their city's public market (Vey and Althaus 2011). By integrating library services into their community the Market Branch contributes to Pittsburgh's efforts to create an economically successful and livable city. Ultimately, as the PPS has said, "Libraries will sink or swim based on how well they serve the needs of their respective communities—whether they are truly great places, not just eye-catching buildings" (Nikitin and Johnson 2012).

Embracing ABCD principles for your public library is an exciting move. Kretzmann and McKnight (1993) conclude, "The local library can become a central facilitator for continuing community development that is organized and driven by the talents and energies of the widest possible range of community residents" (202). We couldn't agree more. By building social capital and strengthening the other types of community assets, libraries can have a dramatic effect on the lives of their communities. As potentially great public places, libraries can bring together community members, revitalize neighborhoods, and help bring about positive community change. We are unapologetically optimistic about the many ways libraries can improve lives and contribute to community building, but we do not think libraries can solve all social ills. Instead we believe libraries can do what community activist Lily Yeh does. Yeh, the artist and founder of Barefoot Arts, an organization that uses art to revitalize neighborhoods globally, has said, "I can't solve these huge social problems, but I can open up new possibilities and spaces where, through creativity and working together, we might come to new solutions" (Pompilio 2012, 37).

BIBLIOGRAPHY

Alberto, Luis. 2006. "Kankakee Gets Its Groove Back." *New York Times*, June 11.
Borrup, Tom. 2011. *The Creative Community Builder's Handbook*. New York: Fieldstone Alliance.
Gauntlett, David. 2011. *Making Is Connecting: The Social Meaning of Creativity, from DIY and Knitting to YouTube and Web 2.0*. Malden, Mass.: Polity Press.
Green, Gary, and Anna Haines. 2012. *Asset Building and Community Development*. Thousand Oaks, Calif.: Sage.
Hamilton-Pennell, Christine. 2008. "Public Libraries and Community Economic Development: Partnering for Success." *Rural Research Report* 18 (10): 1–8.
Hill, Chrystie. 2009. *Inside, Outside, and Online: Building Your Library Community*. Chicago: ALA Editions.
Johnson, Catherine. 2012. "How Do Public Libraries Create Social Capital? An Analysis of Interactions between Library Staff and Patrons." *Library and Information Science Research* 34 (1): 52–62.
Kretzmann, John P., and John L. McKnight. 1993. *Building Communities from Inside Out: A Path toward Finding and Mobilizing Communities' Assets*. Evanston, Ill.: Northwestern University Center for Urban Affairs and Policy Research.

McCabe, Ronald. 2001. "Civic Librarianship." In *Libraries and Democracy: The Cornerstones of Liberty*, edited by Nancy Kranich, 60–69. Chicago: ALA Editions.

Nikitin, Cynthia, and Josh Jackson. 2012. "Libraries That Matter." Project for Public Spaces. Accessed December 13. http://www.pps.org/reference/libraries thatmatter-2/.

Pompilio, Natalie. 2012. "Lily Yeh: Beauty in Broken Places." *Yes!*, Winter: 35–37.

Project for Public Spaces. 2012a. "Eleven Principles for Creating Great Community Places." Project for Public Spaces. Accessed October 28. http://www.pps.org/reference/11steps/.

———. 2012b. "What Is Placemaking?" Project for Public Spaces. Accessed October 28. http://www.pps.org/reference/what_is_placemaking/.

Putnam, Robert D. 2000. *Bowling Alone: The Collapse and Revival of American Community*. New York: Simon & Schuster.

Putnam, Robert D., and Lewis Feldstein. 2003. *Better Together: Restoring the American Community*. New York: Simon & Schuster.

Senville, Wayne. 2009. "Libraries at the Heart of Our Communities." *Planning Commissioners Journal* 75: 12–18.

Urban Libraries Council. 2005. "The Engaged Library: Chicago Stories of Community Building." Urban Libraries Council. http://www.urbanlibraries.org/filebin/pdfs/Engaged_Library_Full_Report.pdf.

———. 2010. "Partners for the Future: Public Libraries & Local Governments Creating Sustainable Futures." Urban Libraries Council. http://www.urban libraries.org/filebin/pdfs/Sustainability_Report_2010.pdf.

Vey, Jason, and Elena Althaus. 2011. "Libraries without Walls: The Opening of the Carnegie Library at Pittsburgh's Public Market Branch." *Public Libraries* 50 (2): 30–36.

Williment, Kenneth, and Tracey Jones-Grant. 2012. "Asset Mapping at Halifax Public Libraries: A Tool for Beginning to Discover the Library's Role with the Immigrant Community in Halifax." *Partnership: The Canadian Journal of Library and Information Practice and Research* 7 (1): 1–11.

CHAPTER 3

The Future of Libraries, Now

We should start off by saying that, really, none of us can accurately predict the future of libraries. And, while it is an interesting mental exercise, it is ultimately something that we don't spend a lot of time on. In fact, we'd argue that the community-centered library is one that focuses on the *now* (hence the chapter title). This is a fine line, of course. Focusing too much on the present state of our institutions doesn't give us much room to think about the ways in which we want to grow and might need to adapt. But looking too far into a future that is beyond our ability to predict puts us in danger of missing the opportunities and needs that present themselves in our communities at this very moment. Our philosophy is fairly simple. We do believe that, to adapt and stay relevant, the future of public libraries will demand that they are centered in their communities in ways that build individual and community assets. But achieving this requires that libraries focus on the present and work in the moment. Building community, and repositioning the library, is long-range work, as we will see in part II. But the best way to make these changes, to adapt and to stay relevant, is to adopt this long-range goal (being community centered) while understanding that the way to achieve it is to work in the now, building relationships, strengthening social bonds, and addressing the community in innovative ways. It may seem contradictory or counterintuitive, but the best way to adapt for the future is to work in the present with a mind toward your community.

Of course, a lot of people do focus very serious energy and very smart minds on the future of libraries. There seems to be a general consensus that libraries will need to adapt and prove their worth in the ever-expanding digital age. But whether or not libraries are *defined* by the digital age seems to us to be up to debate. The article that sparked this book was written in response to another article (a very good one, in fact) that looked at the ways in which the library is still relevant in the digital age. But what if we were to acknowledge that we live in a digital age, and acknowledge (gratefully) that the proliferation of technology and expanding universe of information has allowed us to connect with patrons in new ways, without actually defining ourselves either as *part of* or *in opposition to* the digital age? This isn't to say that we don't need to adapt and to prove our worth—we do. But our worth is defined, we think, by the role we play in our communities and the ways in which we can build community and individual assets, not necessarily by how well we compete with an expanding Internet and increasingly wired world. Technology, like everything else in our buildings, is a tool with which we can reach out to our patrons and help them meet their potential. It isn't an end in itself any more than the amorphous idea of "information" is an end itself. The value of libraries will be proven when libraries demonstrate that they can use the tools that they provide to help strengthen and sustain their communities.

The community-centered library is not about information. It isn't about how many computers we have, how many e-books (or print books) we circulate, or how many databases we have. All of these things are important. But they are all, as we said, tools. The community-centered library is about how we can leverage those and other tools in our communities to build assets. This distinction is essential, and it is why we so strongly believe in libraries as partners in community development and capital building. As Chrystie Hill has noted, "We've neglected to recognize our role as organizers and keepers of information access as primarily a *social* role" (Hill 2009a, 18). Our "essential role," she argues, should be as "[purveyors] of both *content* and *connection* for the communities we serve" (xiii). Scott (2011) sums it up thus: "Understanding our role in community building and being able to articulate this role is essential to the work we do" (224).

When we define ourselves in opposition to the digital age—or worse, as desperately trying to keep pace with it—we run the very real risk of defining ourselves out of existence. Think about it: Why would a community continue to fund a library if the members of that community are convinced that information needs can be met by Google searches? Why would anyone vote to increase library funding if the library itself can't articulate its value in a compelling way? This is the point that we made in the introduction—as long as we try to demonstrate our worth by saying that "it's not all on the Internet" or that "librarians do it better than Google" we're not making a convincing argument. Don't get us wrong—we believe that both of these statements are true. But when we look critically at these kinds of arguments—and librarians make them all the time—we have to honestly admit that they just aren't very interesting. Each of us has had the experience of a well-meaning person saying something like this: "I mean, I love libraries and everything. I had a great one when I was a kid. But don't you think that they'll disappear sooner or later? Don't you ever worry about your job? Don't you think that print books are just going to go away?" And each of us, when trying to answer these questions with the statements that we mentioned above, is usually met with a sympathetic but unconvinced look. We lose interest in our own arguments half the time. If we're honest, we have to admit that an awful lot *is* on the Internet (including, with digitization, a lot of those things that account for what Knuth calls our "idiosyncrasies") and that Google does a lot of things *really, really* well. Does that mean that libraries are an endangered species?

Obviously, by this point in the book you know that we think that the answer is no. Libraries are not an endangered species, but they are an evolving species and we must adapt our institutions to the changes around us or—like any other organism, biological or social—we won't survive. Survival means taking steps to deeply understand our communities, as we mentioned in the previous chapter. It means basing our services on what we learn from our communities. And it means shifting away from information as an end in itself to a broader understanding of what the library in the twenty-first century exists to do—which is to imagine, build, sustain, and support our local communities. At the turn of the century, ALA president Sarah Ann Long (1999) wrote that "every day, in every institution I know about, the existing structure, purpose, and ways of working are challenged. Institutions that will survive today and tomorrow continuously renew themselves to meet these challenges" (32). Over a dozen years later, her words ring as true as ever. If meeting these challenges means reallocating budgets, revisioning mission statements, or reconceptualizing services, then that is what we must do. This kind of adaptation means that if patrons want to use our buildings in new ways, then we should support their needs. It means that if patrons want to go beyond consuming content to creating content, we should enable them with the means to accomplish their goals. It means advocating for those in our community who most need our—or other—services. It means taking a seat at the table and actively working to influence local perceptions of and support for the library.

All of this is important, but we don't mean to say that the community-centered library should be in the business of simply giving patrons what they want. This kind of consumer model, when taken without critical examination, doesn't serve libraries well. While always striving to understand and then to meet our community needs, we have to remember that "community" is not homogenous, and that sometimes those who are most vocal about their desires—or those who have the most power—are not necessarily holding the interests of the entire community in mind. The first step for any library considering its role in the twenty-first-century community should be to make a commitment to the community as a whole—including those who are disenfranchised. Likewise, the library exists not just to meet patron needs or to fulfill patron expectations, but to make members of the community aware of the world beyond what they need or expect. In this way the library can help the community understand itself better, imagine itself in new and perhaps previously unconsidered ways, and appreciate its own nuances. The community-centered library isn't a passive provider of entertainment, it isn't a consumer-driven service provider, and it isn't the old information provider of yesteryear. It is a responsive, constantly changing, social institution that exists to support individual and community assets.

In supporting individual assets, the library builds community assets. Hill, one of the leading voices on libraries and communities in recent years, has written and spoken about the ways in which libraries support both individuals and communities. In a TEDxColumbus lecture in 2009 she argued passionately that librarians must

> broaden our focus so that it is not just about the authoritated [sic] content that we are providing access to and distributing, but instead [focus] on the reason why we distribute that content, so that people can make that human connection. Whether it is a reader to a book, or a peer to peer, whatever it may be—the reason why we do that is so that everyone has equal opportunity to learn and ultimately enrich their [sic] lives. (Hill 2009b)

She refined this statement at another TEDx lecture in 2011 when she said simply, "With access to content, space, and service, the library helps individuals become effective members of their community. And when the library provides that opportunity to anyone, it becomes opportunity for all" (Hill 2011). This is the role of the community-centered library—to provide opportunities to individuals in order to strengthen individual and community capital. Librarians have always been committed to providing information access to individuals. We are not giving that up, but are asking librarians to consider how the individual fits into the overall community, and to look at each act of patron service as an act of community asset building.

Throughout this book we will examine in more detail the ways in which you can reposition your library so that it is truly a community-centered institution. But before we consider activities such as networking, collaborating, and programming, we have to start at a more foundational level. The roots of all successful community-centered libraries are the vision and mission statements, which Hill defines as follows: "A vision statement tells your audience about the future you see for your community and library. Your mission statement describes how you plan to achieve that vision. Strong vision and mission statements are typically short, direct, and emotionally compelling" (Hill 2009a, 53). Because your mission statement will be at the core of grant funding efforts, marketing, and services, it must succinctly and accurately convey to your community the goals of the library within that community. Often, your mission statement will evolve with the times, adapting itself to your changing institution and community. Occasionally, though, a library will craft a mission statement that endures for years or, in the case of the Peabody Institute Library, for over a century and a half. When philanthropist George Peabody bequeathed funds to found the institute that bears his name, he requested simply that it be open to everyone and serve the educational, informational, and recreational needs of the community. More than 160 years later, the Peabody Library's mission remains unchanged. This is, in our opinion, a fine example of an elegant, adaptive mission statement. Although it was the charge laid out for us by the library's founder, it has proved to be remarkably enduring. Descriptive, yet not prescriptive, it has provided us with both a vision and a mission that has served the library and the community well. Such a statement gives the library a clear set of goals—meeting the educational, informational, and recreational needs of our patrons—while at the same time allowing for the flexibility in interpreting these goals as the times and resources change.

Furthermore, the explicit inclusion of "community" in this statement reinforces for whom we exist to serve while allowing that community is an organic, dynamic, and heterogeneous collective. Such a statement becomes even more remarkable when one considers that, in 1852, when Peabody charged the institute with this mission, it would have been more in keeping with the times to more narrowly define the scope of the both the institution and its patron base. Did Peabody know that the Yankee community of the nineteenth century would become today's bustling, multiracial, multiethnic city? No. But his trust in the institution, in the simplicity of its mission, served both iterations of the community—and all those in between—very well.

Our library was extremely lucky in being gifted with such a simple and elegant mission. Not all libraries are so fortunate. But, while we see no benefit in changing our mission statement, we recommend that you take a look at what your library offers your community by way of a mission and revise and rewrite it as necessary. Some libraries do this every few years or so. Others operate under outdated or overly complex statements that don't reflect the library, its services, or the community at all. Still others don't have a mission statement or, if they do have one, don't know it. So, before you get started on anything else in this book—begin at the beginning. Look at your mission statement and see if it really says anything about what your library is and does. If it works for you, excellent. If it doesn't, revise, or start from scratch. Just remember to keep it simple and strive for flexibility. Aim at crafting something that can be easily communicated and simply grasped by people within and outside of the library. Find the phrase that will allow your librarians and other staff the latitude of interpretation when telling the library's story. And remember—put the focus on the community. The Peabody Library's statement is about what the library does *in* the community and *for* the community. It is not about the library, per se, but about what the library will accomplish in Peabody. If you make the community the center of your mission statement, it will be that much easier to adapt your library so that it is centered on, and becomes the center of, the community.

In her book, Hill has some good advice for libraries seeking to become community builders—with an important focus on how to successfully outreach to the community in order to better market the library. Her focus boils down to one thing, though. As she said in her TEDxColumbus lecture, "Libraries should be about the people, not about the books, not about the services that we think they need. When you pay attention to the people, you're really in tune with what their needs are. Find the needs, fill the library" (Hill 2009b). Once you find those needs and fill the library, you have a vibrant patron base that can help you tell your story to community stakeholders. This might mean that traditional statistics like gate counts and number of items circulated might begin to carry less weight than web hits and program participants (particularly if the library partners to host programs outside of the building). But these people, filling your library, are the very basis of what will help you tell your story. And telling your story well can play a large part in helping you maintain and secure funding.

Hill notes that "[libraries] struggle with funding. Institutionally our culture is one of deprivation. We never have enough funding. It is a real threat all over the country—in fact, the world—this lack of support for our libraries" (Hill 2009b). This lack of funding has forced libraries to take steps that dramatically move them away from what we believe to be the essence of the public library—which is that it is community controlled as much as it is community centered. In recent years, library systems in several states have been privatized as a way to either make up for poor funding or as a way to hedge against ever-weakening economies. The ALA (2011) defines privatization as "the shifting of library service from the public to the private sector through transference of library management and operations from a government agency to a commercial company," and has come out in opposition to this practice, citing the quality of services, loss of community control, loss of control of tax dollars, and loss of community involvement in foundations, nonprofits, and Friends groups as potential major issues with privatization (5–6). In their foreword to the *ALA Special Report: Privatizing Libraries*, Patricia A. Tumulty and Marci Merola encourage those considering privatization to ask difficult questions about what privatization will do not only to the library, but also to the community. Such questions include "Does the relationship between a public library and its community change when a library is privatized?" and "Does the role of the library as a public good change when the library is privatized?" (Jerrard et al. 2012, vii).

In 2010, the *New York Times* ran an article about the privatization of libraries in California, where the Santa Clarita library system was turned over to a company called Library Systems & Services Inc. in a $4 million deal (Streitfeld 2010). Though there is much debate and back-and-forth over the pros and cons of privatizing libraries, and though those in favor of this practice focus on saving struggling libraries, cutting costs, and keeping buildings open longer, we believe that there are fundamental problems with such a model that no amount of private sector efficiency can solve. Not ignoring the very real concerns over patron privacy, tiered service models, and the professional value of librarians, we would point to the loss of local, community control as the main reason that libraries shouldn't be owned and operated by private corporations. While many tout the private sector's ability to react quickly to, or to anticipate, market need and demand, we believe, in line with the ALA, which "affirms that publicly funded libraries should remain directly accountable to the public they serve," that to be a truly community-centered library one must be accountable to the community, not to a parent company (Jerrard et al. 2012, 2). The library should spring from the community and respond to the community—and here we reiterate that we mean the community *in full*, not just the elements of it who speak the loudest or who hold the most control.

It remains to be seen whether or not privatization of public libraries will be a growing trend. Certainly one of the most worrisome elements of privatization is that, in the case of Santa Clarita, "opposition has faded with time" (Streitfeld 2010). This makes it all the more essential for libraries to become community-centered institutions that can articulate their value, tell their own stories, and retain local control and accountability.

In their book about the future of public library use and employment, José-Marie Griffiths and Donald W. King (2011) note that public library revenue shifted between 2002 and 2007, with federal and state revenue decreasing and local sources making up the bulk of the loss (53). Library budgets are being slashed by states, forcing libraries to close or consider privatization. A 2008 OCLC (Online Community Library Center) report on library funding notes that "over 80% of public library funding comes from local tax receipts" and follows that by stating that "dependence on the local purse for public library funding is high, and increasing" even while taxpayers are contributing to other services like police, schools, and parks (DeRosa and Johnson 2008, 9). It continues to note that "for many public libraries, the need to grow awareness and mindshare is intensifying as library annual operating funds are not keeping pace with the services and resources needed to meet their mission" and reports that the findings of their study on how marketing and advocacy can increase library funding "suggest that there is sufficient, but latent, support for increased library funding among the voting population" (9).

Focusing on elected officials in your community is one way to approach questions of funding. The OCLC report notes that while "elected official [survey] respondents are higher-than-average users of the library and believe that the library is an important community resource," the majority also "feel that their libraries have sufficient funds to meet their day-to-day operational needs" (23). "Elected officials are knowledgeable about libraries and their value, but they often do not see the library as a necessity for the community. The library is seen as a community 'amenity' rather than a 'must have'" (132). This is a problem that will be familiar to many public librarians, who have become adept at doing more with less. It can be a difficult task to convince city or county governments that the library needs more funds when it seems to be operating just fine without additional revenue. It can likewise be difficult to convince elected officials that not everyone can afford to go to a bookstore, or that not everyone has access to the Internet, a computer, or a smartphone. These kinds of divides are often not part of people's perceptions of their own communities, particularly when technology is so seemingly ubiquitous. It is up to the library to tell this part of the community's story, and to advocate for those people who would truly be without access should the library not exist.

Elected officials do provide advice for libraries, though, some of which we discuss in detail later in this book. Such advice includes stressing the library's return on investment, building strategic partnerships, being proactive, engaging voters, and stressing the broad appeal of the library (142). When providing advice on what libraries can do to market themselves in a community they offered additional points, many of which, again, we tackle later in the book. A successful push for library funding will include the following:

- Messaging that focuses on the broader value of the library to the community, specifically a community gathering place, access to technology and programs for teenagers and other groups.
- A passionate, committed, and active champion(s) who can rally support among the elected officials and community influencers.
- Civic engagement, including a commitment to speak with every relevant group in the community to encourage grassroots support.
- A willingness to partner with other public services in a joint effort where strategically advantageous.

• The ability to ask for the right support at the right time: Voter turnout is greater for general elections than local elections. It is often easier to campaign for a new building than for operating funds. (143)

Clearly, in order to maintain what little budgets libraries have—and to grow those budgets for the future—it will be key to make the argument that libraries provide more than books, computers, or information. Program-oriented services will bring people into the building and can help create citizen champions for the library. Librarians should be able to articulate what their budgets fund and be able to talk about how the community benefits when the library is funded. Indeed, the dollars spent at the library can be seen as dollars given directly back to the community in the form of programs and services that meet community members' needs that aren't being met by other agencies or institutions. The library must be able to clearly and compellingly articulate that the community actually has needs that are only met at the library—and then be able to talk about the ways in which the library meets those needs.

In their survey, the OCLC report identifies eight drivers of library funding:

1. Most people claim they would support the library at the ballot box— fewer are firmly committed to it.
2. There is a lot that people don't know about their public library.
3. Library support is only marginally related to visitation. Advocating for library support to library users focuses effort and energy on the wrong target group.
4. Perceptions of the librarian are highly related to support. "Passionate librarians" who are involved in the community make a difference.
5. The library occupies a very clear position in people's minds as a provider of practical answers and information. This is a very crowded space, and to remain relevant in today's information landscape, repositioning will be required.
6. Belief that the library is a transformational force in people's lives is directly related to their level of funding support.
7. Increasing support for libraries may not necessarily mean a trade-off of financial support for other public services.
8. Elected officials are supportive of the library—but not fully committed to increasing funding. Engaging Probable Supporters and Super Supporters to help elevate library funding needs is required. (24)

For our purposes, points 4–6 are most relevant. Survey respondents noted that strong ratings for the librarian equaled strong support for the library. A "passionate librarian" is

1. [A] true advocate for lifelong learning,
2. Passionate about making the library relevant again,
3. Knowledgeable about every aspect of the library,
4. Well-educated, and
5. Knowledgeable about the community. (152)

We would say that all of these, though particularly points 2 and 5, are attributes of a community-centered librarian. Survey respondents also noted that "the library is perceived as a service that provides 'information with a purpose,'" but that, increasingly, that role is shared with many other entities who are "spending significant financial resources to solidify their positioning" (156). The findings support our claim, earlier in this chapter, that the library needs to be about more than information, and that focusing on libraries solely as information resources is not a compelling narrative—especially considering the scant financial resources that *we* have to support this narrative. The research found that those most likely to fund libraries—the "super supporters"—"do not view the library as a source of information, but rather as a source for transformation" (157). This is a beautiful concept and a very elegant phrasing of what a community-centered library does, at its heart. By serving as a source for personal transformation, the library is building individual assets. These individual assets, in turn, strengthen the community as a whole.

The report indicates that "library funding behavior is driven by attitudes and beliefs, not by demographics. Voters' perceptions of the role the library plays in their lives and in their communities are more important determinants of their willingness to increase funding than their age, gender, race, political affiliation, life stage or income level" (145). However, even among the "probable supporters" of library funding, there was a general sense that libraries are becoming obsolete—and this sense was met with "pragmatic acceptance" (171). Those who most passionately support library funding, on the other hand, felt that the loss of a library would lead "to the dissolution of the residential community as we now know it" (172). It is worth highlighting the fears of these survey respondents in some detail:

The loss of the community gathering place or social center was also cited as a critical loss if the library were to close. The result, [respondents] feared, would be an increase in isolation within their communities. Participants perceived that a world without the library would suffer from a reduction in social interaction, a trend they attributed to the rise in use of the Internet. Focus group members articulated concerns that their community would lose a safe, neutral and open meeting place if the library were closed. This loss would lead to a reduction in the community's moral and social values. . . . Ultimately, the group projected, the fabric of their communities would disintegrate because the heart of the community, the library, would be gone. Discussion often followed that this loss would lead to a decline of their community's relative stature to other towns and cities with a library. "Who would want to live in a place without a public library?" (172–73)

The report

identified four compelling arguments that can drive support for public libraries and public library funding: (1) The library provides equal access. (2) The library teaches important and shared community values. (3) The library holds an important, even sacred, place in the community. (4) The library is a community symbol of freedom of thought and progress; the library creates status for its community. . . . They did not equate the library's value to the library's book collection or materials. The objects themselves were not seen as the compelling reason to financially support the library. The impact and value of the library to individual lives and communities are what matters most to library funders. (184)

Ultimately:

an effective library advocacy and marketing campaign in support of increased library funding must ensure that the library is positioned or, if necessary, repositioned as both a unique and essential part of the community infrastructure. The library cannot be viewed as a place of information, an institution that is "nice to have" but not essential, or more important to the past than to the future. Instead, an effective messaging platform must present today's library as a place of transformation. The library is a vital part of the community infrastructure, as vital as fire departments, police, schools, and parks. It is a necessity, not a "nice to have," for a community prepared to compete in the future. The library offers a return to individuals as well as to the community. (187)

If libraries reposition themselves so that they are truly community-centered institutions, if we leave behind the notion of the library as simply an information provider, and if we look at our tools as tools rather than as ends in themselves, we become better able to envision and create the future of our libraries. If we can conceptualize libraries in a new way and focus not on where we can't compete, but on where we can excel, we stand a better chance of demonstrating our worth in more compelling ways. Long recognized that this would be essential work for librarians, but notes that "community building is hard work. It means being bold and taking risks. It means listening and working with diverse groups. And it never stops" (Long 1999, 32). She was correct on all counts—and indeed the work doesn't stop. And truly, when a community-centered library focuses on creating a transformational place that will meet local community needs as a way of making itself relevant for the future, the work *won't* ever stop. And while challenging, we see this kind of work as exciting. When we work with our communities and for our communities, we create the libraries of the future little by little, day by day, ensuring that our institutions will continue to fulfill their missions for years to come.

BIBLIOGRAPHY

American Library Association. 2011. "Keeping Public Libraries Public: A Checklist for Communities Considering Privatization of Public Libraries." American Library Association Office of Library Advocacy. http://www.ala .org/tools/files/outsourcing/REVISEDSEPT2011_ALAKeepingPublic Libraries%20PublicFINAL2.pdf.
DeRosa, Cathy, and Jenny Johnson. 2008. *From Awareness to Funding: A Study of Library Support in America*. Dublin, Ohio: OCLC.
Griffiths, José-Marie, and Donald W. King. 2011. *A Strong Future for Public Library Use and Employment*. Chicago: American Library Association.
Hill, Chrystie. 2009a. *Inside, Outside, and Online: Building Your Library Community*. Chicago: ALA Editions.
———. 2009b. "TEDxColumbus: Chrystie Hill." Online video clip, 21:06. October 20. http://www.youtube.com/watch?v=5fhZPPdrYyQ.
———. 2011. "TEDxRainier: Libraries Present and Future." Online video clip, 12:39. December 28. http://www.youtube.com/watch?feature=player_ embedded&v=ohKEWTXk0F8.

Jerrard, Jane, Nancy Bolt, and Karen Strege. 2012. *ALA Special Report: Privatizing Libraries*. Chicago: American Library Association.

Long, Sarah Ann. 1999. "Planning for the Next Century." *American Libraries* 30 (10): 32.

Scott, Rachel. 2011. "The Role of Public Libraries in Community Building." *Public Library Quarterly* 30 (3): 191–227.

Streitfeld, David. 2010. "Anger as a Private Company Takes Over Libraries." *New York Times*, September 26.

Part II

HOW TO CREATE COMMUNITY-CENTERED LIBRARIES

CHAPTER 4

Allocate the Resources

When a library makes the decision to become more community centered, it is imperative that it evaluate its resources. When contemplating increased programs and services for a given community's diverse populations, and the personal touch that a truly effective library's community services require, librarians may begin to realize that current library responsibilities need to be restructured, physical spaces reevaluated, and mission statements reexamined. These changes require a commitment from library boards, administration, and general staff members. In order to thrive, community-centered library services call for the same basic nourishment that traditional library services require: money, personnel, time, and physical spaces and equipment. While these resources won't appear overnight, we're confident that any committed and enthusiastic library staff can bring about the necessary changes over time. This chapter will examine why and how to allocate these resources with a focus on advocacy, fund-raising, volunteers, and creative use of the library's existing physical resources.

WHY

The allocation of resources is the foundation of community-centered library services, and is a strong indicator of a library's commitment to its community. In the quest to best serve our patrons, and maintain relevance in changing times, these building blocks are essential. Although putting these cornerstones in place may seem daunting at first, both the library and the community will yield generous long-term benefits from these initial investments. Allocating resources communicates that the library is committed to responsive services and community-centered programming. When a library provides the means for new responsive programs and services, library use increases, user satisfaction increases, and the public library itself gains relevance and respect in the community.

The Adams County (Colorado) Library's Anythink initiative is a shining example of what can happen when a library allocates the necessary resources to rethink old and implement new programs and services. Previously dubbed the worst library system in the state (Oder 2010), this library system overhauled everything, including its classification system, public relations plan, buildings, and job titles and descriptions for librarians. The result of Adams County's creativity and forward-thinking approach is a library system where "usage statistics . . . have vaulted, and building openings make for community celebration. Job applicants line up. Anythink has joined the short list of must-see libraries for those thinking ahead" (Oder 2010, 18).

While Anythink is an extreme example of resource allocation and reallocation, it's important to recognize that even very minor changes can still make a big difference in your community. For instance, when a library adds a teen librarian position, that library is able to better serve a large segment of the population with the addition of just one staff member (see chapter 15 for more about the importance of having a youth services librarian). An even simpler idea, and one employed at the Reading and Peabody (Massachusetts) Public Libraries, is to offer a small bookcase of popular adult titles in the children's room. With this very simple collection move, the library better serves parents who might find themselves unable to make frequent visits to the adult collection when they are accompanied by children. As you can see, community-centered libraries cast broad nets to serve as many community members as possible, and gather fans and supporters along the way.

WHAT

As mentioned earlier in the chapter, the key resources required for community-centered libraries are money, personnel, time, and physical spaces and equipment. Depending on the changes a library wishes to make, it may be necessary to implement as few as one or as many as all of these elements. Implementing new services, developing new programs, hiring more staff, and reimagining the building all require searches for new capital (through grants, gifts, or base budget increases), or the rearrangement of already existing budgets. Issues of personnel and time are closely connected. Obviously, every library has a staff, but those staff members are probably already quite busy with their regular duties, which brings us to the need for time. In addition, all libraries have physical spaces, but are those buildings and rooms set up to best serve your patrons? The same goes for equipment. Looking to new models for patron service, libraries may find that they need new equipment to meet community needs, or that they need to repurpose or rethink uses of existing equipment. Access to all of these necessary resources begins with the support of the library board and the library director.

As the library's chief advocates, the board and especially the library director need to fight for the monetary resources necessary for the library to best serve the community. Additional personnel, extended hours for current employees, and new equipment cost money. A director has many duties, one of which is to advocate for the funds necessary for resources like these. Sometimes advocacy means talking to the mayor or town manager, sometimes it involves presentations at local organizations that might monetarily support the library's new vision, and sometimes this type of advocacy happens one-on-one with patrons who might be able to make a difference either by word of mouth, volunteerism, or through their own generosity. In chapters 6 through 8, we will discuss networking, collaborations, and grants in more depth, but you can already see that these concepts are key tools for strong and effective administrators who strive to raise the necessary funds to make their communities' libraries the best that they can be.

As we noted in our PLA (Public Library Association) presentation, "Trustee and director support is fundamental to programming success" (Edwards et al. 2008). If you are a director, you have the ability to grant your staff the time and flexibility necessary to make positive changes. If you are not a library director, you have an opportunity to present your supervisors with new and exciting ideas for consideration. In Peabody, as with many other public libraries, library programs in all departments have increased dramatically over the past ten years. This means that librarians spend far more time planning, promoting, and running events than they ever have in the past. Because of the time required for programming, the jobs of Peabody's department heads have evolved quite a bit from those of traditional collection management and circulation-based library services. While some of this evolution happened very slowly and naturally, at other times the director and our staff had to revisit the way we do things and make changes.

A key example of a time when we had to make a significant change occurred just recently. As the primary programming librarian for adults, Kelley is responsible for much of the library's public relations and marketing needs. In the past, each department promoted its own events separately via various combinations of press releases, flyers, an online events calendar, an e-newsletter, and program brochures. In response to patron requests to see all events for adults listed in one place, the library director asked Kelley to work with the reference librarian, the archivist, and the two branch librarians to coordinate a unified marketing plan for adult events library-wide. The new plan required a good deal more of Kelley's time than the promotion of her department's programs alone. The library director recognized this challenge and solved the problem by redistributing some of Kelley's collection management responsibilities to another librarian. Thanks to the support of her director, Kelley was able to work with other Peabody librarians to plan and implement a new event marketing strategy that responds to patron needs and brings Peabody's librarians together to create a stronger, more unified host of services.

In the case described above, the library was able to make changes with existing staff, but sometimes community-centered change might require the creation of a new position, or the recruitment of skilled volunteers. We all know how difficult it can be to find funding for new positions, or even extra staff hours, so advocacy on the part of the library director is essential here. Being able to clearly demonstrate what your library does for the community, and being able to communicate why new personnel are essential for keeping your library community centered, is key. Many people think that librarians' sole duties are to check out and shelve books—it is up to the library director to effectively sell what professional and paraprofessional staff actually do, not only for the library, but for the community. Consider approaching a new position in this way—not as another person to work in the library, but as another person to work *for* the community. And when it comes to volunteers, think outside the box. Shelving and weeding projects are all well and good, but a community-centered library not only offers responsive and forward-thinking services, it offers volunteers rewarding opportunities to share their unique skills with their communities. In California, "The Get Involved: Powered by Your Library program began in 2008. At that time the state library was running an initiative to better serve and involve Baby Boomers. After trainings and local needs assessments, more than half of the libraries in the state asked for funding for volunteer programs—this is what the Boomers were asking for!" ("Nonprofit Spotlight" 2012). A win-win, this unique program provides the opportunities that the area's boomers want, and provides the library with volunteers skilled in areas such as fine art, graphic design, digital storytelling, photography, fund-raising, and more.

In addition to money, personnel, and time, a community-centered library requires physical resources in the form of building space and equipment. For example, many libraries already have meeting room spaces available, but others do not. In the absence of traditional meeting rooms, it may be time for a library to revisit the use of existing library spaces, look into local meeting rooms available for library use, or even consider a building construction proposal for an addition to an outdated building. In the case of equipment, funding is the primary issue, and it could be time for fund-raising, possibly through the library's Friends group or Foundation, if those organizations are already in place.

HOW

Once you know what you need in terms of money, personnel, time, and physical spaces and equipment, it's time to get to work and allocate those resources! Remember that new programs and services take time and coordination to implement, so don't feel daunted when you consider your list of needs. With a combination of fund-raising, a flexible view of current job descriptions, volunteer help, and creative use of physical spaces, you will be well on your way to offering the community-centered services your library envisions.

Fund-Raising

For the purposes of this chapter, the term *fund-raising* encompasses all the ways in which libraries seek the funds necessary to fulfill their goals. Fund-raising efforts include advocacy within the community, campaigns by Friends groups and/or Foundations, and taking advantage of grant application opportunities. The fruits of these labors can support anything from library programs to equipment and supplies for new services to a new program space for the children's room.

In the quest for funds, a library's first stop is often a look at its principal municipal budget. As many libraries have received decreased budgets in recent years, advocacy is of the utmost importance if a library director hopes to increase, or sometimes even simply maintain, the public library's percentage of the municipal budget. Advocacy is a powerful tool, and has saved more than one library from closing its doors entirely. In an excellent example of the power of strong library advocacy, when the Troy (Michigan) Public Library faced potential closure, they created a satirical Book Burning Party campaign to get public attention:

> Troy Public Library would close for good unless voters approved a tax increase. With little money, six weeks until the election, facing a well organized anti-tax group who'd managed to get two previous library-saving tax increases to fail, we had to be bold. We posed as a clandestine group who urged people to vote to close the library so they could have a book burning party. Public outcry over the idea drowned out the anti-tax opposition and created a ground-swell of support for the library, which won by a landslide. (Doctorow 2012)

In another excellent example of library advocacy the Friends of the Fargo (North Dakota) Public Library got a ballot measure initiated for a tax increase to support library expansion (Reed and Nawalinski 2008). In this case, the library wasn't in danger of closing, but needed more space to offer services to its growing number of community members.

In addition to the principal municipal budget, many public libraries survive on small-scale fund-raising. Library Friends groups are often the primary generators of public library fund-raising efforts. "For almost a century, Friends groups have been helping libraries purchase furniture and equipment, supporting programs, donating to special collections, and working to get bond issues passed and budgets increased" (Reed and Nawalinski 2008, 177). In Peabody, the Friends of the Peabody Institute Libraries provide funding for the majority of events on the library's busy program calendar. Through book and flower sales, applications for grant funds, and general membership donations, the Friends provide the library with upwards of $8,000 annually to support programs and services. Some libraries also have specialized Friends groups to support particular library initiatives or departments. For instance, the Library of Congress has Friends groups to support the Asian Division, Folk Archive, Music, Law Library, Hispanic Division, and Geography and Map Division, and the Pequot (Connecticut) Public Library has a special Friends of Music group to support the library's musical programming.

For larger donations and estate gifts, some public libraries also have Foundations. According to King County (Washington) Library System Foundation executive director, Jeanne Thorsen, "By raising private dollars, library foundations are able to leverage and stretch public dollars. Donors may have a strong belief in the value of the public library yet do not wish to give their philanthropic gift to a public entity. They will, however, contribute to a non-profit, tax-exempt private organization: a library foundation" (Thorsen 2012). From Andrew Carnegie to the Peabody Institute Library's beloved George Peabody, philanthropists have a history of generosity when it comes to public libraries. Lee Price asserts, "In most communities, whether poor or wealthy, the distribution of wealth forms the traditional bell curve. Public Libraries should not neglect the 10 percent at the wealthy end of the curve. This is where your potential major donors reside. Identify them. Pay attention to them. Educate them. Cultivate them. Ask them for support" (Price 2011, 28). And the library Foundation is the perfect organization to make the approach.

In Peabody, the Peabody Institute Library Foundation enabled the library to purchase new furniture for its historic main room, supports an annual fall concert series, and recently began plans for a fund-raiser to benefit the restoration of the library's John James Audubon *Birds of America* collection. Programs and services like these would be impossible with the library's municipal budget alone, so the library counts on the Foundation's support to make possible things beyond the library's standard operating budget.

Aside from internal fund-raising sources, many libraries also look for grant opportunities to support programming and services. We will discuss grants in detail in chapter 8, but it would be remiss to neglect to mention them here as they can be a substantial resource for libraries.

Flexible Job Descriptions

No matter how much money a library raises through Friends groups, Foundations, and grants, funding can't benefit the community without the staff to put it to good use in the form of programs and services. The implementation of these efforts often requires some changes in a librarian's day-to-day duties, and it is essential that library administrators recognize and support the changes necessary to make the job fit the desired outcomes. For example, librarians assigned new programming responsibilities will require time away from their usual activities, such as ordering materials or an afternoon reference desk shift, so that they have time to plan, coordinate, promote, and run events. At the same time, that new recording equipment in the teen room is likely to increase afternoon foot traffic in the Young Adult Department, requiring the YA librarian to request the help of a part-time aide or volunteer. When a library responds to the community's needs with new programs and services, it's time to reconsider current job descriptions and explore the possibility of creating new positions.

As in any workplace, thanks to new initiatives, technology, and the changing needs of patrons, library jobs evolve with the times. There was a time when technical services librarians maintained a physical card catalog to keep track of materials, but today those same librarians catalog and order books through computerized acquisitions systems, making it easier for both librarians and patrons to find out what items are available in the collection. In the same way, community-centered public services librarians, who once spent the majority of their time involved in collection management projects, may now find themselves primarily wearing their "event planner" caps. When changes like these occur, it's important that a balance is found between employees' current responsibilities and the new duties requested of them. While librarians may be able to maintain some of the activities they have always done, other responsibilities will have to be eliminated or passed on to other staff members, so that time to implement the new services becomes available. In the case of the technical services librarian, one method of getting the job done replaced another, so while workflow may have changed, the elimination of the card catalog allowed the time to work with the new system. However, in the case of the public services librarian, this librarian has been asked to take on added responsibilities, not just replace an old responsibility, so the job must adapt.

In some cases, a new program or service might require a skill not possessed by any librarians currently on staff. In these cases, administrators might decide to offer current librarians the opportunity to attend classes or training to prepare them for new responsibilities, or they might decide to hire a new employee who already has the necessary skills to hit the ground running. In Peabody, when the library needed a new website to promote its growing programs and services, the director offered Kelley the opportunity to take on the project. Kelley knew that her HTML skills were basic and that she would need to take a class to increase her knowledge before tackling the new site. By allowing her time to learn more about web design as part of her job, the director supported Kelley's continuing education. Rather than hiring a temporary outside web design consultant, the director chose to increase the knowledge of her current staff, and now the library is able to maintain its entire website in-house.

While current staff was able to handle the changes in Peabody, when the Fayetteville (Illinois) Public Library wanted to start a Fab Lab, they created a new position: director of transliteracy development. Hired to fill the role, Lauren Bitton Smedley explains that "transliteracy aims to help people communicate across this wide expanse of new technology" (Reeder 2011). In a climate where information delivery changes rapidly, transliteracy addresses digital and visual literacy. In addition to her work in the Fab Lab, Smedley's job is to help patrons understand these new and exciting literacies. As libraries seek to reinforce their relevance in changing times, employees like Smedley, with diverse educational backgrounds and specialized skills, will become increasingly valued in libraries.

Volunteers

In addition to paid employees with specialized skills, strong community-centered libraries offer these unique "job" opportunities to volunteers. Volunteer opportunities are one of the best services a community-centered library can offer, as they provide the library with needed resources to implement services and at the same time offer rewarding experiences for the individuals involved. In public libraries, volunteers shelve books, run programs, sort materials for book sales, teach teens to use new computer software, and so much more. In Peabody, volunteers even assist the archivist with the digitization of historic newspapers and yearbooks. After a positive experience, many volunteers move on to become library employees, and most become strong supporters of and advocates for the library.

Carla Lehn, manager of California's statewide library volunteer program, stresses the importance of "volunteer engagement" versus "volunteer management," emphasizing that "many of the volunteers connecting with the library through the VolunteerMatch hub are people who haven't set foot in a library in a long time . . . when they do come in they are amazed and excited to see how libraries have evolved with the times" ("Nonprofit Spotlight" 2012). When a library is able to match people with meaningful work, which may mean accepting ideas and initiatives from the volunteers themselves, volunteer connections introduce new users to the library, and each connection strengthens the library's place in the center of the community.

Creative Space

When the average person thinks about the public library, the first image that comes to mind is shelves and shelves of books. We argue that, while the library will always be a home for books, it is first and foremost a home for people. To make room for people, who by their very nature want to communicate and share ideas, many libraries have begun to refocus their buildings' purposes so that they serve as gathering places rather than storage spaces. These gathering places take many forms, including cafes, library program spaces, media labs, and public meeting rooms, and all of them are central components in the creation of today's community-centered libraries.

New York Public Library's (NYPL) controversial Central Library Plan is a hotly debated example of a library's effort to create a community gathering place. "The project would convert the main library, now strictly a reference operation, into a hybrid that would also contain a circulating library, many computer terminals and possibly a café" (Pogrebin 2012). The cost of this project is the sale of two branch libraries, and has many critics concerned about the NYPL's role as a highly regarded reference library. Despite criticism, the NYPL's plan reflects the scene in many other public libraries today. Public computer access is generally the standard in today's public libraries, and more and more libraries offer some form of café or snack station for patrons. Even in the tiny town of Jackson, New Hampshire (population 835), the library offers a K-Cup coffee and tea machine for library users. For just $1, patrons get to fill one of the library mugs with a warm drink and, when they are done, the librarians take care of the dishes in the kitchen. While a simple service to offer, Jackson's "café" fosters a warm and welcoming atmosphere that encourages patrons to enjoy the library and the time to connect with each other.

Back in Colorado, at Anythink's Wright Farms branch the library even utilizes outdoor space as an opportunity to connect with the community. According to Pam Sandlian Smith, the Wright Farms branch will offer "community gardens at two branches, enabling Anythink 'to get to know our communities in a way we haven't before'" (Oder 2010, 23). While a community garden may not be a traditional library service, it is most definitely the service of a library that is community centered. The gardens will ignite new interest in the library and beautify the grounds, and at the same time fulfill a need for neighborhood gardening space.

In order to find a home for new services, sometimes a library space has to multitask. In Peabody, the library's archives, which is a beautiful historic room available to the public by appointment only, doubles as a popular program space for lectures and concerts. Because of the dual nature of the room's purpose, in an effort to accommodate both researchers and concert-goers, the librarians who use the space must work together to coordinate a mutually agreeable schedule. The result is that, each year, hundreds of people attend events in a room they never knew existed, and in the process gain a new appreciation for their library. This creative use of space isn't just limited to the archives; during the school year, morning craft programs for adults meet in the library's Young Adult Department, a space much more conducive to painting and stamping than the historic archives.

Sometimes a library's need for space goes far beyond the need for a lecture or craft area. When the Chicago Public Library created the YOU-media Lab, they dedicated the "first ever discrete space devoted to teens at the Chicago Public Library, occupying an open, 5,500-square-foot space on the ground floor of the Chicago Public Library's downtown Harold Washington Library Center" ("Philosophy" 2012). Providing access to computers and media creation tools such as music recording equipment and software, the YOUmedia space not only encourages teens to think creatively, but also encourages them to think about the library in new and positive ways. On a smaller scale, in Peabody, when Melissa wanted to combine the library's YA Drop-In computer space with the Young Adult Department, the library reduced the size of its print reference collection and relocated the magazine collection to make room for computers, tables for homework and hanging out, and a Play-Station. Now, instead of newspaper readers quietly sipping their coffees at the back of the YA Room, the teens truly own their space and pack the room every afternoon after school.

In addition to creating the space necessary for new library programs and services, libraries should also look to already existing spaces as community building assets in the form of public meeting room use. A good library looks beyond books when seeking to give patrons what they want and need, so it is important to realize that the physical space of the library is also a community resource, just like the library's book collection. When a library makes space available for public meetings, it builds a positive relationship with the community. A library's policies should always be geared to allow librarians to say yes to their patrons as often as possible. So, when the local environmental group, the homeschooling meet-up group, the high school drama club, or the neighborhood condo association ask about meeting space, say yes! Non–library users will come to the library for a public meeting, and many will be pleasantly surprised by what they find in the library itself.

CHALLENGES

As with any change, challenges arise, and there are certainly challenges associated with resource allocation. In the quest to put new services in place, often the first hurdle librarians face is resistance to change. Before the implementation of a new program or service, it is of the utmost importance to openly communicate the details to the library's staff members. If you want the support of your staff or coworkers, they need to identify the project at hand, understand their roles in the creation of the service, and have an opportunity to voice any concerns. Informed, involved people are happier people, and the strong support and interest of the staff in new initiatives will go a long way when the time comes to sell those ideas to potential donors, boards, and volunteers.

A related challenge is resistance to the job description changes that go hand in hand with many new services. Some staff members simply don't want their jobs to change, so it is important to listen to their concerns and provide the training and support that will make them as comfortable as possible in their new roles. In addition, nonadministrative staff are often unionized, and union regulations can make job description and requirement changes difficult to implement. It is the job of administrators to work with unions to come to mutually agreeable terms that will provide the best resolutions for both the library staff and the community the library serves.

Another potential challenge is the time required to organize and promote Friends and Foundation groups. Ideally, these groups will come to largely run themselves with little librarian involvement in day-to-day business, but generally a library liaison needs to help with member recruitment and promotion. As with other aspects of resource allocation, it may be time to redistribute some regular library duties, so that a specific librarian has the time to work with these critical fund-raising groups. For more information about starting a Friends group or Foundation, see the Association of Library Trustees, Advocates, Friends and Foundations website (http://www.ala.org/united/).

In addition to time, the economy also affects fund-raising efforts. "In tough economic times, it is critical for organizations to find ways for constituents to give—conveniently and easily" (Lowman and Bixby 2011, 217). In order to make giving as simple as possible for potential donors, a library should offer many ways to give. Cash and check are generally accepted in libraries, but with PayPal accounts so easy to set up, library fund-raising groups should seriously consider opportunities for online donation receipt via credit card. The easier the process for your patrons, the more donations the library will see.

As with fund-raising groups, volunteer organization takes time. Volunteers require recruiting and training, and someone on the library staff needs to be responsible for these tasks. If your library doesn't have a volunteer coordinator, and most don't, it's time to make some job description changes. Although working with volunteers is time consuming, the benefits outweigh the challenges.

In regard to physical space, many libraries don't have the space they need for day-to-day operations, let alone space to offer for public meetings. In these cases, creative thinking can go a long way. Think about the library, and try to look at the space as though you've never seen the building before. You may find that a particular space can serve multiple purposes given just a slight rearrangement before an event. After-hours events also allow libraries flexibility in space utilization. For instance, if the reference area can fit fifty chairs for a lecture when the study carrels are moved to storage, consider hosting an event when the library is closed for regular services. And keep in mind, if you open meeting rooms to outside groups, a meeting room policy is essential. Without a policy, as a public building, the library's meeting rooms have no protection against hate groups and other controversial organizations that might want to reserve a room in the building.

As a final, but very important, note regarding resource allocation, choose your library's mission statement carefully. A well-chosen mission statement will go a long way to support your requests for resources. As we mentioned in chapter 3, the best mission statements leave a lot of room for creative interpretation, and allow for progressive evolution of library services. Think about your community's vision for the library, look to other libraries for examples, and choose words that you can work with. A solid mission statement is something that you can refer to in grant applications, board meetings, and meetings with other important stakeholders.

A library with a strong idea of the resources necessary to implement community-centered services is well on its way to making those services a reality. While there will be challenges, we're confident that libraries and their communities only stand to gain when the public library consciously decides to allocate the resources essential to centralizing its place in the community. With a combination of fund-raising, job flexibility, volunteer help, and creative use of physical spaces, anything is possible.

BIBLIOGRAPHY

"Concert Series." 2012. Pequot Library. Accessed October 4. http://www.pequot library.org/index.php/calendar-events/annual-events-series/concert-series.

Doctorow, Cory. 2012. "Award-Winning Book-Burning Hoax Saves Troy, MI Libraries." BoingBoing. Accessed October 4. http://boingboing.net/2012/06/16/award-winning-book-burning-hoa.html.

Edwards, Julie Biando, Melissa S. Rauseo, and Kelley Rae Unger. 2008. "Running the One Woman (or Man) Show: Successful Adult Programming When You Have a Million Things to Do!" Presentation at Public Library Association National Conference, March 27.

"Friends Groups." 2012. Library of Congress. Accessed October 4. https://wwws.loc.gov/philanthropy/index.php?m=cMain.cFriendsGroups.

"Jackson Library." 2012. Town of Jackson, NH. Accessed October 4. http://www.jacksonvillage.net/Public_Documents/JacksonNH_Library/index.

Lowman, Sarah S., and Mary D. Bixby. 2011. "Working with Friends Groups: Enhancing Participation through Cultivation and Planning." *Journal of Library Administration* 51 (2): 209–20.

"Nonprofit Spotlight." 2012. VolunteerMatch. Accessed October 4. http://www .volunteermatch.org/nonprofits/stories/spotlight.jsp?id=79.

Oder, Norman. 2010. "In the Country of Anythink." *Library Journal* 135 (19): 18–23.

"Philosophy." 2012. YOUmedia Chicago. Accessed October 4. http://youmedia chicago.org/10-philosophy/pages/56 philosophy.

Pogrebin, Robin. 2012. "New York Public Library Defends Plan to Renovate." *New York Times*, April 15.

Price, Lee. 2011. "Wanted: High Net Worth Donors." *Public Libraries* 50 (2): 28–31.

Reed, Sally Gardner, and Beth Nawalinski. 2008. *Even More Great Ideas for Libraries and Friends.* New York: Friends of Libraries, U.S.A.

Reeder, Jessica. 2011. "Are Maker Spaces the Future of Public Libraries?" *Shareable* (blog). November 21. http://www.shareable.net/blog/the-future-of -public-libraries-maker-spaces.

Thorsen, Jeanne. 2012. "Establishing a Library Foundation: Planning, Persistence, Progress." Friends of Libraries, U.S.A. Accessed October 4. http://www.folusa .org/sharing/establishing-a-library-foundation.pdf.

"United for Libraries." 2012. Association of Library Trustees, Advocates, Friends and Foundations. Accessed December 17. http://www.ala.org/united/.

CHAPTER 5

Think Like a Programmer

Once you've evaluated your library's resources, and have a plan in place to strengthen the resources you have and begin building new ones, it's time to get busy! Of all the services necessary to any community-centered library, perhaps the most important are programs. Programs encourage the use of the library as a gathering space, and also provide ways for libraries to demonstrate that they are responsive to communities' needs. According to an article in *Library Journal,*

> Programs have transformed many public libraries into true community centers. They have magnified the importance of the public library to those communities and attracted thousands of new regular visitors who want to participate. Library programs have helped citizens solve all kinds of problems, learn new skills, and even enjoy an evening of entertainment. There is no doubt that a much-expanded and varied array of programs will be one of the key services of the successful public library of the future. (Berry 2012)

Programs enable librarians to get to know their patrons better, and when librarians know their patrons well, they can respond to patron needs more effectively. Also, as we mentioned in the introduction, programming is fun! Programs allow librarians to get creative with their jobs and present nontraditional offerings that put the library on the map in new ways. This, in turn, allows the library to gain greater relevance and importance to a wider variety of patrons in the community.

In this chapter, we will discuss just why programs are so important to your library's future, what you need to do to make regular programming a job element that is every bit as important as collection development, and how you can make programming happen for your library. By the end of this chapter, we hope that new programmers will feel inspired to break out their event calendars and start booking, and that seasoned programmers will walk away with renewed energy and new resources for future event plans. In addition, we hope you use the following information to help administrators and board members understand the importance of a real commitment to programming in their libraries. And, if you're a library director or board member, we hope that you will understand the importance of programming for your library and focus energy on funding programs and supporting programming librarians.

WHY

A community-centered library is not just a building; the people who utilize, gather, create in, work in, and support that library make it what it is. The importance of programming lies in its ability to bring people together. It is this aspect of library programming that makes it such a powerful tool to build community. Good programming is driven by the community's needs and interests, makes potential new users aware of the library's importance, and can even boost staff morale with the excitement of new offerings. The diversity of library programs offered means that programs are a way that libraries can strengthen all sorts of community capital. When community-centered libraries respond to community needs, everyone wins.

When the San Diego County Library (SDCL) saw a steep rise in area home foreclosures, the library began to offer *Home* Owners Mobile Education (HOME) Clinics to help area residents navigate the world of mortgages, real estate, and credit (Berry 2012). A partnership with the U.S. Department of Housing and Urban Development's Housing Opportunities Collaborative, HOME is an award-winning program that has served 3,100 families. Programs like HOME may not be considered "traditional" library services, but just like book-lending and reference services, they serve to educate and inform constituents; the added bonus is that programs like HOME also bring people together and raise library awareness at the same time.

According to Berry's article, since increasing its level of innovative library programming, SDCL has seen a circulation jump of 300 percent in the last five years. Numbers like those at the SDCL prove the ability of programs to increase traditional library use, which in turn reinforces the library's position as an essential service provider in the community. In the digital age, when library relevance is a hotly debated topic, programs that can generate such results, traditional or not, should most certainly be viewed as priorities in library service.

In addition to the attraction of new library users and increased circulation, the SDCL has also reenergized its staff through programming. "The staff of 290 have been energized by a management team and style . . . that empowers them to take risks, come up with new ideas, and offer levels of service that meet people's needs and solve their problems" (Berry 2012). Another important aspect of library programming, the involvement of library staff in both brainstorming and execution can generate levels of enthusiasm that infect every department, not just those directly involved with program planning. Programming is fun, and fun generates fans— from both outside of and within the library.

WHAT

Before a library jumps into event planning, it is important to understand the role of the programming librarian. The programming librarian wears many hats, from event planner to public relations coordinator to host/hostess on the night of the big event. For the purposes of this chapter, we have divided the programming librarian's roles into four categories: planner, promoter, implementer, and library representative.

Planners

As planners, programming librarians research, organize, and schedule events. Research begins with gauging your community's assets, needs, and interests. As a programming librarian, you'll find that research also takes a lot of creative turns. Program ideas are everywhere, and a good librarian looks beyond libraries to find them. Cast a wide net. Sometimes research is leafing through college catalogs for lecture ideas, sometimes research involves surfing the Internet for presenters who have expertise in your community's interests, and sometimes "research" even happens when you're on vacation! Remember that great skateboarding demonstration that you saw at the Warped Tour? Your library's teens would love that; why not contact the local skate shop and put something together?

In addition to researchers, planners also have to be organizers. Once a planner has an idea, he or she needs to find and book a presenter, reserve a meeting room, and take care of other small details that need attention as well. For instance, as an organizer, you might have to keep track of event registration, make sure there are enough chairs set up for everyone in the audience, and attend to details such as making sure there is water available for the speaker or extra pencils for taking notes. A day or two before an event that requires registration, it is also a good idea to make reminder calls or send a reminder e-mail to registered patrons. As you can see, as planners, programming librarians have two very distinct responsibilities: as a researcher, you get to enjoy the "big picture" experience, but as an organizer it's time to take care of all of the practical but necessary detail work.

Promoters

Even with a wonderful idea and all the careful attention to detail you can muster, no program will succeed unless people know about it and, given that the average library doesn't have a marketing department, most programming librarians must become event promoters as well as planners. Programming librarians write press releases, create event flyers and newsletters, and use websites and social networking to get the word out about library events. According to Judith Gibbons (2009) in her foreword to *The Accidental Library Marketer*, "Accidental marketers start out developing handy program fliers or developing attractive computer graphics. Then, wham! Marketing, or what passes for marketing, begins to take up 30 percent, 50 percent, or possibly 100 percent of their day" (ix). And, in our experience, those accidental marketers are usually programming librarians. As you can tell from Gibbons's description, promotion is an extremely time-consuming aspect of programming, and later in this chapter we will address ideas to effectively and efficiently promote your library's events.

Implementers

In addition to planning and promotion, some programming librarians also run their own programs. In the case of youth services librarians, this is particularly common as these librarians plan, implement, and are usually the central figures in story times, craft programs, and other children's events. While not all programming librarians will implement their own events, those who do assume this role have additional responsibilities as performers and presenters. In addition to the planning and promotion previously discussed, these librarians must plan the content of their programs and then present that content to an audience. Librarians who choose to implement their own programs often draw from skills learned outside of library school, personal interests, or unique talents like storytelling or specialized computer skills. Although running a program like this takes time, librarians who implement their own programs don't cost any money above and beyond their regular salary. This makes implementers very valuable people to have on staff.

Library Representatives

Even when they don't implement their own programs, every programming librarian is also a library representative. When librarians host events, patrons get to know them and begin to associate them with the library. Just as customer service is important at the reference and circulation desks, the impression a programming librarian makes is a direct reflection on the library. Especially in discussion-based events, programming librarians have unique opportunities to get to know patrons better than staff members at public desks because, while a circulation transaction might take just a moment, a book discussion could go on for an hour and allows participants the opportunity to connect with each other and the librarian in ways not possible at a public desk. These opportunities allow a programming librarian to be a key social capital builder in a library. As Kelley can attest, even when they're "off duty," programming librarians are recognized everywhere from the grocery store to the highway rest stop as "the one who runs the library events." The good news is that as patrons come to recognize you and develop a rapport with you, they will also tell you what they honestly want from the library. The bad news is they'll also know what brand of salad dressing you buy and what you look like after a six-hour car ride! Whether at the library or "on the road," a good programming librarian develops important relationships with patrons that directly influence the library's program offerings in community-responsive ways.

HOW

Programming requires focused effort from both the administration and the staff members responsible for planning and executing events. Now that you understand the roles of the programming librarian, it's time to discuss how to put those ideas into action. When it comes time to plan, promote, implement, and represent the library, there are many techniques that will help you offer the most effective programs possible to strengthen your library's assets and meet your community's needs. In addition, this section will address specific ways that administrators can support and foster innovative programming for their communities.

Plan

First and foremost, programming librarians need on-the-job time to plan events. Planning includes all of that organizational detail work previously mentioned, but also means unstructured time to brainstorm those creative and unconventional ideas that will position your library as a truly community-driven center. With established time to plan, a programming librarian can then explore a diverse array of resources to obtain event ideas.

Many librarians are familiar with traditional programs such as book groups, author readings, and story times, but for the purposes of this chapter we will focus on unconventional programs and where to find ideas that will please new audiences. A community-centered library offers patron-driven programs and, to do this, a programming librarian needs to know what patrons want. Most importantly, a programming librarian needs to have excellent communication with patrons and members of the wider community. Once you begin to offer programs, you will no doubt get direct patron feedback and requests regarding future events and, often, these suggestions will lead to some of a library's most popular offerings.

In addition to this word-of-mouth approach, surveys and focus groups also help programming librarians determine the events that will best serve their communities. Surveys can be offered to any interested participants via the library's website, or as a printed form available at the circulation desk. Surveys can also be handed out at the end of a program, and these surveys serve as both an evaluation and an opportunity to suggest future events. The advantage of the first type of survey is that it casts a broader net, and you may hear from patrons who might not attend current event offerings. The advantage of the latter is that you have a captive audience more likely to respond thoughtfully to the questions asked. Whatever type of survey you decide to offer, make sure to keep it simple. If a survey is long or complicated, patrons are less likely to actually fill it out. A simple survey with carefully chosen questions provides librarians with the information they need to best serve the community without inconveniencing the intended audience (see table 5.1).

Focus groups require more time and greater organization than surveys, but are wonderful ways to build relationships with community members. When the Peabody Institute Library wanted to attract more library users in their twenties and thirties, Kelley hosted the NeXt Library Café, a focus group to determine events most likely to encourage library use among patrons of this age group. As with any other library event, the focus group was advertised with flyers, press releases, and other standard library promotion techniques. In addition, and this is the case with many focus groups, some participants were directly approached by librarians and asked to participate. It can be difficult to convince people to attend a focus group, but a personalized "ask" is often effective when a passive invitation is not. The result of this group was a long list of event suggestions, including cooking classes, fine arts programs, meditation classes, and a request for a film discussion group that formed in January 2010 and still meets today. In addition, while adult program attendance is still dominated by patrons fifty years of age or older, a core group of younger participants developed as a result of NeXt Library, and this group continues to be very involved at the library.

Another way to involve community members in the planning of library events is through advisory councils. Teen librarians have long known the power of a good advisory board, and we'll discuss their importance for teen community members in chapter 15, but librarians outside the youth services world should consider bringing together residents on a regular basis to advise librarians and plan library events. Just as with focus groups, it can be a challenge to recruit and retain advisory board members. From her work with a teen advisory council, Melissa has learned that it's important to get a group immediately involved in a project of their choosing. This shows members that the library takes their advice seriously and that their work will have tangible results. Other libraries have found that

Table 5.1. Sample Program Evaluation

We need your feedback! Before leaving today, please complete the following evaluation.

Rate your overall satisfaction with the program.

Excellent   Very Good   Average   Poor   Very Poor

Did the program help you to enrich your understanding of the subject?

Yes   No

Did the program help you develop your skill or interest in this area?

Yes   No

How did you hear about the program?

What is the best time for you to attend library programs?

Mornings   Afternoons   Evenings

Are there other programs that you would like the library to host?

Demographic information (optional):

What is your gender?

Male   Female

What is your age group?

21–35   36–50   51–65   66–80   81+

Use the reverse side to comment on the class or library programs in general.

Thank you for taking the time to complete this evaluation. We will use your responses for future program planning.

asking adults to commit to a specific and fairly short time frame (six months, for example) can make it more manageable for those with busy schedules. While this means that librarians will constantly need to recruit, "term limits" can ensure that libraries always have fresh voices to bring new ideas to their councils. Libraries may decide to have one general advisory board, or they may wish to have several, based on specific areas of interest. The Port Washington (New York) Public Library lists on their website an Art Advisory Council, a Health Advisory Council, a Music Advisory Council, and a Nautical Advisory Council. Each council has a different staff liaison, which helps spread out the responsibility and time commitments. These groups not only help with collection development, but they also plan and run events and exhibits at the library. There is virtually an unlimited number of boards of this type that a library could form, and like selecting programs and other services, deciding which councils to establish should be driven by the community. Advisory councils are a great way to leverage community members' assets and interests to benefit the library and the community.

Surveys, focus groups, and advisory councils have their place in planning for services, but they have their limits as well. These methods tend to focus on current library users or new patrons who are demographically similar to those we already serve. To address this gap, in addition to outreach to current library patrons, programming librarians need to communicate with other community organizations who not only have patrons in common with the library, but who serve harder-to-reach community groups. By doing this, local organizations can work together so that they complement each other's services rather than duplicate them. We discuss these types of collaborations further in chapters 7 and 12, but it would be remiss not to mention this concept here.

Another extremely useful tool for library event planners is a connection with other area librarians. To address this need to share ideas, librarians in southern New Hampshire and eastern Massachusetts formed the Library Program Planners Group. This group meets quarterly to share successful (and unsuccessful) library event experiences, make recommendations in regard to local presenters, and discuss issues that pertain to all aspects of a library program planner's job. Most meetings begin with an opportunity for each participant to share the details of a few recommended events and end with opportunities to discuss other program-related issues. Past discussions have included the benefits and problems associated with event registration, relationships with local newspapers, and how to address the needs of local authors in the library. To many, the most useful aspect of these meetings is the compilation of recommended programs. After every meeting, each librarian, even those who are unable to physically attend, contributes to a list of successful events complete with the presenters' contact information. These lists provide library event planners not only a list of great ideas, but also the assurance that other librarians believe that these presenters are easy to work with and offer high-quality programs. In the absence of an area program planners group, librarians can also connect through the "Programming Librarian: An Initiative of the American Library Association Public Programs Office" website (programminglibrarian.org). The site not only provides a place for librarians to share program ideas, but also offers information about grant opportunities and library advocacy.

Although communication with library patrons, the wider community, and other librarians is essential to a good library program plan, some programs are born from pure brainstorming and creative thinking. Cast a wide net. If your community enjoys educational programs, look through college course catalogs or adult education class brochures for innumerable ideas. As you embrace the concept that everyone is a community asset, you'll learn to see everyone you meet as a potential library program presenter; everyone has a special talent and many people would love the opportunity to share that talent with others. Surf the Internet to see what other libraries around the world offer for programs. We've also found that nonlibrary organizations can provide great ideas. For instance, Melissa's Earn-a-Bike program for teens was inspired by Boston-based nonprofit Bikes Not Bombs (n.d.). Also, make it a point to keep up with a few nonlibrary blogs. Shareable.net is an example of a blog community that recognizes the importance of libraries and also promotes an important foundational value of public libraries: sharing. Tuning in to groups that have the same goals as libraries can help a programming librarian expand his or her concept of what a library can do. Train yourself to see program ideas wherever you go. Once you start thinking like a programmer, you'll find yourself always pondering, "How can we do this at the library?"

Promote

According to Kathy Dempsey (2009), "Proven, well-planned promotional techniques can raise the public's awareness of and respect for the libraries we all love" (xvi). Unfortunately, as mentioned earlier in the chapter, event promotion can be the most time-consuming aspect of a programming librarian's job. Given the importance of promotion and the amount of time it takes to be successful at it, it is of the utmost importance to have an organized promotion plan in place.

To begin with, you will need a comprehensive and up-to-date list of local media outlets and their contact information. Most news outlets accept press releases via e-mail, so consider saving all of your public relations contacts as a group in your address book. With that group in place, you'll be able to send press releases to as many local news outlets as you like with just one e-mail. As time goes by, make sure to confirm these contacts periodically. Reporters come and go, and you want to be sure that your announcements get to the right people to make sure they make it into print or onto the web. Also, don't forget your fellow staff members. When you e-mail press releases, consider sending them to all library staff; this will keep staff members up to date about library events and encourage them to participate themselves. A frontline staff well versed in the library's event schedule can provide some of your best word-of-mouth advertising.

In addition, make a list of promotional resources not reached by a traditional press release. For instance, does your library have an online event calendar? If so, be sure that all events are listed with accurate information and plenty of advance notice. Social networking is another excellent way to promote library events, so consider assigning a librarian to manage postings on these outlets. Because of the varied ways in which people obtain information, it is important to maintain a balance of print and web promotional techniques in order to reach all members of the community.

Flyers and event brochures are also excellent ways to promote library events. Even in the age of smartphones, Facebook, and online event registration software, many people still prefer something they can pick up at the library and stick on the refrigerator at home. These print resources also make excellent handouts for board members and administrators, and help raise their awareness of the quality, variety, and importance of library programs. As event promoters, programming librarians often design these promotional flyers and brochures themselves, so some basic familiarity with desktop publishing software is an asset. In order to get their jobs done, programming librarians often need to call on skills, including web design, graphic design, and writing, learned outside of library school.

Another popular event promotion technique is the library e-newsletter. When patrons apply for a new library card, consider asking them to opt in to an e-mail list for library announcements. Subscriptions to services like Constant Contact and MailChimp are relatively inexpensive and allow libraries to reach broad audiences. When the Peabody Institute Library started to offer an e-newsletter, online event registration jumped dramatically. Because of this change, most patrons receive event reminders via e-mail, so instead of having to make fifty reminder phone calls for each event, the library only needs to make five or ten. Patrons love the service, and because they make the programming librarian's job easier, e-newsletters are a win-win.

With so many publicity outlets to update and maintain, it can be difficult to be sure that you've covered all the promotional bases for every event. We highly recommend the development of an "Event Planning Checklist" (table 5.2) to keep track of everything you need to do for each program. In addition to a list of publicity outlets, the "Event Planning Checklist" can include details such as "Send presenter directions to the library," or "Request payment disbursement for performer." Anything you might forget should be included and kept up to date for reference on those days when you just can't remember what has already been done. With a solid plan in place, library programmers can set themselves up to be extremely effective and efficient promoters.

Implement

The most essential ingredient in implementing an event is time. Just as librarians need time to plan and coordinate events with hired presenters, they also need scheduled time to plan events that they implement on their own. In addition, librarians who implement their own events will need time to actually run these events. Sometimes, the same librarian who works at the circulation or reference desk also implements programs. In order to plan and run events, the library needs to carefully schedule employee time so that public desks are covered during librarian-run events.

In addition to time, an event implementer might require training. The typical library thinks nothing of allowing reference librarians to attend database training workshops, so why not let the programming librarian attend a basic course to gain certification in skills that patrons want to learn? For instance, when demand for children's yoga classes in Peabody grew,

Table 5.2. Event Planning Checklist

Event title:
Presenter name/organization:
Phone:
E-mail:
Tax ID for payment purposes:
Cost of event:
Brief description of event:
Special room set-up or equipment?
Will presenter allow photos and/or video for library website and/or local cable TV station?
Publicity:
Library's Online Events Calendar
☐ Reserve Meeting Room   ☐ Post to Public and Adult Services Calendars
Press Release
☐ Created   ☐ Sent
Flyer
☐ Created   ☐ Posted
☐ Constant Contact
☐ Facebook
☐ Include event in Adult Services Events Brochure
Payment and Funding Requests:
☐ Submit funding request to library director
☐ Submit payment disbursement form and invoice to accounting
Pre-Event Confirmation:
☐ Send presenter directions to the library
☐ Confirm one week prior to event (arrival time, final details, etc.)

it made more sense to pay for a librarian to attend yoga teacher certification classes rather than pay an outside presenter every time the library wanted to offer a yoga class. The initial investment for training like this might seem costly at first, but in the long run libraries save money, and increase their popularity with patrons, when they train staff members to run high-demand programs.

Librarians who are willing and able to implement their own programs are very valuable staff members. In addition to greeting people as they arrive for programs, these librarians teach, learn, and actively engage with patrons for the entire length of the event. Talk about a great way to get to know your community, build community capital, and generate library fans at the same time!

Represent Your Library

As we mentioned, all programming librarians are library representatives, and it is important to present a positive image to the public. While excellent customer service is important for any librarian, perhaps even more important to the programming librarian is the cultivation of relationships. Trying to learn the names of program attendees and engage them in conversation goes a long way toward making patrons feel welcome at the library. According to ALA past president Molly Raphael, "Transformation happens . . . when libraries engage in new behaviors and develop programs to support the priorities and aspirations of those communities" (Editors 2012). Through something as simple as friendly engagement, you will learn what your patrons want, need, and already enjoy about the library.

Programming librarians also represent the library when they build relationships with presenters and local organizations. Get to know local college professors and the leaders of area cultural organizations. Many professors and local organizations also have the potential to become regular speakers at the library, or even grant partners at a future date. Your initial impression can make or break a lasting relationship, so you want it to be a good one. As you can see, a programming librarian's role as a library representative is probably the least concrete, but possibly the most important, aspect of the job.

Be an Administrative Program Champion

Up to this point, we have talked specifically about the roles and duties of the programming librarian, but administrative support and enthusiasm are essential to the success of any library's programming mission. As an administrator, you have the opportunity to support this unique work in simple, but incredibly powerful, ways.

Programming librarians, who often have other responsibilities in the library, need time to plan, promote, and implement events. As an administrator, think about ways to adjust staff work time to foster creativity. For instance, allow programming librarians to surf the Internet for ideas, or visit other local venues that offer strong cultural programming. While these activities may seem like "goofing off," they can be effective ways for programming librarians to develop unique ideas that bring community members to the library. In addition, programming librarians need to host and run events. This means time spent away from public desk duties, and may require adjustments to current schedules. And remember that—especially in a small library, where you may not have a dedicated programming librarian—programming should be a standard part of your librarians' jobs. Julie remembers one library where a librarian who wanted to host a book group in the library had to do it, uncompensated, on her own time. This is a surefire way to burn out your librarians and to stifle any creativity that they might bring to the job. As we said earlier in this chapter, programs are fun—but they are also work. A librarian who wants to initiate a program to bring more people to the library, or to offer a new service to the community, should be encouraged to do so on library time, as a part of the job. Other duties such as collection development and management don't go away, of course, but programming should be given priority in the community-centered library.

If a programming librarian's current job doesn't allow time for such activities in addition to current duties, as an administrator, you have the power to rethink the distribution of staff responsibilities. While programming and all it entails may not have been part of a librarian's original job description, a good administrator knows that no job description is set in stone. As you move to bring community-centered programs to your library, it is a good time to make some adjustments that will move your library toward positive changes for the future. As we saw in the SDCL example, a management team that encourages staff members to explore and implement new ideas is an essential core to innovative and effective program development.

Administrators also have the power to raise awareness of and support for library programs among other community groups. When administrators show enthusiasm for library programming at city government meetings, library board meetings, and meetings of other local organizations and clubs, that enthusiasm has the potential to become contagious. When other groups in the community become aware of the library's program mission, the library becomes a potential partner for their own projects, and a place where they can refer members and clients potentially interested in the library's offerings. In addition to raised awareness, when administrators communicate the benefits of library programs to the community, the library's programming mission gains wider support, which is essential to continued success.

As an administrator, take a look at your budget and see what kinds of resources can be redistributed to support programming. While many programs are free or low cost, to sustain quality programming you need funding. Allocating funding to programming ensures that your library will continue to develop responsive services for the community and communicates, as we said in chapter 4, your library's commitment to being community centered. Consider working with your Friends groups and Foundations to funnel the resources they bring in toward your library programs. And of course, as you sit in on local meetings with people who have the power to influence your budget, make sure that you not only communicate your enthusiasm for library programs, but that you also express the need for funds to maintain them.

Finally, as a library director or member of a library board, an important way to show support for your librarians and library programs is to simply show up! Julie remembers that the director, the assistant director, and a library trustee all attended her first program at the Peabody Institute Library. Trustees often attended subsequent programs and it sent a strong message to the librarians in Peabody that their efforts were both supported and appreciated.

CHALLENGES

Perhaps the biggest challenge to library programmers is that most libraries don't have a staff member whose sole responsibility is programming.

That means that all the time necessary to plan, promote, implement, and represent the library needs to happen in addition to all of your other duties. Feeling daunted yet? Don't. Programmers can start small, with just one or two events each month. Bring success stories to administrators and encourage them to adjust your job description to make time for programming. Administrators, pay attention to the feedback you receive from your librarians and patrons, and take the initiative in reviewing and adapting job descriptions in collaboration with your librarians. In addition, look for events that can run themselves. Events such as patron-run book groups, sewing circles, or local meet-up groups are all valuable additions to your library's event calendar, and require little work on the part of librarians. As Boulder (Colorado) Public Library outreach librarian, Ghada Elturk (2003), wrote, self-sufficient library events should be a library's goal: "We should start programs, services and projects that can take on lives of their own and that we are able to let go of after a while" (6). While many library programs will not become independent, the programs that do are great examples of how librarians can facilitate connections between community members. Programs don't have to be productions; they just need to encourage the community to gather at the library.

Another common challenge for programming librarians is the typical lack of event funding in libraries. To solve this problem, programming librarians can look to inexpensive events like the sewing circle mentioned above, or they can look to grants and fund-raising, which we will discuss further in the next chapter. In addition, always remember that it never hurts to send an invitation. The worst a pricey presenter can say is no, and some might just say yes! Many folks are library lovers and are willing to work with the limited budgets of public libraries. And again, don't forget your library's Friends group; many libraries request Friends funding for special events. Ultimately, as we mentioned earlier, we hope that it will become common practice for libraries to include program funding as a line item in their budgets, but until then these are just some of the ways programming librarians and directors can seek financial support for library programs.

In addition to a lack of program funds, most libraries don't have funding for employees with professional marketing and PR skills. According to Dempsey (2009), "Library schools don't prepare their students to do professional-level promotion, and most libraries don't have the extra money to hire those who do have the necessary education. Consequently, there are lots of accidental marketers out there" (6). Programming librarians need to seek out opportunities for continuing education in these fields, and encourage library administrators to support these pursuits. In addition, programming librarians may find other staff members with the necessary skills to offer effective event promotion. Administrators should encourage the use of these skills to properly advertise library events and effectively promote the library itself. Libraries can also consider tapping into the marketing skills of community members who are eager to help the library in a meaningful way.

Proper promotion and outreach are especially important when it comes to community groups that are particularly difficult to reach. For instance, teens, community members who speak languages other than English, and adults in their twenties and thirties are often the minority at library events. Through collaborations with other community groups, which we will further discuss in chapter 7, and an honest outreach effort, library programmers should be able to overcome this challenge at least to some degree. There will always be groups that are too busy (e.g., young parents with full-time jobs), or too involved in other community groups (e.g., teens involved in after-school sports) to have time for library events, but with effective event promotion, programming librarians can at the very least ensure that these groups are aware of the opportunities that await them at the library.

Programming can be the most creative and exciting part of work at the library and, more importantly, programming is one of the most effective ways to raise community awareness of the library's role as a place of participation and connection. As we saw in the SDCL example, programming has the potential to address urgent community needs, boost the use of traditional library services, and bring people together. What better arguments to convince stakeholders of the value of program support? As libraries move forward and evolve with changing times, they should look to programs as the essential service that will ensure their roles as relevant, engaged, and responsive community centers.

BIBLIOGRAPHY

"Advisory Councils." 2012. Port Washington Public Library. Accessed December 17. http://www.pwpl.org/information/advisory/.

Berry, John N., III. 2012. "2012 Gale/LJ Library of the Year: San Diego County Library, Empowering the Public." *Library Journal*, June 5. http://lj.libraryjournal.com/2012/06/libraryservices/2012-galelj-library-of-the-year-san-diego-county-library-empowering-the-public/.

"Bikes Not Bombs: Using the Bicycle as a Vehicle for Social Change." n.d. Bikes Not Bombs. https://bikesnotbombs.org.

Dempsey, Kathy. 2009. *The Accidental Library Marketer*. Medford, N.J.: Information Today.

Editors. 2012. "Transforming Libraries . . . Continued." *American Libraries*, June 6. http://americanlibrariesmagazine.org/features/06062012/transforming-libraries-continued.

Elturk, Ghada. 2003. "Diversity and Cultural Competency." *Colorado Libraries* 29 (4): 5–7.

Gibbons, Judith. 2009. Foreword to *The Accidental Library Marketer*, by Kathy Dempsey, ix. Medford, N.J.: Information Today.

CHAPTER 6

Networking

Now that you've read through the chapters on allocating resources and thinking like a programmer, the next question is, how do you actually start making connections within your community? In chapter 7, we will discuss how to form collaborative partnerships with key community stakeholders outside of the library, but before you can begin to form those partnerships, you first have to find potential partners. It is impossible to be truly community centered without taking the time to invest in building relationships outside the library, so in this chapter we will look at networking. Many librarians are used to networking with others in the profession, primarily through consortia and at conferences. While this chapter will take a look at some of ways in which librarians can network with each other, the principal focus will be on networking with nonlibrarian stakeholders in the community.

Although it is time intensive, networking should, ultimately, serve to reinforce the library as an important element of the community at large. Networking should also reinforce the role of the library as a community-centered institution in the mind of librarians and other staff. Eventually, the outcome of thoughtful relationship building will be the formation of collaborations with a variety of partners in order to develop new library or community services.

WHY

Librarians have been writing about the importance of networking for years. A dozen years ago, Kathleen de la Peña McCook (2000) wrote that librarians need to have a "place at the table" in order to facilitate community building and highlight the value that libraries add to communities. Throughout the book she argues that librarians need to consciously make an effort to leave the library, maintains that librarians must be community members first and librarians second, and asserts that making connections between the library and the community is a responsibility (98–99, 101). In order to make the connections that establish the library as a relevant stakeholder in the community building process, McCook allows practicing public librarians to make the point directly, quoting a librarian who states that "keeping close contact with the trends and needs in [the] community, networking with major players, and finding out about the needs of [the] population are critical" (58). It is this focus on networking toward the goal of community engagement that helps the library stay relevant.

Networking for relevance is a key theme in libraries and community engagement. The focus of the article that launched this book is, essentially, how libraries can demonstrate value in order to remain relevant. As Carolyn Bourke (2005) notes, "It is time that librarians looked beyond simply keeping pace with technology and considered the broader picture of the public library's relevance to its community" (71). Relevance, we know, is about more than providing information access. Many librarians are considering new ways to be relevant already, and progressive public libraries across the country are constantly looking at the broader picture in their communities. However, with the limited staffs and budgets that are all too familiar to public libraries, it becomes difficult to look at the broader picture and adapt for relevance without partners. Networking with others in the community is essential for librarians interested in being community centered. And by reaching out to partners beyond the library doors, the library and the community benefit in multiple ways.

Networking allows librarians to see the world outside of the library. Although most public librarians see a wide cross section of the community in their buildings, there are people in every community who don't use the library. These will include average citizens, of course, but also politicians, local business owners, local religious leaders, members of service organizations, and many others. All of these groups interact with segments of the community that the library may or may not have direct contact with. At the very least, each of these groups interacts with community members in a *different* way than the public library does. A business owner, for example, will have a different sort of relationship with her customer than a librarian will have with the same person as a patron. Each person—business owner and librarian—will interact with and understand the same person's needs from different perspectives. Networking with these members of the community will help librarians develop a more holistic understanding of their communities, simply because others in the community will see local needs, issues, and opportunities from a fresh perspective. These perspectives are important—they help librarians realize that they are not the only people in the community interested in community building and social capital, and "when libraries build networks they will also discover that many other people in the community have dreams about how social capital can be increased" (Bourke 2005, 75).

For this reason, networking has tremendous value for libraries as they meet present needs and plan for the future. A community-centered library must root its services in the needs, desires, and aspirations of its community. To do this, libraries need to ensure that community members have a meaningful role in planning library services. Libraries commonly employ surveys to attempt to include public opinion. Distributed in the library, in the community, and online, these surveys are often the most relied upon method of including public feedback in library planning. Unfortunately, they cannot create a truly accurate picture of your community, nor—more importantly—do they provide a mechanism for substantial community involvement. Most often filled out by those who already use the library, library surveys paint an incomplete picture of your community and its existing assets and needs. Instead, augment surveys by learning about your community from outside the library building, and by building relationships with community stakeholders and community members, you can ensure that your services provide the greatest possible value to your community.

Will networking with people and groups outside of the library necessarily mean that different stakeholders will end up on the same page regarding a local issue or prospective service? No. But the process of building relationships is important to a community-centered library, and though networking might not result in immediate collaborations, growing a list of local contacts is critical for two reasons—such a list of contacts provides resources upon which a librarian can call when he or she plans future programs and services, and such a list allows a librarian to put other members of the community in touch with each other. A well-connected librarian is in an excellent position to foster contacts and collaborations between two entities entirely separate from the library. In this way, a community-centered librarian is addressing social needs by tapping into the most relevant stakeholders and connecting them with each other. This is good for the community and good for the library, as it becomes known as a place that can serve as a catalyst and facilitator for relationship building. As Mary Beth Sancomb-Moran (2005) notes in an article about community networking, "The library is entering a new era, and is making itself indispensible in the best way possible—by proving it is literally an invaluable resource in [the community]" (38).

The other benefit of networking is one more directly felt by the library. Developing a wide network of contacts outside of the library has the potential to result in new library allies and funding opportunities. Many people in the community may not be familiar with the library, what it does, and who it serves. Networking allows librarians the chance to tell the library's story to people who may have no concept of what a progressive, community-centered institution does. Telling these stories is a way of counteracting myths or stereotypes that some stakeholders might still have about public libraries. It also provides an opportunity for people in the community to meet with and interact with librarians on committees, boards, or in service organizations. The library director, and other key staff members, should be very public people in the community and should engage in deliberate networking so that people across the community come to know both the people and the institution. Telling the library's story and putting a face to an institution helps the library become better known by key stakeholders and decision makers in the community. The library can position itself within that group of stakeholders and decision makers by consistently and carefully building a network. Members of that network, as they learn more about the library and the people who run it, may be more likely to collaborate with the library, fund special library or community initiatives or projects, or vote on its behalf. Bourke (2007) outlines the projected benefits of networking and partnerships:

> As libraries have partnered with other agencies, government, and business, they have also been able to expand their programs and services without undermining precarious budgets. Libraries have also used these partnerships and nontraditional funding models to demonstrate the value of programs which have not previously been considered core business . . . community enthusiasm has built a momentum which encourages funding

bodies to make these programs core business and set them within normal operating budgets. (138)

Networking can lead to partnerships, which can lead to new programs or services funded by partners, which can lead to a compelling case on behalf of the library for more secure and consistent funding from local government.

WHO

Libraries who engage in networking opportunities must consider the question from two directions—whom in the community should the library network with, and who from the library should be engaged in networking on behalf of the institution?

The (seemingly) simple answer to the first question is everyone! Of course, networking with *all* community stakeholders isn't possible, even for a library with a large staff. Indeed, one of the points of networking is that it creates a web of contacts, so that one individual or institution doesn't have to have direct contact with all relevant stakeholders and decision makers. The library that is interested in networking should look carefully at local service organizations, business groups, religious groups, nonprofits, and educational institutions. It should also consider communities within the community, which may include ethnic or cultural associations and societies or homes for elderly citizens. Librarians should pay special attention to local governments, and should interact regularly with the mayor, the city council, and other municipal entities. The OCLC report on library support in America notes that, while "seventy-one percent (71%) [of elected officials] have a positive impression of the leadership at their local library . . . just half (53%) believe that their local librarian works closely with local politicians and community leaders to find ways to better the community" (DeRosa and Johnson 2008, 137). This is an area in which active participation on the part of the library director and board can yield great benefits for both the library and the community.

The key is to connect first with individuals or organizations who have similar missions, common funding sources, or who serve similar populations. This can take many forms. For example, libraries, museums, and schools all have similar missions of educating and enriching individuals. They have shared interests in culture and literacy. Likewise, some public libraries share funding sources with other local institutions such as fire departments and other city services. And though their clientele might not overlap, libraries often serve the same populations as local businesses and nonprofits, and all three (libraries, businesses, and nonprofits) have an interest in the economic stability and growth of a community. Taking a look at local businesses, organizations, and institutions and figuring out who is doing what is often a good place to start. Another smart way to begin networking is to figure out who in the library (staff, librarians, Friends, board members) has personal contacts with others in the community. Beginning with people you know is an excellent way to figure out how to plug in to the community in new ways. From there, broader connections can be made.

Successful "libraries have found that forming partnerships with area businesses, public radio, museums, and other institutions has revitalized patronage of their libraries. It has also restored a once flagging interest in their libraries" (Sancomb-Moran 2005, 37). Ashley Parker (2012), a library director in Arkansas who wrote recently about the importance of networking, outlines her contacts in her community, and what benefits the library reaps as a result:

> Our library is a member of the Chamber of Commerce, and I am active in Chamber of Commerce activities. I regularly visit with the mayor, city attorney, fire chief, county judge, quorum court members, local business leaders, teachers, and other community leaders. Our library seeks to be involved in many local fundraisers by donating prizes (library related of course), and is constantly looking for community partnerships. By being involved in our community and actively reaching out to key citizens, I have created a persona for our library that reflects us as a caring, well-rounded, and devoted institution. I know that if I need a heavy piece of furniture moved, a last minute Santa, an emergency donation, or just warm bodies, I have a large pool of people to ask for help and a whole community of people to help me solve problems and create solutions. (6)

Once you figure out who you want to start networking with, it is imperative to figure out who will be representing the library in each specific capacity. We strongly believe that the job of networking in the community, and representing the library in the community, belongs to everyone in the library. The director should always take the lead in representing the library—particularly within city government, where he or she should be a fixture on committees and advisory boards—but others in the building, particularly other librarians and board members, should take an active role in community networking. As we mentioned in the previous chapter, this is especially true for librarians who have programming responsibilities, as networking can lead directly to collaborations that result in new programs and services.

McCook (2000) is direct in her perspective on the role of library administrators in community building. She writes that, because building community is "all encompassing," administrators should "authorize and encourage staff to help build community" through education and development opportunities, which are then followed up by a performance review process that includes community building as an element of job performance (101). Librarians and library staff should be encouraged to form relations with other organizations in the community and should feel empowered to represent the library in public (keeping in mind, as we mentioned in chapter 3, that it is essential that anyone representing the library be familiar with and believe in the library's mission, as well as be able to articulate that mission to others). Where possible, the library should pick up the cost of membership in local organizations. In Peabody, for example, the library picks up the cost of membership to local organizations such as the Rotary and identifies a librarian willing to serve in such organizations. Librarians in Peabody are expected to be interacting continually with community members and organizations outside of the library. It is not uncommon, for example, for Melissa to be deeply involved with things going on in the local school system, or for Kelley to be in regular contact with local organizations and colleges. Indeed, librarians are encouraged to become involved locally and to network with an eye toward what will best serve the library and the community.

Similarly, library administration should encourage library board members to become more involved in networking on behalf of the library. Aside from governing the library, board members should be expected to actively engage in the community as representatives of the library. As ALA president Sarah Ann Long says, "Public library trustees represent serious community contacts" (2000, 7). And everyone—director, librarians, board members, Friends—should be encouraged to sit on committees, advisory boards, chambers of commerce, and service and volunteer organizations as representatives of the library. Even in a small- or medium-sized library, if the director, librarians or staff, and board members can each individually network with one other group or organization in a community, the web of contacts grows—and from that growth can emerge new opportunities for collaborations, partnerships, services, and programs.

HOW

"Librarians who build community must be involved in the community. This means attending civic association meetings, community development corporation meetings, civic networking meetings, comprehensive community collaboration meetings, visioning focus group meetings, town meetings, or neighborhood council meetings" (McCook 2000, 98). Clearly, networking takes time, people, and persistence. There are a few ways in which you can easily begin networking so that it is something manageable for you and your library, rather than something that needs to be done on top of everything else that librarians already do.

One of the best ways to get your feet wet with networking, particularly if it is something that doesn't come naturally to you, is to get involved in library consortia or professional organizations and groups. This enables you to have a ready-made group of individuals with similar interests and concerns with whom to interact. Becoming involved in state or regional library associations is a good way to begin making new contacts and sharing old contacts with new people. Sometimes, these formal groups and associations will lead to more informal opportunities for information and resource sharing and exchange.

It is important, however, not to stop there. Librarians need to work with nonlibrarians if they are to build truly community-centered libraries. The best way to become involved in local community networks is to sit as a volunteer on local boards and committees. Particularly at the local and nonprofit level, this is an excellent way to meet a variety of people from around the community who all bring different things to the table. You will likely meet people with whom you would otherwise not come into contact—and from those new connections and relationships, new collaborations can grow. Similarly, and as we have mentioned before, the library director or another high-level administrator should routinely be at the table on government committees and advisory boards. If the mayor has a monthly or weekly meeting with important city officials (city councils, police chief, attorney), a representative from the library should be there. Particularly for libraries who are funded primarily through city or county budgeting, maintaining a presence in key decision-making bodies is essential not only for building connections but for keeping the library in the forefront of the minds of the people who can best advocate for the institution at the highest levels.

Of course, at the heart of networking is personal relationships, and it is important to remember that forming these personal relationships, which can lead to collaborations, is a part of networking. There are times when friendships are formed and networking will seem less like work than like hanging out with friends. It is important to remember, though, that friendships, connections, and things that seem like "just fun" can all lead to building social capital and creating collaborations that benefit the library and the community. When you can make networking fun, you are genuinely better at representing your library and might be more likely to share what may seem like far-fetched ideas or concepts. This is why pairing the right person with the right network is so important. If your reference librarian doesn't easily interact with bankers and business owners, sending that person to chamber of commerce meetings isn't a good idea. But if your young adult librarian delights in interacting with teachers and school boards at open houses, that is exactly the person you want out in the community.

One important thing to remember about networking is that it takes time; "participating in community functions is time-consuming, but if the community sees that you are interested in the welfare of the community as a whole, you will gain friends and supporters of the library itself" (Parker 2012, 6). Attending meetings is time consuming in and of itself. Add to that service organization lunches, community organization functions or open houses, and volunteer work and you can easily overwhelm your schedule. Bourke (2005) notes that "the thought of attending extra meetings may well bring a sense of dread to the busy professional. Yet judicious attendance at meetings is a critical factor in building worthwhile partnerships" (71). There are several ways to mitigate the pressure of networking, though. We will discuss three of them here—flexible schedules, networking on library time, and getting compensated for networking.

Ultimately, "to participate in community building activities, the librarian must leave the library. Meaningful involvement requires evening meetings and weekends . . . librarians who wish to be an integral part of community building initiatives must be willing to commit to participation during non-work hours" (McCook 2000, 102). This is simply a fact of networking. From an early-morning breakfast with the mayor to a late-evening school board meeting, there will be many times when networking requires a commitment beyond the typical nine-to-five workday. It is important to remember that library administrators cannot expect their librarians to regularly participate in activities such as these and still work a forty-hour week. Providing flexibility in scheduling is key in these cases. Allowing librarians to work odd hours and providing in-building backup to cover desk shifts is a necessary part of networking. To allow networking librarians flexibility in their schedules is not to favor one group of librarians over another. Rather, it is a necessity if librarians are expected to perform networking duties as part of their jobs. Networking doesn't happen on a nine-to-five basis and, if a librarian is hired to do networking as part of the position description, the library must understand that portions of this individual's schedule will be dictated not by the library but by the schedules of outside groups or organizations.

In addition to having a flexible schedule, it is helpful to allow, where possible, all librarians to network during those nine-to-five work hours. If Melissa needs to meet with the school principal or a group of teachers to plan a program, she is able to leave the library during her normal working hours to attend those meetings. Similarly, when Kelley attends program planners meetings, she does this on the clock—often in the middle of the afternoon. Attending service organization lunches, meeting with local religious groups during their morning coffee hours, or attending another meeting during work time should be considered work. Additionally, networking opportunities spring up outside of formally scheduled meetings. For instance, a new business owner might set up shop across the street from the library. This provides a great opportunity for a librarian to meet his or her new neighbor over coffee or lunch and talk about the community, the library, the neighborhood, and to learn about the business and its owner. This should all be done as part and parcel of the job—not as something that a librarian has to schedule after work. If you are going to network, and if you are going to legitimatize networking as a part of the role of the community-centered librarian, allowing people to meet with others during the workday is essential.

Finally, compensating librarians for networking time is a nice way to mitigate the stress of networking. This can be done with compensatory time, with a flexible schedule, with encouraging librarians to meet with others during the workday, and by paying for membership in local organizations or clubs.

CHALLENGES

Networking is essential for the community-centered library, but there are challenges that come along with this type of work. One of those challenges might be a certain amount of criticism or resistance from the community itself. It is not unheard of to be criticized for engagement in networking outside of the library—particularly by people who think that it is the job of a librarian to check out books and sit at a desk. However, we believe—and know through experience—that the best way to have a great library is to spend time *outside* of the library, building local connections that eventually get people *inside* your building, using your collections, and attending your programs. As Parker (2012) notes, "While community outreach and involvement takes time and energy away from library buildings and internal services, providing that extra initiative within the local community is very important" (6).

Once you are outside of the library, another challenge might be the weariness and frustration that can come from having to tell the library's story over and over again. Although this is one of the great opportunities of networking, it can become tiresome and disheartening to have to constantly communicate and demonstrate the library's worth in the community. Particularly with groups who might not be familiar with or sympathetic to what the library has to offer, it can sometimes feel as though your efforts on behalf of the library go unheard—or that you are routinely in a position of having to defend the library. There are several ways to address this challenge. First, be sure that the networking responsibilities are spread out as much as possible. As we mentioned earlier, pairing the appropriate person with the appropriate community organization or group can go a long way toward successful networking. This division of labor also helps ensure that no one person is responsible for making connections throughout the community and can help mitigate the burnout that comes along with this kind of outreach. Second, make sure that all the librarians and staff who are responsible for networking have a clear understanding of what the library does, a compelling way to communicate it, and the freedom to interpret and share the library's mission and activities. This enables everyone to be on the same page but also provides enough latitude for individuals to tailor the library's story so that it is comfortable for them to communicate to others. Third, don't worry about winning over hearts and minds across the board. You may sit on a committee or a service organization for a long time and feel as though no one really understands what you do in the community, but all it takes is one library "convert" to champion your services and programs to others. The key here is showing, rather than telling—if you can find creative ways to demonstrate the value added by the library you can more convincingly tell your story. And if you can find a library convert and get *that* person to tell your story for you, so much the better!

It is very important to remember that, although it is essential to network with power players and decision makers in your community, it is as important to build networks with groups that might be marginalized or less powerful. A challenge, and one that public libraries in diverse communities need to take seriously, involves making sure that your library isn't overlooking minority groups (of any kind) in your community. As Stuart Ferguson (2012) writes, "Attempts on the part of public librarians to bridge the gap between the library and 'at risk' groups require strong networking capacity and partnerships" (30). He goes on, however, to point to research that shows that librarians need to target their networking efforts to specific groups in order to achieve success—a one-size-fits-all style of networking and outreach won't work. Looking carefully at the communities that make up your community is the first place to start. Once you know your community, consider the various cultural, ethnic, and linguistic differences that might make networking a challenge and take steps to educate yourself and your staff about these differences. Don't wait for people to reach out to the library—they may never do so. Instead, connect with these groups in ways that are culturally or linguistically relevant for the group. Where possible, hire librarians and staff from these groups and encourage them to outreach within local communities. Building trust and working toward shared community building goals—especially with the outcome of being a more community-centered library—requires that librarians network with groups that are traditionally underrepresented and marginalized. Relationships with these communities are invaluable for setting up future collaborations that result in programs or services that might be of vital importance.

Networking is a critical first step in building collaborations and partnerships within the community. These collaborations, as you will see in the next chapter, can lead to rich, innovative, and sustainable programs and services that truly meet community needs and interests. Networking allows you to tell the library's story, to become involved locally in your community, to build relationships with key groups in the community, and to position your library as a catalyst for relationship building between groups outside of the library. It takes a tremendous amount of work and time, but strategic and well-thought-out networking will pay dividends for the library and for the community because "collaborative networking provides an opportunity for libraries to reach out to their communities and create an awareness of their services and their importance in the scheme of things locally" (Sancomb-Moran 2005, 52). In other words, it is an important part of building a community-centered library. It may seem that some libraries just have great luck in community building and community-centered programming. But behind what seems like good luck is usually good planning and lots of time building relationships to the benefit of all involved—the library, its partners, and the community. One of the benefits of networking is "the premise of serendipity, good things coming by chance," which "can be assisted by being in the right place at the right time. It takes an ongoing build-up of knowledge to realize where the right place is and when you need to be there. Tapping into local networks and building partnerships is a great way to increase serendipity" (Bourke 2005, 74). From that serendipity can grow programs and services that allow you to reframe your library's story, reposition your institution in the community, and create services and programs that are vital components of the community.

BIBLIOGRAPHY

Bourke, Carolyn. 2005. "Public Libraries: Building Social Capital through Networking." *Aplis* 18 (2): 71–75.

———. 2007. "Public Libraries: Partnerships, Funding, and Relevance." *Aplis* 20 (3): 135–39.

DeRosa, Cathy, and Jenny Johnson. 2008. *From Awareness to Funding: A Study of Library Support in America*. Dublin, Ohio: OCLC.

Ferguson, Stuart. 2012. "Are Public Libraries Developers of Social Capital? A Review of Their Contributions and Attempts to Demonstrate It." *Australian Library Journal* 61 (1): 22–33.

Long, Sarah Ann. 2000. "Trustees Can Be a Powerful Lobbying Force." *American Libraries* 31 (5): 7.

McCook, Kathleen de la Peña. 2000. *A Place at the Table: Participating in Community Building.* Chicago: American Library Association.

Parker, Ashley. 2012. "Community Activism: Yes You Should!" *Arkansas Libraries* 69 (1): 6.

Sancomb-Moran, Mary Beth. 2005. "Community Networking: Making the Connection." *Bookmobile Outreach Service* 8 (1): 37–55.

CHAPTER 7

Collaborations

At the start of her term as president of the American Library Association, Sarah Ann Long chose as her theme "Libraries Building Communities" and noted that this "means collaborating and forming partnerships and alliances. Libraries have always done this to some extent. But times have changed. And we can no longer do our work alone. To be effective, we need to work with other libraries, groups, organizations, and individuals who share our goals" (Long 1999, 39). A truly community-centered library must make collaborating with community partners a top priority. Collaborations are often touted and treated primarily as a way for libraries to publicize their services. While working with others does often introduce people to the wonders of their public library, partnerships that are most valuable to our communities and our patrons are more than just marketing opportunities. Substantive collaborative projects between libraries and community partners should improve a library's connection to and enrich the community in specific, identifiable ways. For the purposes of this book, we can use Julie Todaro's definition: "Collaborations and partnerships are, in the broadest sense, connections between and among people and groups to share interests and concerns, and create visions for the future" (Todaro 2005, 137). In the context of community-centered libraries, these connections should ultimately result in actions, such as the creation of a service or a project to benefit the community.

WHY

Community building by its very nature requires relationship building and connections among individual and organizational community stakeholders.

It cannot be done in a vacuum. This means, of course, that the community-centered library will need to jump into the work of building working relationships with many different groups and individuals, as we mentioned in the previous chapter. Creating collaborations may not be an easy or quick process, but luckily, it can be rewarding, energizing, and even fun. Dream projects that aren't possible with library budgets and staffing can become realities if the work and the benefits are shared with others in our communities. Todaro and others have detailed the long list of the benefits that collaboration can bring to libraries and their partners. Lists like Todaro's are helpful when librarians work to convince boards or administrators of the value of partnership creation. Here, however, we will focus on connections, scale, and resilience, three rewards of partnership we have identified as most relevant for libraries that wish to build community assets.

Connections

Collaborations are a vital way that libraries connect with the larger community. It is through the relationships formed by library/community partners that social capital is built. This development of social capital is a crucial part of community building. As we illustrated in chapter 6, when the library works with allies from the public, private, or nonprofit sector, it is essentially serving as a bridge. Some library partnerships will provide bridges from library patrons to outside groups and resources. Others will bridge the gap between nonusers and libraries. Still others will build bridges directly between individuals within the community. The best collaborations will accomplish more than one of these, building trust and ties among neighbors, their social institutions, and local government, including the library.

While they create bridges between various segments of the community, libraries also strengthen the ties that the collaborators and community members have with their community. For example, one of Melissa's rewarding collaborations involved the local workforce development board, the city's vocational high school, and the library. Vocational school staff identified some of their most promising and hardworking students. They, along with the workforce investment board, coached the students on how to succeed in the workplace. Students learned about filling out applications, interviewing, workplace etiquette, and so forth. The library interviewed and selected teen workers who would be paid minimum wage to perform odd jobs around the library after school. The workforce investment board used federal grant money to pay the teens, while Melissa supervised them during their six-to-eight-week employment and worked with them to complete learning plans provided by the workforce investment board that spelled out the goals of the experience. Vocational school staff checked in periodically with the library and the students to ensure that things were going well.

It was not an elaborate partnership and had fairly modest goals (providing good jobs for teens and providing the library with reliable temporary employees) on the surface, but the benefits were numerous. The library had worked with the workforce investment board previously and this project strengthened the organizations' ties. The workforce investment board appreciated that the library was dependable about filing the required paperwork and that the library provided structured, supervised jobs for youth. Even after this relatively short collaboration was over, they knew they could turn to the library in the future for good placements for teens. At the same time, in the summer when the library needs temporary workers, but rarely has the budget to pay them, the workforce investment board helps out. The vocational school and the library, both equally committed to community collaborations, have gone on to run numerous mutually beneficial projects together. As for the teens, they learned valuable workforce skills, earned a paycheck, and, most importantly from our viewpoint, developed important community connections with the workforce investment board and with the adults they worked with at the library. This one example shows how even simple library partnerships can build human capital (in the form of the teens' increased job readiness) and social capital (in the form of the bonds created among the various players).

Speaking of the importance of community collaborations for teen patrons, Robyn Vittek (2010) says, "It is not always easy, but it is vitally important. Not only does it make life easier for the teens and provide them with learning opportunities, but by investing in the community, they feel stronger ties to stay and improve the community as they grow up, go to college or learn a trade, and have the choice as to whether to stay or to go" (13). It is true that youth benefit tremendously from being brought into contact with a diverse array of community members (see chapter 15 for more about how community-centered libraries collaborate with youth). We go further and contend that in today's world Vittek's logic applies to all the members of our communities. All people, not just youth, are mobile and many are disconnected from their communities. The collaborative efforts of libraries are needed by all segments of our population.

Scale

When libraries collaborate with community partners, they can increase the size and scope of the services they offer. While some collaborative projects and services will require a monetary commitment from the library, and while all of them will require staff time, the fact remains that partnerships can enable your library to offer bigger and better services than you'd be able to offer on your own. Many One Book, One Community reading programs are good examples of how expanding library programs out into the community can work. Partnerships with schools, senior centers, local businesses, city government, and others widen the reach of these reading initiatives.

Resilience

Julie and Melissa have argued elsewhere (Rauseo and Edwards 2012) that collaborations make library services and community projects more resilient to the fluctuations that naturally occur over the course of projects, especially long-term ones. Peabody's Summer Food Service Program, which provides lunches to youth in at-risk neighborhoods during the summer, is a big undertaking, requiring commitments from a variety of groups. The first summer the library partnered with a community substance abuse prevention group, the senior center, a local church, and the workforce investment board. The program also required a variety of volunteers from groups as diverse as the sheriff's department and the city's Rotary Club. During subsequent summers, some partners, including the library, have not been able to play the same roles, due to staffing shortages, renovations, and other constraints. Having so many partners, and being willing to recruit new ones, has allowed the project to carry on despite these obstacles.

When working with nonprofits and other government entities, changes in funding, board members, and staff can all lead to priority, and even mission, changes. Similar changes face private sector partners, with additional variables like economic conditions coming into play. Pair these with the changing conditions within the library itself and it's easy to see why communities need to be deliberate about ensuring the resiliency of projects. Community collaborations are one of the most successful ways to make sure that valuable community services are maintained long term.

Community collaborations have the potential to allow libraries into service areas that expand the traditional roles of literacy and information services. As we will discuss in chapter 9, public libraries are often among the first institutions to recognize new community needs. When unemployment rises, libraries see an increase in job seekers looking for resume help. When homelessness increases, our patrons seek the names of emergency shelters. It was when the librarians in Peabody saw how many children were spending hours in the library each day without snacks or lunch that they began to take the steps that led to the Summer Food Service Program.

Because they are aware of community needs and know how bring people together to solve problems, community-centered librarians often find themselves in the position to create partnerships that expand their sphere of influence. In the area of unemployment, for example, in addition to creating resource guides and running one-time resume workshops, the Philadelphia Public Library goes a step further and actually provides jobs for homeless community members. This project started as a collaboration between the library and the nonprofit organization Project H.O.M.E. to hire homeless individuals as library bathroom attendants. These attendants have dramatically reduced the number of problems library staff have with homeless patrons using the restrooms to bathe. Building on the success of this program, Project H.O.M.E. and the library launched the H.O.M.E. Page Café, located in the main library. The café employs recently homeless adults who are part of Project H.O.M.E.'s jobs programs. Working at the café not only offers full- and part-time work, but it also provides workers with valuable job skills training (Price 2009).

Philadelphia's innovative project shows how public libraries can be proactive in helping their communities build important assets. To do this, libraries will need to broaden their network of relationships and look in untraditional places for collaborators.

WHO

Identifying potential partners should not be challenging for librarians who have put in the effort to network within their community (see chapter 6). Table 7.1 suggests some valuable potential partners, but most libraries

Table 7.1.   Partners to Consider

Public	Private	Nonprofit
• Elementary, secondary, vocational, special education, and charter schools • City/town departments—senior centers, recreation departments, health departments, police, community development, public housing administration, etc. • State agencies • Federal agencies • Community colleges • State colleges and universities • Public health clinics • Veterans hospitals • Court systems • Prisons and juvenile detention centers • Military bases • Public radio • Public television *In your community:* • _____ • _____ • _____ • _____ • _____ • _____ • _____ • _____	• Businesses—of all types • Fitness facilities: gyms, health clubs, dance schools, yoga and karate studios, etc. • Group homes (may be private or public) • Business cooperatives • Nursing homes • Private colleges and universities • Local sports teams (amateur and professional) • Chamber of commerce • Doctors/hospitals • Women's groups • Local artists, writers, musicians *In your community:* • _____ • _____ • _____ • _____ • _____ • _____ • _____ • _____ • _____ • _____	• Private and parochial elementary and secondary schools • Homeschooling groups • Soup kitchens and food pantries • Homeless shelters • Places of worship • Parent/teacher associations • Labor unions • Professional associations • YMCAs • Meals on Wheels • Time banks • AARP • Museums • Cultural organizations • Community action programs • Fraternal organizations: Rotary, Lions, Elks • Community Development Corporations • County/state fairs • Local festivals • Support groups • Community theaters • Historical societies • Social service agencies • Community clubs • Community television stations • Community radio stations

should be able to generate a community-specific list twice as long. Almost any local group is a potential valuable ally for a community-centered library with creative and open-minded staff. Once librarians begin exploring their cities and towns for organizations that are also seeking to build assets and strengthen communities, they may well find some unusual allies. In fact, when faced with an especially challenging or perplexing community need, it can be important to have some new types of partners. As Borrup (2011) has said, "If you bring together the usual people, you'll get the usual results" (155). For a fresh perspective and a new supply of ideas, mix your partnerships up. Opening up the door to working with new groups can reap valuable rewards for libraries, patrons, and communities.

It is also worth noting that, while collaborations can and should be created with organizations, libraries should remember that partners needn't be groups at all. Individuals within your community are valuable assets as well. Libraries often make use of the time of volunteers, but it is less frequent that they truly leverage specific talents of their community members. This can be a bit of a leap of faith, since community collaborations with individuals involve ceding some control to your fellow collaborators. Your traditional volunteers may shelve books or dust shelves, but a community partner will assume some (maybe even most) of the responsibility for a project. The national TimeBanks movement (www.timebanks.org) takes as one of their guiding principles the belief that *we are all assets* and we all have something to contribute to our communities. Community-centered libraries would do well to adopt this mantra. Once librarians start looking at community members with this in mind, a whole world of potential will open up. Local artists, schoolteachers, retired tradespeople, unemployed human resource workers, homemakers skilled at cooking or gardening, and others can all add value to their libraries and communities. A local farmer may not be a traditional partner for a public library, but Kelley tapped into the considerable knowledge base of one and was able to offer a popular introductory program on community-supported agriculture.

To return for just a moment to time banks, it is worth pointing out that these community groups, which are catching on across the United States, are a treasure trove of potential collaborators. Time bank members are, by nature, inherently community oriented. They join these networks to exchange services with one another on the basis of hours. All work is valued equally, so one hour of babysitting is treated as equal to one hour of tax preparation assistance. Members earn "time dollars" by providing services and can then "spend" these credits receiving services provided by other members. Many time banks allow organizations to join as institutional members and then provide and receive services. The Peabody Library is an organizational member of the Time Exchange of the North Shore. The library can earn time dollars by allowing the Time Exchange to host some of their committee meetings in the library's community rooms and having staff run informational sessions and orientations for new members. Time bank members are a talented group offering services ranging from running after-school drop-in crafts for teens to offering resume assistance, to running line dancing classes. Participating in a local time bank can put libraries in touch with many potential partners.

HOW

Once a library has decided to join the rewarding world of community collaborations and has identified long lists of potential partners, it's time to figure out how to make the potential partnerships actual collaborations. On some lovely occasions, libraries will be approached by other community organizations and invited to work on a project. Librarians in this enviable situation need only respond with a cheerful yes! We highly advocate adopting the policy of saying yes first and figuring out the details later. Especially when working with a new partner, it is important that library staff bring flexibility and enthusiasm to collaborations. Making a habit of responding in a positive way to new projects will make community partners eager to work with the library again in the future.

Many times, however, especially if a library is new to the work of community building through collaborations, it will be up to library staff to take the lead on a project. Before a library approaches a new partner, it is helpful to spend some time thinking about three specific things. First, what do you want this project to be or accomplish? Second, what assets does your library bring to the partnership (see table 7.2)? Third, what do you want your collaborators to bring to the partnership?

Once you have a general proposal (that you realize will be tweaked and changed with your partners) fleshed out, you are ready to reach out to your desired collaborators. While many people and groups will love being approached and will be eager to work with you, others may be reti-

Table 7.2.   Assets Public Libraries Bring to Community Collaborations

• Physical space (indoor and outdoor) • Research skills • Information resources • Technology • Literacy knowledge • Flexibility • Community trust • Strong dedication to the values of equal access, privacy, intellectual freedom, and more • Staff time • Money • Library volunteers, Friends groups • Individual staff skills • Enthusiasm • Knowledge of the community • Patrons • Grant writing skills • Marketing/publicity experience	*Assets your library brings to partnerships:* • _____ • _____ • _____ • _____ • _____ • _____ • _____ • _____ • _____ • _____ • _____ • _____ • _____ • _____ • _____ • _____ • _____

cent and will need you to explain the benefits of working together. More commonly, people will like the idea of collaborating but might not be responsive to your overtures, because of the busyness of their schedules. If this happens, the first thing to do is to assess who on your staff is the best person to make contact with the organization. It may not be the most obvious choice of the library director, youth services librarian, or outreach librarian. Melissa tried for several years to reach out to a local private school but never had much success. Instead, it was a part-time library aide who had graduated from the school who mentioned to the school principal that the library is an excellent resource for their students. That was the start of a great library/school relationship.

Another consideration may be who in the potential partner organization you (or another staff person) approach. Directors, owners, CEOs, school superintendents, principals, and other high-level leaders may appreciate the benefits of collaborating in theory, but are too busy to do the legwork. It may be someone lower down the chain of command who will go all out to make your project a success. If the boss isn't responding to your e-mails, try another employee before you give up hope.

Remember, when you are first working with a new group, it may be best for all parties that you start out small. Your wonderfully creative new service may not be the best first partnership with a new group. Try something a little smaller and give it your all. Once your new community colleagues see how beneficial and easy it is to work with the library, they will be eager to take on new projects.

Once you have the buy-in of your community partners and get to work, keep the lines of communication open. In a time when we can all be too isolated by technology, one of the wonderful benefits of library partnerships is that they put community members in touch face-to-face. That does not mean, however, that you have to send telegraphs to communicate with your partners or run programs that ignore the best tech innovations. As Todaro (2005) points out to librarians, "[The best collaborations] find ways to involve people face-to-face but make maximum use of emerging and existing technologies" (140). In part III, we will highlight a number of library projects that successfully leverage technology to the benefit of the library and the community. It's worth having a conversation with your partners about what technology will help you meet your goals.

As you begin to get the word out to the general public about your community-centered project, remember to always acknowledge the contributions of your partners. In all marketing materials, flyers, press releases, and so forth, list all the parties that worked together to bring about the great service. When talking to reporters, stress how valuable your fellow collaborators are. If an organization, business, or group went above and beyond in their contributions, consider sending a letter to the editor of your local papers publicly thanking all those involved. After the Peabody Institute Library ran its first Earn-a-Bike program for teens, Melissa sent such a letter acknowledging the Peabody Police Department for supplying the bikes our teens worked on and the local bike shop for donating time, expertise, tools, and parts. Such publicity helps generate goodwill and/ or an increase in business for your partners, and everyone likes to hear a thank-you for a job well done.

CHALLENGES

Not all community-centered collaborations will run smoothly from beginning to end. You will face some challenges before you even begin to implement a new project, while others will pop up along the way. Anticipating what these may be and working through them in advance will help a great deal.

A few potential sticking points that should absolutely be addressed before all parties agree to participate are

- Time
- Money
- Organizational values—intellectual freedom, ethic of free services, etc.
- Need to share facilities, control, money (Berry 1997, 6).

John Berry (1997) has pointed out that many of our great potential partners have fundamentally different core beliefs and missions from a public library. Schools, for example, have a different charge within the community when it comes to intellectual freedom and privacy, and businesses may need to be reminded of the commitment public libraries have to equal access and free services (6). These differences should be able to be worked out if addressed immediately and respectfully.

Some of the challenges community-centered librarians will face, especially those that require libraries to cede control to partners or allocate library funds in a new way, are similar to the ones libraries faced when they began partnering with each other to form networks for resource sharing. Libraries overcame these obstacles to create consortia that have had tremendous benefits for patrons. We believe that community collaborations have the potential to be just as valuable to a twenty-first-century library for librarians who are willing to work through the new issues presented.

Despite our best efforts, some collaborations will not work out. Librarians should take heart if one of their efforts to create a new community partnership doesn't end in the creation of a successful program. While of course that is the aim of the community-centered librarian, Todaro (2005) reminds us that when participating in the hard work of community building, "Even if a few original or even lofty goals are not met in the end, the process of bringing people together to discuss the critical issues can be the single most important element of the process" (156). If a project fails to come to fruition or flops soon after implementation, librarians must remember to be forward thinking and immediately start to consider how the relationship building that took place can be channeled into making the community's vision become a reality.

As they go about their daily routines of working with others committed to improving their communities, librarians must remember that the work in which they are engaged is important. Berry (1997) sees the high stakes and even higher rewards of working together: "If the movement toward collaboration survives, it could mean restored faith in public institutions, new civic pride, and new evidence that government has the power to solve problems. Those are such compelling needs in our self-absorbed American society" (6). They are also needs that community-centered libraries can help meet through collaborations.

BIBLIOGRAPHY

Berry, John, III. 1997. "Why Risk a Community Mission?" *Library Journal* 122 (16): 6.

Borrup, Tom. 2011. *The Creative Community Builder's Handbook*. New York: Fieldstone Alliance.

Long, Sarah Ann. 1999. "Building Communities Is Our Business." *American Libraries* 30 (7): 39.

Price, Lee. 2009. "The Story of the H.O.M.E. Page Café." *Public Libraries* 48 (4): 32–40.

Rauseo, Melissa S., and Julie Biando Edwards. 2012. "*Summer Foods, Libraries and Resiliency: Creative Problem Solving and Community Partnership in Massachusetts*." In *Public Libraries and Resilient Cities*, edited by Michael Dudley, 89–100. Chicago: ALA Editions.

Todaro, Julie Beth. 2005. "Community Collaborations at Work and in Practice Today: An A to Z Overview." *Resource Sharing & Information Networks* 18 (1–2): 137–56.

Vittek, Robyn. 2010. "The People in Your Neighborhood: Using Local Collaboration to Advocate for Teen Patrons." *Young Adult Library Services* 9 (1): 13–14.

CHAPTER 8

Get Grants

As we mentioned in chapters 4 and 5, community-centered library services require money, and all too often those funds don't come out of the library's standard operating budget. In a time when libraries struggle just to maintain their buildings, pay staff salaries, and build collections, new programs and services can seem far out of reach. After reading this far in the book, you have the resources, the ideas, and a long list of eager community partners, but you might be starting to wonder, "Where will I find the money for all of these wonderful programs and services?" This is where grants come in. According to Julie Flanders (2010), "Despite these difficult economic times, philanthropy is alive and kicking. Foundations, businesses, and government agencies are still giving, and persistent grant writers can still find opportunities to secure funding for their projects" (472).

Just when you thought you were wearing enough hats—programmer, networker, collaborator, librarian—we're going to ask you to don one more: grant writer. If you have never written a grant before, don't feel daunted. According to Herbert Landau (2010), "Librarians are their own best grant proposal writers. No outsider can write a proposal as effectively as a 'library insider' who fully understands the institution's mission and priorities as well as the needs of the community it serves" (35). In this chapter, we will examine why grants are such an important resource for public libraries, what grants fund, the types of grants available to libraries, how you can identify appropriate grants for your programs, and how to write winning applications.

WHY

Effective libraries learn very quickly how to do a lot with a little, but sometimes we find we need a little more. If a library is to offer community-centered programs and services, librarians must become grant writers. We realize that many librarians have never written a grant, but we firmly believe that anyone can learn the necessary skills. Ideally, all library schools would offer grant-writing classes, and administrators would include this important duty in job descriptions for key staff members. Grants enable libraries to expand current programs and services, as well as offer new programs and services that would otherwise go unfunded and unrealized. In turn, these grant-funded programs and services, which should respond directly to patron needs and desires, increase the library's relevance in the community. By forcing librarians to look at their funding requests with fresh and critical eyes, grants encourage librarians to create stronger programs. When librarians examine grant application questions and requirements, they think seriously about the essence of the new program's or service's purpose in relation to the library's long-range plan, possibilities for collaboration, and how to evaluate the success of the new program. This kind of examination generates stronger and more effective library services that expand the library's presence among other community organizations, and increases patron interest and satisfaction with library offerings. In addition, because larger grants often require multiple staff members to work together to plan programs and services, grants inspire creativity, enthusiasm, and teamwork.

When King County (Washington) Library System saw a need for Adult Basic Education (ABE) classes in its communities, the library made these services an "institutional priority" (Cavinta 2012). To make ABE possible for the library, in addition to partnering with a number of other community organizations, the library system applied to AmeriCorps for assistance. "Currently, the programs are managed by a Diversity Program Coordinator, two Literacy AmeriCorps members, one support staff, and thirty Literacy Advocate Designates (LAD)—librarians that represent the forty-six branches in the library system. Literacy AmeriCorps members are the only staff whose time is dedicated 100% to these services" (Cavinta 2012). There are times when the greatest obstacle to new programs and services is inadequate staffing, and grants are an excellent way to remedy this problem. In the case of King County, a grant provided the library with two extra staff members to execute new services that directly respond to a community need.

Like King County, the Kootenai-Shoshone Area (Idaho) Libraries also responded to a community need with the help of a grant. With a Library Services and Technology Act (LSTA) grant, the library offered "From Your Library," a program "to provide library service to people who do not have access to walk-in libraries" (MacKellar and Gerding 2010, 184). As part of the grant project, the library partnered with the City Parks Department and the Food Service at the school district. Through the combination of great partnerships, a Sprinter van equipped for circulation and other library services, and targeted deposit collections, the library achieved its program goal. According to the library, "The most important elements of a successful grant are strong partnerships and community support. Because we have strong partnerships we have strong programs, because we have strong programs we have strong partnerships" (MacKellar and Gerding 2010, 185). With the help of the LSTA grant, the library provided resources for underserved community members, built relationships with community partners, and in turn strengthened the library's position in the community.

In 2008, when the Peabody Institute Library received an LSTA "On the Same Page" grant to offer Play by the Book, a baseball-themed community reading program, we too built relationships with community partners and patrons, but also built stronger relationships among staff members. The library decided to offer programs for all ages, requiring the efforts of the children's, young adult, and adult services librarians. Branch librarians also got involved, and offered events at the library's south and west branch locations. In addition, the reference librarian compiled an event bibliography, and the assistant director was active in the grant writing and evaluation processes. Through Play by the Book, all of these librarians came together to plan and execute a very successful program, as well as a winning grant application.

Programs like those at King County, the Kootenai-Shoshone Area Libraries, and the Peabody Institute Library are just three of thousands of possible examples of grants' positive impacts on libraries. Given the time to plan and write, any librarian can become a successful grant writer who makes new services possible for the surrounding community.

WHAT

Before you consider the possibility of a grant for your library, it is important to know about the different types of grants available. In the previous examples, we focused on grants as funding sources for programs, but grants also provide resources for needs such as new equipment, collection building, capital projects, preservation, and more. In this section, we will focus on three specific grant categories: government grants, library-specific grants, and private foundation grants. We will also offer examples of what these grants provide for libraries. This is by no means a comprehensive list (for a more complete perspective, please see Kepler's *The ALA Book of Library Grant Money* [2012]), but it should provide a helpful introduction for those getting started with grant research.

Government Grants

Government grants provide libraries with funding for a wide variety of programs and services. From large federally run organizations like the National Endowment for the Humanities (NEH) to small organizations like Local Cultural Councils (LCC), these grants add value to libraries all over the country. Four types of government grants relevant to libraries are LCC grants, NEH grants, Institute of Museum and Library Services (IMLS) grants, and LSTA grants.

Many states offer Cultural Council grants, often managed by town- or county-specific LCCs. In Massachusetts the Local Cultural Council (LCC) Program, according to their website, "is the largest grassroots cultural funding network in the nation supporting thousands of community-based projects in the arts, humanities, and sciences annually." Thanks to LCC grants, Kelley and Melissa have both been able to offer numerous literature- and art-related programs to Peabody Institute Library patrons. Although these grants are not large (they are usually $1,000 or less), they contribute enormously to the support of the library's busy program schedule.

Managed on a federal level, NEH grants also provide exciting opportunities for libraries. Depending on the project, NEH grant awards vary widely, from $2,500 for their Small Grants to Libraries Programs to as much as $50,000 for Digital Humanities Start-Up grants. Popular in public and academic libraries, "the NEH Small Grants to Libraries and Other Nonprofit Institutions program brings humanities public programming to libraries and other eligible nonprofit institutions across the country" (National Endowment for the Humanities). The most recent Small Grants to Libraries opportunity was *America's Music: A Film History of Our Popular Music from Blues to Bluegrass to Broadway*, a scholar-facilitated film discussion series that focused on American music. Previous Small Grants included discussion series on Louisa May Alcott and Abraham Lincoln. Digital Humanities Start-Up grants are more flexible and based on a library's needs. *What's on the Menu?*, a project of the New York Public Library, used this NEH grant to fund an online transcription tool to facilitate "the process of transcribing the 10,000 menus in the library's online gallery to turn it into a fully searchable database that can be browsed by dish, beverage or price as well as name and date" (Mainland 2011).

According to their website, "The mission of IMLS is to inspire libraries and museums to advance innovation, lifelong learning, and cultural and civic engagement. [They] provide leadership through research, policy development, and grant making." The website for Learning Labs in Libraries and Museums, a popular opportunity of the IMLS grants to libraries, provides libraries and museums with the resources to plan and implement labs "intended to engage middle- and high-school youth in mentor-led, interest-based, youth-centered, collaborative learning using digital and traditional media." Supporting grant applications of up to $100,000, Learning Labs grants support major projects.

Under the umbrella of the IMLS, the LSTA "authorizes the Institute of Museum and Library Services to administer several grant programs including: Grants to States, National Leadership Grants, Contracts and Cooperative Agreements, and Library Services for Native Americans and Native Hawaiians" (Manjarrez et al. 2009). These LSTA grants help libraries provide programs and services for patrons of all ages. In Wilmington, Massachusetts, a LSTA "Serving Tweens and Teens" grant allowed the library to strengthen the teen science collection, add new technology, and develop a series of science-related discussion programs for teens (Manjarrez et al. 2009, 14). At the Henderson District (Nevada) Public Libraries, a $100,000 LSTA grant allowed the library to offer Bright Beginnings, "a series of events that would incorporate community partners and parents into encouraging a child's early exposure to reading" (18). And at the New York Public Library, the LSTA-funded "'Hispanic Community Outreach' is a project focused on providing programming for the Hispanic community of the New York Public Library (NYPL) service area" (15).

Library-Specific Grants

Some organizations, foundations, and states provide grants specifically for libraries. Like government grants, awards range in value greatly, and opportunities are available for programs and services to patrons of all ages.

The American Library Association's (ALA) Public Programs Office (PPO) offers a variety of grants to both public and academic libraries. Their website states that "through professional development activities, programming resources, model programs and grant opportunities, PPO supports libraries as they fill their role as community cultural center, a place of cultural and civic engagement, where people of all backgrounds gather for reflection, discovery, participation and growth." PPO grants provide opportunities which include scholar-led discussion programs, traveling exhibitions in conjunction with related programming, and even collection development. Some of these grants are targeted for youth populations, so they are a resource for youth services librarians as well.

Divisions of the ALA can also be a source of grant opportunities. The Young Adult Library Services Association (YALSA) and the Association for Library Service to Children (ALSC) both have sections on their websites with information about grants that benefit children and teens. YALSA sponsors a Great Ideas Contest, a grant to provide new books to at-risk teens from communities with high poverty rates, and a grant with Dollar General to support summer reading programs. ALSC also has summer reading program grants, offers a Bookapalooza grant, and a grant for library outreach to underserved children.

Awarded annually, the $2,500 Baker & Taylor Entertainment Audio Music/Video Product Award provides libraries with an opportunity to develop collections. According to their website the purpose of the award "is to promote the development of a circulating audio music/video product collection in public libraries and increase the exposure of the format within the community. The grant was established in 1997 and is sponsored by Baker & Taylor."

For libraries in need of new technology, the Gates Foundation supports "efforts to supply and sustain free public access to computers and the Internet through local public libraries" (Bill & Melinda Gates Foundation 2012). With the Gates/LSTA-funded program, Renew Washington, the Washington State Library awarded grants "to help public libraries initiate new services, enhance existing services, conduct outreach and partnership efforts, or complete other activities that are identified as important to the library in addressing the needs of people searching for employment-related information, resources, and services," according to the state's website.

On a larger scale, some states offer library-specific grants that support capital projects. For example, "Since 1990, the Massachusetts Public Library Construction Program (MPLCP) has awarded grants to more than 200 cities and towns throughout the Commonwealth for construction of new library buildings, addition/renovations, special projects and the preliminary planning activities essential to building projects" (Massachusetts Board of Library Commissioners 2012). Over $10 million in MPLCP funds contributed to the award-winning renovation of the Cambridge (Massachusetts) Public Library, a project, according to the MLBC Notes website, that included a new addition as well as renovation of the existing building. Further south, a similar program, Maryland County Capital Grants, provides "$5,000,000 annually for a grant program to assist in the funding of public library capital projects. Since the grant program was implemented in FY 2008, 17 library systems have received funding for 29 capital projects" (Maryland State Department of Education 2003).

Private Foundation Grants

In addition to government and library-specific grants, libraries are eligible for many grants from private foundations. There are two primary advantages to grants from private foundations: grant opportunities are often less prescribed, so a library can be truly creative with program ideas, and private foundation grants often serve a local area, thereby cutting down on competition and increasing the library's chances of a winning grant application. Private foundations are often found at local banks, local businesses, local clubs, and organizations; some families have small foundations as well. At the Peabody Institute Library, the McCarthy Family Foundation supports an annual concert series, and the local Rotary Club recently funded "Explore, Play, Create," a series of programs "centered on creativity and technology." If you take the time to look into local grant opportunities, you will find that opportunities like these exist in many communities across the country.

HOW

As you can see, there are many grant opportunities available for motivated library applicants. To get started with grants, you first need to know two things: where to find available grants, and how to fill out grant applications.

Where to Find Grant Opportunities

Thanks to the Internet, tracking down grant opportunities has never been easier. Many grantors offer grant announcements, information, and even applications right on their websites, making it simple for applicants to quickly determine if a grant is right for their library. While annually published print grant listings are still available, we find that the majority of this information can be found online, without the need for the purchase of an expensive grant directory.

For government grants, Grants.gov is a wonderful resource. This site is one-stop shopping for all federal grants and includes grant announcements, information, applications, and samples of past successful grant application submissions for your reference. Perhaps the most useful aspect of this site is the option for e-mail notifications. Once registered, all federal grant announcements get sent to your e-mail account, so there is no need to frequently remind yourself to check the site for updates. LSTA grant information can be found on your state or county's resource page.

There are a number of resources for library-specific grants, and we'll go over some of the more popular options here. The Programming Librarian website has a "Library Awards and Grants by Deadline" page that is very useful. The list includes grants that serve patrons of all ages. Another place to find a variety of library-related grant announcements is the *American Libraries Direct* newsletter. This newsletter is automatically sent via e-mail to ALA members, but anyone can register at http:// americanlibrariesmagazine.org/aladirect. The PPO also offers grants to libraries, and information about these opportunities and the previously discussed Gates Foundation grants, can be found on their websites.

Grants from private foundations are a little trickier to track down, but are well worth the effort. The Foundation Center (http://foundationcenter. org) website includes a Foundation Finder that helps applicants match their projects to appropriate grant opportunities. There are also e-mail newsletters that you can sign up for to receive notice of private foundation grants. For example, *Youth Service America* offers a monthly newsletter that advertises their grants and others targeted to youth volunteer projects. This newsletter is a great resource for teen librarians who want to do volunteer projects with their teens. To locate lists like this, look for organizations that provide technical support for nonprofit organizations. Grants are the lifeblood of most nonprofits, so they know where to find this money. For more localized opportunities, check to see if community banks in your area have foundations, contact the local Rotary Club or other service organizations, and make sure to keep your ears open. Word of mouth is a powerful way to find out about less publicized opportunities that can make a difference for your library. According to MacKellar and Gerding (2010), "You never know where a great contact might come from or who might be on a foundation board or know just the right funding opportunity" (143). Here's where all of those relationships you cultivated by networking in your community can literally pay off. Make sure that people know you are looking for funding for a special project, and with any luck they might just be able to help you find what you need.

How to Write a Successful Grant Application

Once you identify a grant that meets your library's needs, it's time to write the application. Grant application requirements can be as simple as a mere business letter that includes a funding request, or as complicated as a multiple-page form that requires a narrative, attached budgets, tax forms, resumes, and other information relevant to the project. No matter how easy or difficult the application, it is important to approach any grant with a clear vision of your project and an understanding of the grant-writing process itself. "Grant seeking requires you to develop and apply skills in marketing, writing, and project management, tempered with creativity and a bit of a gambler's spirit" (Landau 2010, 36). Here we divide the process into eight basic steps.

Plan Your Project

Before you identify an appropriate grant opportunity, you need a clear understanding of the program, service, or project for which you plan to use the grant funds. According to the Non-Profit Guides website, "Preparation is vital to the grant-writing process. Solid planning and research will simplify the writing stage." Know what you want to do and how you plan to do it, and make sure you can describe the project clearly and compellingly. In addition, your proposal should directly relate to the library's mission statement. According to Landau, "Your strategic plan should be the basis for clarifying your library's potentially grantable needs" (Landau 2010, 35). Finally, identify just what community need your project serves. Funders want to help people, so the stronger the benefit of your project to the community, the greater the chances that your grant application will be successful.

Identify Staff Members, Community Partners, and Your Target Audience

People are at the heart of every successful grant application. Library staff plan, write, and execute the grant. Community partners support the library with related programs and resources. And, most importantly, your target audience participates in, evaluates the success of, and benefits from your grant-funded program. First, decide which library staff members will be involved in the grant. You need staff to write the grant, plan the programs and/or services that the grant will fund, and manage those programs and services once they are in place. Remember, all librarians, not just directors, can and should write grants. Sometimes, more successfully than anyone else in the library, a teen or programming librarian can better speak to the needs of projects that affect their patrons. As you plan your grant project, look outside the library to the wider community. Make sure your grant project has the support of community partners and the interest of your patrons and potential patrons. Determine the best community partners for your project, get commitments from them, and finally, determine your target audience within your community. "Programs that are designed in isolation from the community they serve and devoid of partners are inclined to fail" (MacKellar and Gerding 2010, 142). Remember, community-centered library services serve the community. That means the community should be at the heart of and included in the grant-planning process.

Identify the Right Grant for the Project

Once you have a well-defined project with clear goals, you need to find the right grant to fund the project. The majority of grants have eligibility requirements, and you should read these requirements carefully before you decide to apply for a grant. For example, if the grant is only offered to academic libraries, you want to know that fact before you spend hours filling out the application for a public library. Aside from organizational eligibility requirements, pay close attention to the types of projects that grants fund. You want to be sure that your project matches the grantor's expectations and mission. According to Landau, you should "use your stated mission, objectives, goals, and strategic tasks to guide your grant shopping" (Landau 2010, 35). When the library's mission aligns with the grantor's mission, the application is probably a good fit.

Manage Your Time Wisely

Some grantors provide grant writers with a lot of time to collect information and fill out the application, but other grants offer much less time to prepare a winning proposal. As you get ready to write the grant application, keep an eye on the calendar, set deadlines for yourself and the rest of the grant-writing team, and make sure that the application goes out on time. It is important to submit your application on time or early. If a funding agency receives the proposal past the closing date, many will reject your application without a look. Remember that the grant-writing process is essential to ensure funding for community-centered programs and services. If you are an administrator, be sure that staff members have the support they need in order to take time away from regular duties to write grants.

Write the Grant (aka Follow Directions)

Recently, when Kelley discussed a grant application with a supervisor who serves on a grant review committee, her supervisor said that the biggest mistakes that grant writers make are that they neglect to answer the questions as asked and they neglect to follow instructions. Some grants look complicated, but if you break them down into parts, they are made up of clear lists of questions and instructions. Read the questions carefully, and answer them clearly and comprehensively. Remember that it's okay to write a grant as a team. If one staff member is great at narrative writing, and another is comfortable working with budgets, why not work together to build the strongest possible application? If attached documentation is required, such as tax forms, budgets, and resumes, organize those documents and be sure to include all of them with your final submission. When available, review examples of applications that succeeded in the past, and adjust your writing style accordingly. Also, show your enthusiasm! Don't get so bogged down in the grant-writing details that you forget to show how much you care about the project you propose. According to MacKellar and Gerding (2010), "Attitude, perception, and public opinion make a difference. Decisions to give (like most human decisions) are emotional" (143).

Compile a Grant Toolkit

Once you fill out your first grant application and then move on to the next, you might notice that different grant applications contain a number of common elements. You'll save a lot of grant-writing time if you compile a grant toolkit, a folder of information commonly requested in grant applications. For example, many grants ask for tax forms, resumes, library history, and community data. If you keep all of this information in one place, you'll have a solid set of boilerplate information to begin any new grant applications. Trust us, a grant toolkit will save you a lot of time and a lot of frustration (see table 8.1).

Complete a Final Report

Most large grants require a final report or evaluation. Gathering data and statistics as you implement your grant will make the reporting process

Table 8.1.   The Grant Toolkit

The following is a list of items to consider as you compile your grant toolkit:
1. Community census data 2. Resumes of staff members who frequently direct grant-funded projects 3. Relevant tax forms for Foundation and Friends groups 4. Your library's mission statement 5. A copy of the library's long-range plan 6. A document with information about the library's history 7. A list of potential community partners and their contact information 8. Draft letter of support 9. Draft grant cover letter 10. A list of locally available grants, including a record of when you last applied and which librarian(s)/department(s) submitted the application

much easier. Make sure you complete this process on time, and include all required information. When it comes to grants from small foundations, a thank-you note is always a nice gesture. If you hope an organization will support your library's future endeavors, you want to make the best impression possible. Gratitude goes a long way.

Have a Back-Up Plan

While we hope that all of your grant applications are successful, we know from experience that scenario is not likely. In the event that your application is rejected, try again with a different funder. Or, contact the original grantor to find out why your application was not accepted. You might find that, with a little tweaking, your proposal might be reconsidered in the future. Grant writing requires a lot of work with no guarantees in terms of payoff, but in our experience, it's definitely worth the effort.

CHALLENGES

As with any new project the library decides to explore, grant writing is not without challenges. The first hurdle that many librarians face is that they are not grant writers. We're going to tell you a secret: you do not have to be a professional grant writer, or even a library director, to write a successful grant. If you know your project, know your community's needs, know how to answer questions, and know how to follow directions, you can write a grant. Also, don't be afraid to ask for help, advice, and proofreaders. Chances are, a supervisor or coworker has written a grant before and would be happy to offer assistance.

Once librarians realize that they are capable of writing grants, many then realize that they have no time to write a grant. As with other elements of community-centered library services previously discussed, you need to work with your supervisor to make time in your job for grant writing. If you are a supervisor yourself, guarantee your staff the support that they need to take on this new and important work. Grant writing often makes possible the community-centered programs and services that ultimately strengthen and position the library as a central force in the community.

In some cases, eligibility can also be a challenge. Many grantors only accept applications from 501(c)(3) organizations, and many public libraries do not fall under that designation. In Peabody, we solve this problem by working with the library's Friends group and the Foundation. The librarians are the architects of the grants, but the Friends, or Foundation, submit the grant and manage the funds.

Staffing is another potential grant challenge. In some cases, even if a library receives grant funding, staffing is too limited to support the execution of new programs and services. In cases like these, community partners and volunteers can be a big help. Also, if the initial program is successful, use that success as a strong argument for increased library staffing. Grant-funded programs not only meet community demands, sometimes they increase community demand for a given program or service. Keep in mind that this is an excellent problem to have, and libraries need to prepare for this possibility at the time of grant planning.

Librarians always have to consider the sustainability of the grant-funded project. Most grant applications ask questions about how you'll sustain the project after the grant is over. Don't gloss over this in planning. Come up with a plan for sustainability. Once the community embraces new programs and services, the library needs to continue to offer those services. The library must consider what happens with funding and staffing resources after the grant expires. If a library is not prepared to at least consider committing to the project in the long term, it should not apply for the grant in the first place. But successful grant applications, and their successful programs, are excellent tools with which to advocate for increased budgets or resources. Share the news of your success with your patrons and with decision makers in your communities, such as the mayor and the city council. After all—as we said in chapter 3—money to the library is money to the community, and what is good for the library is often good for the entire town.

As libraries look to implement community-centered programs and services, grants are extremely important resources. Whether you're a small rural library or a large library system, grants make possible projects that strengthen communities, strengthen libraries, and offer countless valuable opportunities for their patrons. As you approach your first grant application, or even your second or third, remember that you are the best possible person to write that application. So, make the time, identify the right grant, and start writing! Who knows where your library's grant program will lead.

BIBLIOGRAPHY

"About Us." 2012. Institute of Museum and Library Services. Accessed August 20. http://www.imls.gov/about/default.aspx.

"Awards, Grants, Stipends." 2012. Young Adult Library Services Association. Accessed September 25. http://www.ala.org/yalsa/awardsandgrants/yalsaawards grants.

"Baker & Taylor Entertainment Audio Music/Video Product Award." 2012. Public Library Association. Accessed August 18. http://www.ala.org/pla/awards/btaudiomusicvideoproductaward/.

Bill & Melinda Gates Foundation. 2012. "United States Program." Accessed August 20. http://www.gatesfoundation.org/united-states/Pages/program-over view.aspx.

"Cambridge Wins Its 11th Design Award." 2012. MBLC Notes. Accessed December 17. http://mblc.state.ma.us/mblc/publications/notes/v29n3/page9.htm.

Cavinta, Jo Anderson. 2012. "Partnering to Serve Immigrants and ESL Learners." Programming Librarian. http://www.programminglibrarian.org/library/plan ning/partnering-to-serve-immigrants-and-esl-learners.html#.UH2EHFHF28A.

"Explore, Play, Create." 2012. Peabody Institute Library. Accessed August 21. http://www.peabodylibrary.org/teens/epc.pdf.

Flanders, Julie. 2010. "Grant Writing on the Web." *College & Research Libraries News* 71 (9): 472–79.

"Guidelines." 2012. Non-Profit Guides. Accessed August 21. http://www.np guides.org/guide/index.html.

Kepler, Ann, ed. 2012. *The ALA Book of Library Grant Money*. 8th ed. Chicago: American Library Association.

Landau, Herbert. 2010. "Winning Grants: A Game Plan." *American Libraries* 41 (9): 34–36.

"Learning Labs in Libraries and Museums." 2012. Institute of Museum and Library Services. Accessed August 20. http://www.imls.gov/about/learning_labs.aspx.

"Library Awards and Grants by Deadline." 2012. Programming Librarian. Accessed December 17. http://www.programminglibrarian.org/library-grants.html.

"Local Cultural Council Program." 2012. Massachusetts Cultural Council. Accessed August 20. http://www.massculturalcouncil.org/programs/lccgrants.asp.

MacKellar, Pamela H., and Stephanie K. Gerding. 2010. *Winning Grants: A How-to-Do-It Manual for Librarians with Multimedia Tutorials and Grant Development Tools*. New York: Neal Schuman.

Mainland, Alexis. 2011. "The Library Hands Out Menus to Thousands of Volunteers." *New York Times: Diner's Journal*, April 4.

Manjarrez, C., L. Langa, and K. Miller. 2009. "A Catalyst for Change: LSTA Grants to States Program Activities and the Transformation of Library Services

to the Public." Institute of Museum and Library Services. http://www.imls
.gov/assets/1/AssetManager/CatalystForChange1.pdf.

Maryland State Department of Education. 2003. "County Library Capital Grants."
http://www.marylandpublicschools.org/MSDE/divisions/library/grants/clcg.

"Play by the Book." 2012. Peabody Institute Library. Accessed August 20. http://
www.peabodylibrary.org/pbtb/index.html.

"Professional Awards and Grants." 2012. Association for Library Service to Children. Accessed September 25. http://www.ala.org/alsc/awardsgrants/profawards.

"Public Library Construction." 2012. Massachusetts Board of Library Commissioners. Accessed August 15. http://mblc.state.ma.us/grants/construction/
index.php.

"Public Programs Office (PPO)." 2012. American Library Association. Accessed
August 20. http://www.ala.org/offices/ppo/.

"Renew Washington." 2012. Washington State Library. Accessed August 20.
http://www.sos.wa.gov/library/libraries/projects/renewwashington/.

"Small Grants to Libraries and Other Nonprofit Institutions: *America's Music:
A Film History of Our Popular Music from Blues to Bluegrass to Broadway.*"
2012. National Endowment for the Humanities. Accessed August 20. http://www
.neh.gov/grants/public/small-grants-libraries-and-other-nonprofit-institutions
-americas-music-film-history-ou.

Part III

INSPIRATION FOR COMMUNITY-CENTERED LIBRARIES

CHAPTER 9

Libraries as Centers of Civic Action

Lady Bird Johnson is known in the library world for her famous quote, "Perhaps no place in any community is so totally democratic as the town library. The only entrance requirement is interest." At the time, she probably didn't realize the extent of just how right she was. Because libraries in the United States are public buildings with services and materials offered free to all, they have been associated with democratic ideals since their inception. These days, many libraries go far beyond the basic public services of the original "free libraries" and become key players in their communities' political lives.

In this chapter we will look at the ways in which public libraries have met some of the challenges that Michael Baldwin (2002) sets forth in his article about remaking libraries. We will illustrate how public libraries nurture political capital in a community, look at the ways in which libraries promote civil discourse, and focus on how libraries can creatively address social issues in their communities. We will explore big initiatives such as Banned Books Week, the September Project, and Building Common Ground and highlight individual libraries that help their patrons participate in democracy and civic life by coordinating voter registration and education programs, hosting political debates, and planning civic engagement programming.

MAJOR LIBRARY INITIATIVES

There are several major initiatives that libraries across the United States have undertaken in order to address issues of democracy and civic engagement. We will examine two here—Banned Books Week and the September Project.

Banned Books Week is perhaps the most popular fall program for public libraries. Founded in 1982, the displays, events, and programs around Banned Books Week highlight First Amendment issues surrounding the freedom to access and read materials that have been banned or challenged in communities, schools, and libraries. Sponsored by eleven organizations, including the ALA, Banned Books Week is held each September and "highlights the benefits of free and open access to information while drawing attention to the harms of censorship by spotlighting actual or attempted book banning incidents across the United States." The ALA offers suggested events and graphics for individual libraries each year and has hosted a "Read Out" of banned books in Chicago every year since 2000. In 2011, with the launch of the ALA's Banned Books Week YouTube channel, the "Read Out" went virtual. Local public libraries host similar read outs, set up displays, and provide education for patrons and the public about the role of libraries and communities in protecting an individual's right to read. Community members are often encouraged to participate in or contribute to events and displays by talking about their favorite banned books or their experiences with censorship. In this way Banned Books Week events open up a space for dialogue about individual rights, community values, and the roles of the library in protecting freedom of access and inquiry.

Another fall event that promotes civic mindedness and can strengthen local political capital is the September Project, whose tagline is "Connecting the World, One Library at a Time." The September Project "is a grassroots effort to encourage events about freedom in all libraries in all countries. Events explore and exercise freedom, justice, democracy, and community and include book displays, community book readings, children's art projects, film screenings, theatrical performances, civic deliberations, voter registrations, gardens, murals, panel discussions, and puppet shows." According to cofounder David Silver, "Participating libraries, mostly public and academic, organize events about issues that matter to their communities." Silver also notes that although the initial purpose of the September Project was for libraries to host events on September 11 in order to reflect upon the world since the 2001 terrorist attacks, the program has grown and now focuses on broader issues. He has also publicly stated that an event, or series of events, like this one has no political agenda but is nonetheless inherently political:

> It is, of course, political. These days, to exercise any form of public discourse is political, eh? To publicly assemble is political. To organize anything free is definitely political. To talk about issues that matter—to talk about the war, to talk about human rights, to talk about the Earth—that's political. In our times, any idea that encourages us to be citizens rather than consumers is highly political.

Libraries can foster this kind of discourse by providing programs that encourage discussions of this nature. The library space provides people with a safe place in which to discuss ideas, issues, and problems that have become contentious and partisan in our world of twenty-four-hour news cycles and specialized media outlets. Encouraging people to gather and to talk about what freedom, democracy, and politics mean is indeed a political act that can ideally help foster a more politically savvy and engaged community (Fister 2007).

HELPING PATRONS PARTICIPATE IN POLITICAL AND CIVIC LIFE

Public libraries have played an important role in helping patrons participate in local political life. One of the most important and elemental ways in which libraries help educate an engaged citizenry is through voter registration and education programs and projects. Many public libraries offer voter registration information on their websites. For example, the Gwinnett (Georgia) County Public Library voter registration page notes that they offer postage paid mail-in registration forms at all library branches. The library offers all new patrons the opportunity to register to vote when they apply for a new library card, and they also offer to help patrons amend their voter registration whenever patrons update their addresses with the library. The Jersey City (New Jersey) Free Public Library offers voter registration forms in both English and Spanish via their website. At the Westmont (Illinois) Public Library citizens can register to vote at the library up to thirty days before every election. In addition to offering information and forms on their websites, these libraries and others also link out to local or state election resources that provide helpful, straight-to-the-source information for patrons and nonpatrons alike.

Of course, registering voters is just one aspect of helping people participate in the democratic process. A democracy is presupposed, as we noted in chapter 1, not just by a citizenry, but by an *informed* citizenry. To that end, public libraries have, to varying degrees, provided resources both online and off to meet the goal of helping to create those informed citizens. Some libraries offer information about local, state, and national elections. Others include information about the process of voting itself. The Hartford (Connecticut) Public Library provides links to voter registration cards and an online registration tutorial and also offers information on how and where to vote as well as lists and contact information for federal, state, and local elected officials. In Minnesota, the Rochester Public Library created a similar website that links to federal, state, and local governments, provides information for Minnesota voters, links to state legislators' voting records, and links out to sites that track political contributions and fact-check politics.

The Athens County (Ohio) Public Libraries partnered with the League of Women Voters of Athens County to create an informational website that includes voter guides, voting resources, and updated information on candidate forums, election and party issues, sample ballots, and election results.

Some libraries go beyond voter registration and information to tackle issues of civic engagement through lectures, discussions, and other programming. In 2012, the Chapel Hill (North Carolina) Public Library, in partnership with the Town of Chapel Hill Justice in Action Committee, launched a series called "Civic Engagement and Social Justice: The Intersection of Rights and Responsibilities." "Combining events, programs, book and film lists to help the community dig deeper into issues of importance and to consider ways of engagement in civic life," this series asks questions and fosters discussions about social justice and action based on the library's belief that "civic reflection builds community connections. [That] libraries are boundary spanning advocates of intellectual freedom. [And that] they are trusted safe spaces for investigation and expression of diverse ideas." Chapel Hill provides a wonderful example of a library that is aware of the way that political and social capital are intertwined (even if their terminology is different) and designs programs that explicitly strengthen these community assets.

Another excellent example of civic engagement programming is the Boulder (Colorado) Public Library's "Geopolitics Series." A partnership with the Boulder Chapter of the United Nations Association, participants in this program read about "current events around a selected geopolitical theme for each month, and [talk] about the topic in the context of the intermix of political, social, ecological and economic factors within a spatial context."

Civic engagement is a learned practice, and public libraries are one of a few institutions that are equipped to engage community members who aren't old enough to vote in meaningful political dialogue. In the months leading up to a recent mayoral election, the Peabody Institute Library's staff and teen advisory board put together a Teen Mayoral Forum that gave local teens the opportunity to pose their questions to the two candidates for office. Teens asked questions about local flooding issues, public school funding, the environment, libraries, public safety and jobs. By creating opportunities for teens to engage in political issues, the library brings new voices into the conversation and shows teens the importance and rewards of being civically engaged. This kind of involvement also legitimizes teens as citizens and members of a community, and provides a public forum for their questions, concerns, and perspectives.

Such democratic engagement by libraries can result in quantifiable results for communities and libraries. In 2011, the Urban Libraries Council noted the contributions to civic engagement made by the Calgary (Alberta) Public Library for their events hosted around local municipal elections in 2010. The series of programs and related materials, including a blog called "Don't Be an Idiot," which used "the ancient Greek term for a person who failed to become involved in civic affairs," garnered media attention for the library, "contributed to increased community interest and participation in the electoral process (voter turnout increased to 53.24%), and raised the profile of the Library during a critical time: all electoral candidates at Library programs discussed, without prompting, the importance of the Library to the community and of maintaining adequate Library funding."

A MODEL FOR CIVIL DISCOURSE

In addition to helping patrons become more politically aware and active, public libraries have also taken a role in helping foster civil discourse. In an age when anyone of any political ideology can find a news or media source tailored specifically to that ideology, it is more important than ever that libraries maintain a space for civil discourse and provide opportunities for people to practice what may seem like a dying art. Like Frances Moore Lappé, Adam Davis, the director of the Project on Civic Reflection, sees the facilitation of civil discourse, necessary in a "living democracy," as an important role for libraries. These skills must be strategically created by communities because "we are not culturally conditioned to nurture the most important democratic practices: asking ourselves hard questions, listening to people we do not know or think we know too well, and trying to look with fresh eyes at what we ourselves hold dear." By providing the space and opportunities for individuals to foster and learn civic skills, libraries can build political capital for their communities and "bring democracy to life" (Davis 2012).

One program designed to do just this is called Building Common Ground. Building Common Ground is a joint collaboration between the ALA and the Fetzer Institute with a focus on engaging "the public in contemplation and discussion of the importance of community, civility and compassion in their daily lives. By bringing adult audiences together for programs and events that include reading, viewing, reflection, discussion and civic engagement initiatives, public libraries will enhance the quality of life and learning in their communities." This program granted thirty public libraries grants of up to $2,500 in order to build a program series around local issues that could benefit from being viewed through the lens of community, civility, and compassion. The project required libraries to collaborate with a community partner on programming and events and the goal was to help participants "reflect on content, engage with issues through discussion, and learn of opportunities to take action on behalf of their communities."

Another program utilized in libraries across the country is the Socrates Café. Founded by Chris Phillips, the Socrates Café aims to gather people together to "exchange thoughtful ideas and experiences while embracing the central theme of Socratizing; [sic] the idea that we learn more when we question and question with others." Individuals are welcome to start local Socrates Cafés in order to build community and "create a more vibrant and participatory democracy and empathetic society." The South Portland (Maine) Public Library hosts a Socrates Café where "participants select a question for discussion by democratic process, which is then examined over the next hour and fifteen minutes for built-in assumptions, embedded concepts and logical consistencies (or inconsistencies)." Noting that "alternative viewpoints are encouraged and explored," the South Portland Public Library Socrates Café encourages people to listen and explore questions in a group setting, and importantly to not expect a consensus on issues. They have built meetings around questions such as "What is free speech?," "What is morality, and who defines it?," and "What is community?"

Libraries have also taken up the challenge of independently promoting civil discourse and encouraging patrons to participate in difficult or complex discussions. The Skokie (Illinois) Public Library hosted a program initiated and organized by the local Indian community in an effort to explore the views of various religious traditions on questions of peace and nonviolence (Anthony 2012). The Chattahoochee (Georgia) Valley Libraries built a program in 2012 called "Building Common Ground: Race, Religion, and Politics in Columbus," which was cosponsored by the Muscogee County Friends of Libraries and Midtown Inc. and asked the question: "Doesn't democracy require more from us?" The library hosted nationally known speakers to "explore the difficulties of race, religion and political discourse in both our community and our country" as part of an election-year attempt to build real conversations made up of real civil discourse. In Maryland, the Calvert Public Library also hosted a 2012 series on civil discourse aimed at encouraging "conversation and understanding among the members of Calvert's diverse population in order to promote a sustainable and peaceful community." One of their programs focused on rights and responsibilities and asked participants to consider what we mean when we talk about rights.

Programs like these show how libraries can do more than just offer information or entertaining programs. Libraries can invite community members in and ask them to think deeply and intelligently about difficult subjects, to consider why they believe what they do, and to explore the ways in which their perspectives may come into conflict or consensus with their neighbors'. In doing so, public libraries can "utilize their special characteristics of bringing together culture and technology, the local and the virtual, different [ethnic] and social groups, different generations and different arenas of interest, and thus further develop their potential as a social meeting place" so that "their democratic role in today's society may be extended" (Aabø 2005, 209).

ADDRESSING SOCIAL PROBLEMS

Libraries promote democracy and civil discourse in programs and projects, but in addition to encouraging people to talk and ask questions, public libraries are also getting more involved in addressing social issues that affect people and groups in their communities. Across the country, libraries are interested in tackling some of the major issues and problems facing communities today. Their efforts strengthen many forms of community capital, including human, financial, environmental, and, by bringing people together, political and social. From environmental degradation to hunger, from affordable housing to domestic violence, and from homeless youth to public health issues and beyond, libraries are providing information and resources, encouraging individual action, and occasionally building partnerships and leading initiatives that help the community build assets and work toward change.

Because public libraries are open to all, many libraries are frequented by homeless citizens. Public librarians in both urban and rural areas meet homeless citizens in their libraries and are often in the position to see social patterns and issues before other municipal agencies. Some libraries have begun offering information and resources for homeless patrons or for those who live on the precarious line between security and homelessness. The San Jose (California) Public Library, in partnership with social worker associations and groups, hosted a panel discussion on homelessness in that community. Their website includes resource information, statistics, and links for referrals, legal advice, and medical care. San Jose Public Library also offers Social Workers in the Library, an information and referral service that helps patrons connect with social work professionals from the California Chapter of the National Association of Social Workers on a variety of issues from employment to immigration. The Washington, D.C., Public Library has targeted information to homeless teens in the community, providing a resource page with information on local homeless shelters and emergency hotlines. This public library also looks at some of the roots of why young adults might not feel welcome at home, including providing information resources on LGBT teens, for example.

In addition to issues of homelessness, libraries are focusing on issues of hunger and food security, sometimes even taking a central role in feeding hungry youth in their communities. In 2012, the Watauga (North

Carolina) County Public Library, as part of the Building Common Ground Project, hosted a series on food security, complete with book groups, films, speakers, local farm tours, and a community service fair in order "to help participants understand the connections between food security, sustainability, and compassion, develop skills to address our area's food security challenges, and cultivate a deeper commitment to the common good of our community."

In other examples of libraries efforts to address the issue of hunger, the Peabody Institute Library developed a series of community partnerships that led to a Summer Foods program, feeding hundreds of local youth over the summer and involving teens in related programming at the same time, and the Saint Paul (Minnesota) Public Library in 2011 partnered with the Saint Paul Public Schools for a similar program designed to provide young people with nutritious meals during the summer months. The Saint Paul Public Library developed this program because "staff noticed how many kids were coming in hungry asking if we had food" and because they wanted "to help kids continue to learn through the summer months and being hungry undermines it all." As Julie and Melissa have written before, these kinds of programs, resulting in direct action on the part of a library, are part and parcel of the responsibilities of any community-centered library (Rauseo and Edwards 2012). Is it within the scope of a library's mission to provide free meals to young people? Not usually. But it is completely in line with the social responsibility a library has when it identifies a local problem. Focusing on these kinds of outreach programs, designed to meet a pressing social need and only tangentially related to the traditional idea of libraries, is one of the most profound ways libraries can redefine themselves and illustrate their worth.

Libraries are also providing information resources and assistance in other areas as well. The Public Library of Cincinnati and Hamilton (Ohio) County partners with the Ohio Benefit Bank to connect "low and moderate income families to tax credits and work supports that help in their day to day lives." The Baltimore (Maryland) Public Library has a web page dedicated to providing resources to citizens dealing with domestic violence, suicide, rape, eating disorders, and more. The Public Libraries of Saginaw (Michigan) provide resources on teen parenting directed to new moms and dads. Libraries are also focusing on sustainability and the environment. The Spokane (Washington) Public Library, under its online Research page, lists links to sustainability resources. In Montana, the

Missoula Public Library provides links to local and nonprofit resources on energy and the environment. And the Kalamazoo (Michigan) Public Library's page on environmental resources provides staff book recommendations, local community resources, and relevant newspapers, magazines, and websites.

YOUR DEMOCRATIC LIBRARY

Even in the digital age, "the purpose of public libraries is still to further democracy, equality, and social justice, increase access to information, disseminate culture and knowledge, contribute to a meaningful and informative leisure time, and act as a communal institution and a social meeting place" (Aabø 2005, 210). By focusing on helping patrons participate in democracy, practice civil discourse, and meet social needs, the repositioned public library can demonstrate the ways in which we add value to our communities and develop that informed citizenry on which democracy depends. Seven decades ago Archibald MacLeish stated that library service in support of democracy is difficult, but sagely added that, indeed, "democracy is difficult" (MacLeish 1940, 422). He was also convinced that libraries and librarians were up to the task. We believe that, though the task has become, if anything, even more difficult, we are capable of meeting it in our own day and age.

MAKE IT HAPPEN

Are you interested in developing library services, programs, and resources that support the democratic process? Here are some tips to get you started:

- Partner with your secretary of state to provide voter registration forms, in English and other languages, for your patrons. Provide access to them in the building and online, provide assistance in filling them out, and offer to cover the postage of mailing them in on behalf of your patrons.
- Collaborate with local civic organizations or nonprofits to develop resources and programs that help voters educate themselves on candidates and issues. Offer the library for a candidate debate or for a

more informal mix and mingle. Contact the city to find out what you need to do to be a neighborhood polling place.

- Don't forget to model democracy by becoming involved, as an institution, in local government. A librarian should sit on important municipal committees and should be involved in any local mayoral advisory groups.
- Consider forming a Socrates Café, hosting a Banned Books Week event, or looking for grants such as those offered by Building Common Ground in order to create opportunities for patrons to learn about and practice civil discourse.
- Create displays that provide a wide range of views on an issue, and remember (and remind your patrons) that the library is still the best place to find information that both supports and challenges their ideas.
- Notice a social issue in your community that needs attention? Build a resource and referral list and provide access to it online and in the building.
- Consider partnering with local social workers to develop referral services for patrons.
- Spearhead partnerships that can lead to programs that directly address local needs, such as hunger and food security. Often the library sees local problems before other municipal agencies—take what you see and what you know and try to find proactive ways to address local problems beyond just providing information.

BIBLIOGRAPHY

Aabø, Svenhild. 2005. "The Role and Value of Public Libraries in the Age of Digital Technologies." *Journal of Librarianship and Information Science* 37: 208–9.
Anthony, Carolyn. 2012. "Building Community through Engaged Discussion at Skokie Public Library." *Programming Librarian* (blog). March 20. http://www.programminglibrarian.org/blog/2012/march-2012/building-community-through-engaged-discussion-at-skokie-public-library.html#.T9elHfFI0y5.
Baldwin, Michael. 2002. "BackTalk: Can Libraries Save Democracy?" *Library Journal* 127 (17): 52.
"Banned Books Week." 2012. YouTube. Accessed June 12. http://www.youtube.com/user/BannedBooksWeek.

"Banned Books Week: Celebrating the Freedom to Read." 2012. American Library Association. Accessed June 12. http://www.ala.org/advocacy/banned/bannedbooksweek.

"Building Common Ground: Discussions of Community, Civility, and Compassion." 2012. Accessed June 12. http://ppo.ala.org/commonground/.

"Building Common Ground: Race, Religion and Politics in Columbus." 2012. Chattahoochee Valley Libraries. Accessed June 13. http://www.cvlga.org/commonground.

"Civic Engagement and Social Justice." 2012. Chapel Hill Public Library. Accessed June 12. http://chapelhillpubliclibrary.org/txp/?s=services&c=0221-civic-engagement.

"Civil Discourse/Community Building." 2012. Calvert Public Library. Accessed June 13. http://calvert.lib.md.us/voices.html.

"Connections: Children, Youth & Family Resources." 2012. Baltimore Public Library. Accessed June 14. http://www.bcpl.info/community/connections.

Davis, Adam. 2012. "Libraries and Democratic Life: Promoting Civic Engagement." Programming Librarian. http://www.programminglibrarian.org/library/planning/libraries-democratic-life.html#.T-s_6VI1z4w.

"Elections and Government." 2012. Rochester Public Library. Accessed June 12. http://www.rochesterpubliclibrary.org/research/resources/elections.html.

"Environment." 2012. Kalamazoo Public Library. Accessed June 14. http://www.kpl.gov/guides/environment/.

"Environment." 2012. Missoula Public Library. Accessed June 14. http://www.missoulapubliclibrary.org/online-resources/environment.

Fister, Barbara. 2007. "The September Project." ACRLog. Accessed December 13, 2012. http://acrlog.org/2007/09/04/the-september-project/.

"Food Security Programming." 2012. Watauga County Public Library. Accessed June 14. http://www.wataugacountylibrary.com/foodsecurity.

"Geopolitics Series." 2012. Boulder Public Library. Accessed June 12. http://bplnow.boulderlibrary.org/event/2012-05-31/15665.

"Homeless." 2012. San Jose Public Library. Accessed June 14. http://sjpl.org/tags/homeless.

"Homeless Youth and Runaways." 2012. DC Public Library. Accessed June 14. http://www.dclibrary.org/node/177.

MacLeish, Archibald. 1940. "The Librarian and the Democratic Process." *ALA Bulletin* 34 (6): 385–88, 421–22.

Rauseo, Melissa S., and Julie Biando Edwards. 2012. "Summer Foods, Libraries and Resiliency: Creative Problem Solving and Community Partnership in Massachusetts." In *Public Libraries and Resilient Cities*, edited by Michael Dudley, 89–100. Chicago: ALA Editions.

"Saint Paul Public Library Provides Free Summer Meals to Youth." 2012. Saint Paul Public Library. Accessed June 14. http://www.sppl.org/about/library -news/saint-paul-public-library-provides-free-summer-meals-youth.

"September Project." 2012. Accessed June 12. http://theseptemberproject.org/ connecting-the-world-one-library-at-a-time/.

"Services, Ohio Benefit Bank." 2012. Public Library of Cincinnati and Hamilton County. Accessed June 14. http://cincinnatilibrary.org/services/ohiobenefit bank.html.

"Socrates Café." 2012. Accessed June 13. http://www.philosopher.org/Socrates_ Cafe.html.

"Socrates Café." 2012. South Portland Public Library. Accessed June 13. http:// southportlandlibrary.com/?page_id=60.

"Sustainability Resources." 2012. Spokane Public Library. Accessed June 14. http://www.spokanelibrary.org/index.php?page=research&cat=findthebest &id=128.

"Teen Parenting." 2012. Public Libraries of Saginaw. Accessed June 14. http:// www.saginawlibrary.org/teens/teen-issues/teen-parenting/.

"21st Century Literacies: Civic Literacy." 2012. Urban Library Council Innovations Initiatives. Accessed June 12. http://urbanlibraries.org/displaycommon .cfm?an=1&subarticlenbr=644.

"Voter & Election Information." 2012. Hartford Public Library. Accessed June 12. http://www.hplct.org/library-services/adults/voter-election-info.

"Voter Registration." 2012. Jersey City Free Public Library. Accessed June 12. http://www.jclibrary.org/resources/voter-registration.

"Voter Registration." 2012. Westmont Public Library. Accessed June 12. http:// westmontlibrary.org/library-services/voter-registration/.

"Voter Registration at the Library." 2012. Gwinnett County Public Library. Accessed June 12. http://www.gwinnettpl.org/usingthelibrary/voter-registration .html.

"Vote Smart." 2012. Athens County Votes. Accessed June 12. http://www.athens countyvotes.org.

CHAPTER 10

Libraries as Centers for Sustainability

To put it kindly, discussions of economic and environmental public policy can be a bit dry. The work that libraries are doing in their communities to contribute to sustainability, though, is anything but dull. Libraries and their patrons are converting old silos and Walmarts into branches, growing plants on the roof, and learning to fix things. They are lending a helping hand to job seekers and are creating spaces and services to nurture small businesses. When librarians embrace sustainable principles with a sense of fun and discovery, they model for residents and decision makers the enjoyment that can be found in embracing a way of living that respects and builds precious environmental, financial, and human capital for our communities. In this chapter, we will focus on ways that libraries strengthen those forms of capital in order to create truly sustainable local economies and communities.

STEWARDS OF ENVIRONMENTAL CAPITAL

Alongside many institutions, organizations, and businesses, libraries are acknowledging their duty to help create communities that are ecologically responsible. The two major contributions libraries can make to the "green" movement is through their buildings and spaces, and by acting as community educators in the area of environmental literacy.

The management of library buildings is an important way that librarians contribute to the physical capital in their communities. If done thoughtfully and carefully, library building and maintenance can protect the natural resources (i.e., the environmental capital) of their local communities.

When a community is lucky enough to undertake a project to create a new library, one of the first decisions that must be made is whether to build a new structure or renovate an existing building. New structures can be designed and built with an eye toward green concerns that simply weren't considered when old buildings went up. Positioning a building to take advantage of passive solar heating, insulating a building to conserve heat, and using sustainable and nontoxic building materials are all options when a library is being built from scratch. The Hennepin (Minnesota) County Central Library is a case in point. While it is a "new" building, 95 percent of the construction materials were recycled. Other environmentally friendly features of the building include automatic lights, efficient heating and cooling systems, and a ventilation system that runs under the floor to reduce energy needed for cooling the building. Most innovative of all, though, is the library's "green" roof, which uses generally wasted space to grow plants. Green roofs have a wide array of environmental benefits, including reducing water waste, improving outdoor air quality, and increasing energy efficiency. Hennepin's Central Library illustrates just a few of the green options open to libraries that construct new buildings.

On the other hand, when Petra Hauke and Klaus Ulrich Werner (2012) examined the reuse of old buildings for libraries around the world, they identified a number of benefits to recycling old buildings. First, cost. A university in Switzerland transformed an existing building on campus into a library for half the price of a new building (62). Second, location. The municipal library in Germany that found its home in a former train station is convenient for all the residents of its community (62). Third, originality. A library in Italy used beautiful existing historical buildings for its expansion, preserved the local character of their place, and created a one-of-a-kind destination for community members (63). Closer to home, the McAllen (Texas) Public Library transformed an abandoned Walmart into the largest single-story library in the United States (Pinter 2012). The act of transforming a building from a Walmart, devoted to consumption, to a public library, whose ethos is one of sharing, is in itself a very green thing to do.

Library buildings are not the only physical capital entrusted to library stewardship. All libraries have outdoor space, even if it is only a sidewalk or a roof. We've already discussed how a library roof can be pressed into servicing the community's natural resources. Other libraries are gifted with significant outdoor space, and some have even been designed to be part of their community's green space. The main branch of the Peabody Library is located downtown and does not have a very large or attractive outdoor space. Still, the library's courtyard hosts a Saturday Market from July through September. This market is a good example of how libraries can support the three areas of sustainability. By providing a market for local artisans, the library is supporting the local economy. By making fresh, local produce and other foods available in the downtown neighborhood, the library is both supporting the environmentally friendly local foods movement and helping create access to healthy foods in a low-income area.

The Northern Onondaga Public Library in Cicero, New York, has taken this type of project to a new level by devoting half an acre of library land to an organic community garden. They encourage community members to "check out" a plot of land at the "Library Farm" and grow anything they'd like on it, as long as they respect the garden's organic guidelines. For residents who don't want their own plot of land, the library has designated some of the garden as a shared space, where anyone can plant, maintain, and pick anything he or she wants. The library has also committed to donating some of the produce from the farm to local food pantries. Library programs at the farm aim to "preserve knowledge that our grandparents might have had but that never got passed down." This educational component to the farm includes workshops on herbs, canning, composting, and cooking with the fresh produce. In this way, Cicero's library is combining an environmentally sustainable use of its physical space while also strengthening environmental and food literacy within the community. According to the Urban Libraries Council, this is what libraries should be aiming to do:

> What makes green building and operations in public libraries particularly valuable is the educational impact. . . . Tours of green roofs, kiosks telling the library's green story, demonstrations on how solar panels on library buildings generate energy, and visible recycling activities raise awareness about the importance of collective community action to preserve environmental resources. (Urban Libraries Council 2010, 19)

The Greensboro (North Carolina) Public Library is also doing this work at its Kathleen Clay Edwards Family branch. Located in a ninety-eight-acre park, the branch library includes a bird and butterfly meadow, reading garden, walking trails, ponds, and wetlands. Its calendar of events shows that the library is devoted to environmental education with garden-ing programs, resource backpacks for children, story times, hikes, and more to introduce visitors to the natural resources around them. Some of the library's ongoing projects are No Impact Week, the Leopold Educa-tion Project, and Biking 101 for Adults.

Another library system dedicated to integrating sustainability into their building, collection and programs is the Arlington County (Virginia) Li-brary. Their green motto is "Bikes, Buildings and Broccoli." Library staff are encouraged to bike to work and a program was offered to conduct a bike tour of the seven library branches. The library also offers bike main-tenance and safety classes. Their physical space has been greened by cut-ting electricity and energy use through solar panels installed on the library roof. To help community members also cut their energy use, the library circulates electricity monitors. Like the Library Farm, Arlington's Central Library has gardening classes and an organic garden that provides veg-etables to the Arlington Food Assistance Center. The gardening project was tied into the library's special events through their annual "Arlington Reads" project that focused on food sustainability.

Some environmental movements, like Transition Towns, believe that the key to a sustainable future lies with individuals and communities re-learning old skills, like cooking, sewing, gardening, rebuilding soil, and repairing things, in order to cut their environmental impact and rely less on nonrenewable energy sources. This is what the Library Farm and the Greensboro and Arlington Libraries are doing with their gardening and food preservation classes. According to Monika Antonelli (2012), editor of *Greening Libraries*, libraries of the future should step up and host more events where people can relearn "more traditional ways of doing things, often by combining these traditional skills with 21st century knowledge. These reskilling abilities can include everything from how to darn a sock to how to cook with a solar oven and from how to raise bees to how to cre-ate a hoop tunnel. Again, with their commitment and ongoing mission to provide community programs, libraries make ideal institutions to host and provide reskilling workshops" (Antonelli 2012, 246). Hennepin County has embraced the idea of reskilling programs with their community wide Fix-It Clinics. These clinics, many of which are held at Hennepin librar-ies, help residents fix a variety of items, including appliances, electronics, mobile devices, clothing, and more. The goal of these events is to "reduce the amount of stuff that gets thrown in the trash, teach valuable trouble-shooting and basic repair skills, and build community connections." Hennepin is just one of many communities around the world embracing the idea of minimizing trash. These repair programs are a great way for libraries to help participants gain skills, free up landfill space, and create stronger social capital by utilizing volunteers from within the community to serve as repair instructors.

The beauty of libraries' green programs and services is how they strengthen communities in multiple ways. Green buildings, beautiful outdoor learning environments, and programs that promote and teach sustainable skills can build physical, environmental, human, and social assets for communities. That is time, space, and talent well spent by community-centered libraries.

SKILLS AND SEEKING JOBS

Today more than ever before, individuals trying to succeed in the workforce need a wide variety of skills. Public libraries play a vital role in providing members of their community with access to the resources and opportunities they need to find work and to develop skills for the twenty-first-century workplace. The two parts of supporting workers in your community, finding a job and developing job skills, are intimately related and libraries are actively involved in both.

For many job seekers, public libraries are an important destination. Every day more than three hundred thousand Americans get job-seeking help at their public library (Hill 2012, 14). A survey of library patrons in Wichita, Kansas, revealed that a full 50 percent of patrons who use the library computers do so in order to look for jobs, prepare resumes, and do other employment-related tasks (Urban Libraries Council 2010, 14). These statistics provide just a snapshot of how vital libraries are to the many community members who are job searching. Community-centered libraries have recognized this importance and have created services to assist these patrons.

Every year the Urban Libraries Council recognizes innovative libraries that serve their communities in new and forward-thinking ways. Their 2012 Top Innovators in the Workforce Development category show the breadth and depth of library services to unemployed and underemployed individuals. One of their innovators is the New York Public Library. As a result of increased demand for assistance for job seekers during the recession, the library partnered with a nonprofit, Workforce1 Career Centers, to expand their existing services for job seekers (resume and interview workshops, computer access and assistance, etc.) to include referrals and placements. Librarians were trained to better assist job seekers by identifying appropriate job placements. Actually finding jobs for patrons may be a new role for librarians, but it is a good fit for institutions dedicated to connecting community assets. The New York partnership was not without challenges. To accommodate each new career center, library branches had to free up one to two thousand square feet of valuable space. Loss of space is a real sacrifice for most libraries. The library system was willing to make this concession in order to provide the best possible service to their community members. The ultimate success of the venture for residents and the goodwill generated by the partnership with city policy makers makes the effort worth it for the library.

As we've pointed out throughout this book, access to library services is a vital consideration for a community-centered library. Many libraries offer remote and electronic access to job-searching databases for patrons to use from home. This, of course, requires community members to have access to computers at home. In order to serve patrons who don't have these capabilities, the Plainfield (Illinois) Library created a partnership with the Mobile Workforce Center, a state-of-the-art RV equipped with a computer lab and satellite Internet that travels to communities to help with job hunting (Hill 2012, 15).

Many patrons seeking help with job searches at their libraries belong to groups that for one reason or another have a harder time finding work than the average individual. In keeping with their dedication to social equity, libraries are developing specific services for these populations. The Pierce County (Washington) Public Library offered targeted help for two groups of residents who sometimes have difficulty finding jobs: older adults and newly discharged veterans. Working with the technical and community colleges, the AARP, Workforce Central, Pierce County Aging and Disability Resource Center, and others, the library hosted a "Recareering at 50+ Expo" that offered workshops, resume assistance, panel discussions, and more. Pierce County librarians also worked with a local military base to provide assistance to soldiers who would soon be reentering the civilian workforce. In a successful outreach effort, librarians went to the military base to introduce library job searching resources to soon-to-be discharged military personnel. The Denver (Colorado) Public Library, meanwhile, reached out to female ex-offenders and offered assistance with computers and resume writing. This project was so well received that Denver is planning to offer similar services to men who have recently been released from prison.

Denver's services to former prisoners actually fall into the categories of job-searching assistance and skill development. Their female students often needed to learn basic computer skills before they could even begin the job search. This is not an unusual situation. The Urban Libraries Council (2007) reported that 92 percent of public libraries offer computer instruction on a monthly basis (5). These classes move libraries into the realm of workforce development/job training. There is certainly a need for this type of assistance for many of our community members. The Urban Libraries Council points out that "new economy jobs call for higher level skills and a willingness to pursue continuing training to stay competitive. . . . Higher wages are strongly linked to some form of post-secondary education. Economic self-sufficiency—the ability to support a family—requires education beyond high school" (13). Many individuals are now getting some of this necessary training and knowledge from their public library.

The discussion of libraries supporting human capital through workforce development is intricately linked to library services we discuss elsewhere in this book. When libraries offer free programs, develop English language classes, teach patrons to use the tools in a digital media or fabrication lab, support early literacy, or hire and train teen employees, they are contributing to the development of a better trained local workforce. Some of this important work is done through community partnerships. The San Jose (Texas) Public Library, for example, worked with local employers to bring English as a Second Language and workplace literacy classes to their employees. The individuals who participated in the project were janitors, preschool teaching assistants, and environmental service workers in health care. Library staff members delivered the initial Work Wise classes. Librarians took their project a step further and engaged the talents of local community members to serve as tutors. After being trained by library staff, these volunteers worked one-on-one with the English language learners in the workplace. Both employers and employees involved in Work Wise saw significant benefits from the skills gained through this collaboration. Helping community members find quality jobs *and* have the necessary skills to succeed in these positions is an important two-pronged approach to strengthening the human capital in local communities.

GROW YOUR OWN ENTREPRENEURS

Intricately connected to workforce development is support for local small businesses. Certainly helping create a more skilled local workforce benefits all businesses in a community, but libraries' contributions to strengthening companies certainly do not stop there. One model of economic growth that is aligned with sustainable development principles (and community-centered library values) is "economic gardening." Christine Hamilton-Pennell, a leading voice in positioning libraries as key economic players, describes economic gardening, which was pioneered in Littleton, Colorado, in the 1980s, as "supporting local entrepreneurs through development of physical infrastructure, human capital, and information resources. It is a 'grow your own' model" (Hamilton-Pennell 2012). As we noted earlier, true sustainability depends on a multifaceted approach that supports a system that fairly distributes economic benefits without damaging a community's natural resources. With its emphasis on supporting local business, economic gardening can be a strategy for supporting a healthy ecosystem. As you will see, many of the library/business partnerships we will discuss in this section have the added benefit of adding to their community's environmental assets.

Running a successful small business is hard. With access to fewer resources than large corporations, small businesses heavily depend on their communities' local assets. Hamilton-Pennell (2008) believes this is why libraries are so valuable to economic gardening efforts: "Public libraries can bring many assets when partnering with business and economic development, including knowledgeable staff; proven return on investment; online and print resources to support business, workforce, and literacy development; and the library building and its technological resources" (2). Libraries across the country, and across the world, are leveraging these assets to provide to local businesspeople information and research help, spaces to support innovation, and connection to other community assets.

The Johnson County (Kansas) Library supports the information needs of its community's entrepreneurs by hosting an annual showcase of government and nonprofit resources available to small businesses (Urban Libraries Council 2010, 15). The Cecil County (Maryland) Public Library takes this approach a step further and has created a small-business information center, staffed by librarians dedicated to helping local entrepreneurs. Their motto is "quality research for your business." A wide range of small businesses have received help from Cecil County librarians, including a candy shop, a web-hosting business, a homemade ice cream shop, a hot dog stand, a thrift store, a handmade soap company, a hair salon, a bakery, a graphic design firm, and an artists' cooperative. In 2011, the library was named the Cecil County Chamber of Commerce Nonprofit Partner in Business.

One of the barriers librarians often cite as to why they don't reach out to the business community is lack of knowledge about the business world (Hamilton-Pennell 2011). The best way to overcome this obstacle is by partnering with other agencies that have deeper knowledge of the needs of small business. Librarians at the Carson City (Nevada) Public Library jumped right into the world of small-business development by spearheading the creation of "BRIC." This Business Resource Innovation Center is a multipurpose facility that nurtures local businesses. Librarians jumpstarted the creation of BRIC by applying for an LSTA state grant and reaching out to other community stakeholders. The original plan was to create a downtown location that would house the Carson City Office of Business Development, the Nevada Small Business Development Center, and a library business resource center. Municipal officials embraced the library's vision and decided to purchase a larger building that ultimately ended up housing Carson City's Building Division, Business Licenses and Permit Center, Planning Division, Engineering Division, the Capital City Arts Initiative, as well as the original trio. A part-time business librarian and the library's adult services librarian staff the Business Library. The library has benefited from their involvement in economic development in myriad ways. They are such an integral part of the city's efforts to revitalize their community that the "City Center Project" was designed around the inclusion of a new sixty-thousand-square-foot library, the Carson City Knowledge and Discovery Center (Hamilton-Pennell 2011).

The Urban Libraries Council (2007) report on local economic development determined that "one of the biggest traditional barriers to small business has been access to current and comprehensive business product, supplier, and financing" (3). Research skills are often one of the strongest assets that libraries can offer their communities. By connecting these skills with other community organizations and local businesses, libraries position themselves as important economic and community development actors in the community.

Innovation is a driving force in today's economy. To be competitive, local businesses need spaces, tools, and technology to create and test cutting-edge new products and services. Forward-thinking libraries have identified this as an opportunity to utilize their spaces to benefit their local economies. Like the libraries that have created green roofs, the Fayetteville (North Carolina) Public Library decided to utilize their roof space for community benefit. They are participating in an experiment with their local tech company, Power Electronics International, to install forty-eight solar panels on the library's roof. The hope is that the solar panels developed by Power Electronics can provide some of the energy for the library (Hadro 2009). Power Electronics is gaining an important opportunity for product testing, and the library is strengthening its ties to the local economy. This project is a perfect example of truly sustainable development since it protects the community's environmental capital by utilizing "green" solar energy, while also strengthening financial capital by supporting an emerging community business.

Other libraries are also catching this spirit of promoting economic in-novation. After the Cecil County Public Library started their business resource center, one of their business librarians loaned a local green technology company space in her garage at home to design and test their products (Hamilton-Pennell 2008, 5). While this speaks to the personal stake that librarians take in their communities, if this company was based in Helsinki, Finland, they would not have needed to rely on a librarian's garage. Instead, they could have made use of the city library's innovative "LABRARY." The LABRARY was developed to serve as a test lab for the products designed by small-time, local inventors and entrepreneurs. The Helsinki Library staff select themes that relate to their public service mission, including sustainability and the environment, health and well-being, and new public services. Community innovators that have devel-oped products that fit into one of these categories are allowed to showcase their creations in the LABRARY. Library patrons are then encouraged to test and try these innovations and provide feedback to the creators. The Helsinki Library is hopeful that this pilot program can evolve into a per-manent library service. In addition to the obvious benefits the LABRARY has for the local economy and entrepreneurs, the library sees the project as benefitting individual community members. Terhi Vilkman, of the Helsinki City Library, in an interview with us noted that "this is a way for libraries to offer a new kind of service to their customers—information in a new form; new, interactive and participatory contents . . . it benefits the libraries as well as their users, who can find information [about] these useful innovations, which they can use in their everyday life." The Helsinki Library's innovative service leverages the library's physical capital to benefit businesses and also to engage and give residents a stake in the economic life of their communities.

The LABRARY project is an excellent example of how libraries can claim the role of "research labs to support innovation." The Urban Libraries Council (2010) describes this as a major way libraries can further sustainable development in their local communities (17). The makerspaces, digital media labs, and other library creation spaces that we discuss in depth in chapter 14 are perfect examples of how libraries are building community spaces and equipping them with the tools that community innovators can use. In the process, libraries are encouraging invention and nurturing design. Community spaces devoted to exploration and design effectively connect creators and innovators from within your community. Connecting potential and existing entrepreneurial minds has real economic benefits for your community. Library spaces like these are crucial to development of a thriving creative local economy. As the Creative Economy Association of the North Shore (Massachusetts) points out, "Creative activity reaches its full economic potential when it is linked to other creative enterprises and activity, markets and to urban life and communities" (ConsultEcon Inc. 2008). The Skokie (Illinois) Library's Digital Media Lab, the Fayetteville Library's MakerSpace, and the Tacoma (Washington) Library's StoryLab are providing these crucial links for their communities (Kroski 2012).

Ultimately, the connections that libraries facilitate for small local businesses is their most important contribution to the economic assets of their communities. Just as networking, relationships, and community connections are fundamental to a community-centered library, they are also the lifeblood of new, small, and local businesses. Connecting local business people with other human and financial capital in the community is a perfect role for public libraries. Community-centered librarians should always be on the lookout for chances to create these links. For example,

Hamilton-Pennell (2008) suggests that public libraries consider developing a project that connects fledgling or aspiring entrepreneurs with retired business mentors (6). Libraries can also facilitate relationships between businesses and organizational or individual investors. One of the major stumbling blocks for many local would-be entrepreneurs is access to financial capital and credit. While libraries aren't banks, credit unions, or other money-lending institutions, they can strengthen community members' access to start-up capital through creative partnerships. The Brooklyn (New York) Public Library, for example, works with the Citi Foundation to host an annual PowerUP Business Plan Competition. All local entrepreneurs can enter and the company with the strongest business plan will win $15,000 to turn their dreams into reality. Four San Diego (California) County Library branches located in low-income or remote areas of the county created a groundbreaking partnership with the Foundation for Women to help female entrepreneurs start their own businesses. The foundation provides women with small loans, the women provide each other with peer support, and the library provides meeting rooms and helps connect women with local business and technology mentors. By designing services that support community entrepreneurs who may otherwise not have access to the resources they need to start up their businesses, libraries support both the economic and the social equity components of sustainable local development.

Ultimately, when a community-centered library dedicates itself to the fundamental principles of sustainable development, it is in a better position to strengthen community capital and help community members create better lives.

MAKE IT HAPPEN

Do you want to bring exciting programs like the ones mentioned in this chapter to your library's community? Here are some tips to get you started:

- If you are responsible for the creation of a new library, carefully weigh the option of reusing an old building or starting from scratch. Either way, make it a point to add as many environmentally friendly features as possible.

- Look for ways to incorporate green features into your existing building. Can you add a green roof to your building? Install more energy efficient windows?
- If your building has green features, look for ways to turn them into learning opportunities for the public.
- Consider tapping the talents of local community members to start reskilling workshops at your library, like quilting, repairing small appliances. or canning.
- To position your library as a destination for job seekers, contact your local employment office or workforce development board about creating a partnership.
- Once you've started offering job-seeking programs, consider how you could tweak them to help groups who face extra barriers to finding work, like older adults, English-language learners, or former prison inmates.
- To start assessing the needs of your local businesses and entrepreneurs, reach out to your chamber of commerce.
- Start arranging networking events or coordinate a mentoring program for small-business owners.
- Host a business plan competition or "petting zoo"–type program where the public can test out products designed by local inventors.

BIBLIOGRAPHY

"About Minneapolis Central Library." 2012. Hennepin County Library. Accessed October 14. http://www.hclib.org/News.cfm?ID=3188.

Antonelli, Monika. 2012. "The Public Library's Role in the Transition Towns Movement." In *Greening Libraries*, edited by Monika Antonelli and Mark McCullough, 241–56. Los Angeles: Library Juice.

"Bikes, Buildings and Broccoli: Integrating Arlington County's Smart Growth and Fresh Aire Principles into Who We Are and What We Do." Urban Libraries Council. 2012. http://www.urbanlibraries.org/bikes--buildings-and-broccoli --integrating-arlington-county---s-smart-growth-and-fresh-aire-principles-into -who-we-are-and-all-we-do-innovation-161.php?page_id=39.

ConsultEcon Inc. 2008. "North Shore Creative Economy Market Analysis and Action Plan." ConsultEcon Inc.: Economic Research and Management Consultants. http://www.ceans.org/documents/Final_Full_Report_041508.pdf.

"Fix-It Clinic." 2012. Hennepin County, Minnesota. Accessed December 17. http://www.hennepin.us/fixitclinic.

"Free to Learn—Public Library Services for Ex-Offenders." 2012. Urban Libraries Council. www.urbanlibraries.org/free-to-learn-----public-library-services -for-ex-offenders-innovation 62.php?page_id=46.

"Green Roof Benefits." 2012. International Green Roof Association. Accessed December 17. http://www.igra-world.com/benefits/index.php.

Hadro, Josh. 2009. "Fayetteville Public Library Going Green and Local with Solar Power." *Library Journal*, March 30. http://www.libraryjournal.com/ lj/community/buildingandfacilities/854585-266/fayetteville_public_library_ going_green.html.csp.

Hamilton-Pennell, Christine. 2008. "Public Libraries and Community Economic Development: Partnering for Success." *Rural Research Report* 18 (10): 1–8.

———. 2011. "Carson City Library, Partner in Economic Revitalization." Supporting Entrepreneurship. May 10 (12:39 a.m.), accessed October 12, 2012. http://supportinglocalentrepreneurship.wordpress.com/2011/05/11/carson -city-library-partner-in-economic-revitalization/.

———. 2012. "Libraries." Growing Local Economies. Accessed October 12. http://growinglocaleconomies.com/libraries.

Hauke, Petra, and Klaus Ulrich Werner. 2012. "The Second Hand Library Building: Sustainable Thinking through Recycling Old Buildings into New Libraries." *IFLA Journal* 38 (1): 60–67.

Hill, Nanci Maloni. 2012. "Public Libraries and Services to the Unemployed." *Public Libraries* 51 (2): 14–21.

"Kathleen Clay Edwards Family Branch." 2012. City of Greensboro North Carolina Library. Accessed October 8. http://www.greensboro-nc.gov/index .aspx?page=824.

Kroski, Ellyssa. 2012. "10 Most Amazing Library Laboratories." Online Education Database. September 26. http://oedb.org/library/beginning-online -learning/10-most-amazing-library-laboratories.

"Library Farm." 2012. Northern Onondaga Public Library. Accessed October 14. http://www.nopl.org/library-farm.

"Micro Enterprise @ the Library: Foundation for Women." 2012. Urban Libraries Council. http://www.urbanlibraries.org/micro-enterprise---the-library --foundation-for-women-innovation-56.php?page_id=46.

Pinter, Dave. 2012. "Abandoned Walmart Transformed into a Functioning Library." PSFK. June 28. http://www.psfk.com/2012/06/abandoned-wal-mart -transformend-into-a-beautifully-designed-library.html.

"PowerUP! Competition." 2012. Brooklyn Public Library. Accessed October 13. http://www.brooklynpubliclibrary.org/locations/business/powerup.

"Preparing Discharged Soldiers for the Job Market." 2012. Urban Libraries Council. http://www.urbanlibraries.org/preparing-discharged-soldiers-for-the-job-market-innovation-175.php?page_id=46.

"Recareering @ 50+ Expo." 2012. Urban Libraries Council. http://www.urbanlibraries.org/recareering---50--expo-innovation-181.php?page_id=46.

"Small Business Success Stories." 2012. Cecil County Public Library. Accessed December 17. http://cecil.ebranch.info/small-business/success-stories.

Urban Libraries Council. 2007. "Making Cities Stronger: Public Library Contributions to Local Economic Development." Urban Libraries Council. http://www.urbanlibraries.org/filebin/pdfs/MakingCitiesStronger_Full_Report.pdf.

———. 2010. "Partners for the Future: Public Libraries & Local Governments Creating Sustainable Futures." Urban Libraries Council. http://www.urbanlibraries.org/filebin/pdfs/Sustainability_Report_2010.pdf.

"Work Wise: Improving Job Performance and Proficiency." 2012. Urban Libraries Council. http://www.urbanlibraries.org/work-wise--improving-job-performance-and-proficiency-innovation-35.php?page_id=45

"Workforce1 Expansion Centers." 2012. Urban Libraries Council. http://www.urbanlibraries.org/workforce-1-expansion-centers-innovation-66.php?page_id=46.

CHAPTER 11

Libraries as Cultural Reflections of the Community

Archives, digital and special collections, and oral history projects are not just within the purview of large academic or research libraries. Many public libraries have collections that extend far beyond what is traditionally associated with a local community library. Archives and unique collections can be found all over—from the largest public library system to small county and tribal libraries. Some archives may be grand in scale, with museum-quality exhibition space or digitization equipment. Others are small-scale initiatives designed to preserve and make accessible local history, which may simply include things such as local yearbooks or newspapers. Some public libraries have developed oral history projects and collections that tell the stories of their communities through the people who live there. Other libraries have created unique circulating collections based on the needs and interests of their patrons. Still other libraries have spent the time and money to either restore traditional buildings or to build sweeping new structures that capture the imagination of patrons and establish the library as a destination.

In all cases, the public libraries featured in this chapter are about more than pleasure reading or traditional programming. Local libraries play important roles in preserving community history, identity, and gathering space. By doing so, they are building new cultural assets and making existing ones more visible. Public libraries are venturing into areas that are more often associated with academic libraries, and they are making great contributions to local genealogists, researchers, and community members in general. This chapter will look at some of the unique ways in which libraries have expanded their collections and services beyond the traditional. We will look at some of the fun and funky circulating collections developed in response to community interests. Then we'll take a look at archives and oral history projects, large and small. Finally, we will spend some time considering library buildings themselves, many of which are not only important physical assets, but are also culturally significant and serve as important cultural and social markers within their communities.

THE FUN AND FUNKY SIDE OF CIRCULATING COLLECTIONS

In 2011, an article in the *Chicago Tribune* asked the question, "You can get *that* at the library?" The article featured a variety of unique circulating collections that libraries had developed to meet patron needs. Focusing on how library services and collections help patrons save money, the article featured fairly standard library offerings such as Internet access and e-books, but also noted that the Oakland (California) Public Library "has some 2,700 tools that it lends. . . . Other libraries will loan fishing poles and tackle boxes. . . . At other libraries you can borrow paintings and sculptures, movie projectors and digital cameras, and karaoke machines and laptop computers." The article quotes ALA president Molly Raphael as saying that while "some could argue that equipment lending is not part of a library's core business, libraries do have a mission of learning and discovery" (Karp 2011).

Of course, these kinds of collections do more than just save people money. They also function as a very visible and tangible way for the library to truly be community centered. We believe that part of the mission of learning and discovery to which Molly Raphael refers involves meeting the needs of the local community. Unique circulating collections encourage librarians to take a look at the social, cultural, and recreational needs and interests of their patrons and then design collections that address these needs and interests in a material way. Creating unique collections also prompts librarians to consider carefully the assets that really do make their communities unique—so what circulates well in one community may not hold much appeal for another. A 2010 forum on LibraryThing asked librarians about the most unusual things their library loans. The responses came in from all over, and the resulting list was as eclectic as one would imagine. Public libraries circulate toys, pedometers, paintings, games and puzzles, umbrellas, and electric guitars! These are just a few of the wild, weird, or wonderful items that libraries provide to their communities, and they meet practical, intellectual, and aesthetic needs. They also help patrons realize that the library is about more than just books, and they help the libraries in question stay responsive to the community in an out-of-the-box way.

Among the most popular special collection items are circulating cake pans. The North Liberty (Iowa) Community Library has a collection of "nearly 200 aluminum cake pans for one-week checkout." Also in Iowa, the Colo Public Library circulates a cake pan collection that was given to the library by a donor. The Keokuk (Iowa) Public Library not only lends cake pans, they've set up a site where patrons can submit photos of their finished cakes. While cake pans aren't necessarily unique to a specific community, they obviously fill a lending niche and, in doing so, meet a community need. Blogger Tina King, upon spotting a collection of cake pans (in the stacks!) in a library in Atkinson, Nebraska, noted sagely that "since most of these towns don't have big box superstores nearby, I can imagine it's very handy. . . . If you haven't been to your local library lately, check it out. You never know what you may find to borrow as branches strive to become community centers" (King 2010).

In 2010, the Merritt (British Columbia) Public Library instituted one such community-centered initiative with their "Extreme Learning" lend-ing program. This yearlong program circulated a variety of outdoor and recreational equipment to local patrons. With a library card, community members could check out a mountain bike, a GPS, snowshoes, tennis racquets, walking sticks, fly-fishing kits (and lessons), and gym passes. Some of these items were purchased by the library while others, like the gym passes and fly-fishing lessons, were donated by local organizations or individuals. "Extreme Learning" served several purposes—it pro-moted an active lifestyle, highlighted what the library can offer patrons beyond books and movies, and helped patrons try new things that they might not have otherwise. Deborha Merrick, branch head of the Merritt Public Library, noted in an interview with Julie that the library likes to keep things "weird and different." The library, with only a handful of staff in a community of about six thousand, encourages users to try different things and also seeks new users with its constantly changing initiatives. A close relationship with local papers keeps the library in the front of people's minds and, as a result, community members routinely vote in support of the library.

Offbeat and creative library collections can also do a lot to build community assets. Oakland's Tool Library, for example, was started with a community development block grant after the community suffered from two natural disasters just two years apart. Residents of Oakland needed tools to physically rebuild their community, and the public library stepped in to fulfill that need. Even when they aren't building community in such a literal sense, offering unusual items for loan can bring other community benefits. Items such as power tools, fishing equipment, and telescopes require upkeep and knowledge that not all librarians have, providing a window of opportunity for libraries to utilize community members' skills and talents. Oakland relies heavily on volunteers to maintain and circulate their tool collection, while the Portsmouth (New Hampshire) Public Library collaborates with the New Hampshire Astronomical Society to offer telescopes for circulation. Individual Astronomical Society members are a crucial part of the "Library Telescope Program." They clean and repair scopes and "act as a local astronomical resource to the library patrons." Club members will even take on "apprentices" at a local library, mentoring the next community telescope expert. When libraries can connect patrons to share knowledge, skills, and interests, as well as materials, it can be a powerful way to build social capital in local communities. A blogger in the online Shareable community was so inspired by some circulating collections that she deemed public libraries "future-forward, locally-focused entities connecting patrons with informative and useful materials to enhance ourselves and the world around us" (Johnson 2011). Now there's a worthy description for a community-centered library!

Another popular circulating item highlights how libraries can collaborate to form partnerships that benefit both local institutions and community members. Many libraries circulate passes to local museums. Partnering with Museums Work for Chicago, the Chicago Public Library offers kids' passes to fourteen city museums and institutions, including the Art Institute, the Field Museum, and the Shedd Aquarium. The Peabody Institute Library, in "cooperation with the library and the community," offers free or discounted passes to over a dozen local and regional institutions. Farther south in New England, the Fairfield (Connecticut) Public Library offers passes to over thirty museums, zoos, aquariums, and historical societies in Connecticut, Massachusetts, and New York. A multiparty partnership between the Friends of the Hampstead Library, the Hampstead Mothers' Club, the Community Resource Association, the Hampstead

Civic Club, and anonymous donors resulted in passes to fifteen museums for library card holders in Hampstead, New Hampshire.

These kinds of collaborations yield multiple benefits—the libraries and institutions involved see new patrons, and community members who might not be able to afford a ticket to a museum or art gallery have an opportunity to explore the historical and cultural assets in their communities. These partnerships are particularly beneficial in that they highlight the important connection between the community, the library, and cultural institutions, and the public benefits by the cultural capital built by the collaboration.

Of course, collaboration doesn't necessarily happen just between institutions, as we see with the Hampstead Public Library. Friends groups, private donors, or other local organizations can partner with both libraries and museums to make passes available for public circulation. Some libraries have partnered with corporations to provide passes, such as the Toronto Public Library, which partnered with Sun Life Financial to create the Museum + Arts Pass providing access to over a dozen local institutions. Whatever the partnership, the result is a circulating collection that fosters both library use and cultural life.

HIDDEN COLLECTIONS BECOME VISIBLE

Archival collections in public libraries focus on what is unique to the surrounding community, both historically and contemporarily, and serve as important places for historical and genealogical research. Similarly, oral history collections record the stories of a community as told by the people who lived them, providing unique first-person perspectives. Libraries large and small are creating or maintaining unique collections that help in preserving and, more importantly for a public library, making accessible, local information.

Several large public libraries have extensive digital and archival collections that speak not only to local community interests but also to national interests. The Birmingham (Alabama) Public Library's Department of Archives & Manuscripts has two dozen archival collections containing more than thirty million documents on subjects ranging from the Civil War to sports history. Given the city's important role in the civil rights movement, their Civil Rights Archives are especially worth noting. The two collections housed at the library focus on civil rights and race relations in Birmingham, and civil rights and race relations in Alabama as a whole. According to their website, the BPL has acquired over one million documents related to civil rights in Birmingham, collected over fifty years. The "BPL librarians compiled scrapbooks, acquired items from the community and created large newspaper clipping files relating to civil rights activities and activists." The library eventually began "systematically [collecting] the records of local, city and county government, area civic and civil rights organizations, individuals and the news media." A major grant in the 1980s enabled the library to preserve city records, which would have otherwise been lost or destroyed, and now this public library "is recognized around the world for holding one of the most comprehensive and heavily used research collections on the Civil Rights Movement."

The San Francisco Public Library is home to the Gay, Lesbian, Bisexual, and Transgender (GLBT) Archives, part of the Gay and Lesbian Center at the library, which was funded in 1991 with a gift from Ambassador James Hormel. The archives "[collect] unpublished materials such as personal papers, organizational records, flyers and other important documents chronicling the history of the GLBT community in Northern California." In addition to this regional focus, other materials in the center are "national and international in scope."

Many large libraries are making their collections available digitally. The Denver Public Library's Western History and Genealogy Digital Collections is a "renowned online collection [containing] a selection of photographs, maps, broadsides, architectural drawings and other documents from the collections of the Western History/Genealogy Department chronicling the people, places, and events that shaped the settlement and growth of the Western United States." Funded by grants and expanded through partnerships, this collection is huge and ambitious in its scope, digitizing photos and historical documents, and also allowing community members themselves to generate and curate content in an extraordinary example of participatory culture. In a similar initiative, the New York Public Library is enlisting the help of the public to make forty thousand historical and contemporary restaurant menus available and searchable digitally. The library's director of strategy, Micah May, says, "There are literally millions of tasks that librarians will never have the time to get to, and there's a great appetite by the public to contribute to something meaningful" (Johnson 2011). This type of project becomes possible when librarians begin to see their role as facilitators of community building instead of information gatekeepers and experts.

Archives and digital collections like these aren't limited to large metropolitan libraries, however. The Peabody Institute Library (2011) holds an archival collection comprised of "thousands of rare volumes, hundreds of maps, photographs, manuscripts and artifacts" focusing on Peabody history, George Peabody, Essex County history, and genealogy. The library is also one of only "134 repositories which own John James Audubon's historic work, *The Birds of America.*" South of Boston, the New Bedford (Massachusetts) Free Public Library Archives has collaborated with the City of New Bedford Management Information Systems Department for a grant-funded Whaling Collection Archives, "a comprehensive index of men and ships on whaling voyages from the New Bedford Customs District from 1807 through 1925" that clearly speaks to a unique local history and culture. Another project of collaboration, materials in this collection come from the New Bedford Free Library, the National Archives in Waltham (Massachusetts), and the New Bedford Whaling Museum/Kendall Institute. In another example of libraries focusing on local interest, the Winter Park (Florida) Public Library has small digital collections focusing on four of the hurricanes to have hit the area. And in an example of a fun digital collection, the Milwaukee (Wisconsin) Public Library has created a file of historic recipes that were published in the *Milwaukee Sentinel* and *Milwaukee Journal* between 1960 and 1980. Aside from being an interesting resource from a local publication, a collection like this provides a fascinating glimpse into local taste and culture at a specific time in history.

Archives and special collections also play an important role in tribal libraries, some of which serve as public, tribal college, and tribal government libraries all at once. The Colorado River Indian Tribes Library/ Archives (Arizona) contains "information from personal correspondence, Bureau of Indian Affairs files, and works of historians, ethnologists, anthropologists, and journalists" for use by all tribal members and approved nontribal members. The Delaware Tribe of Indians (Oklahoma), in collaboration with the Bartlesville Public Library and Bartlesville Area History Museum, and with a Basic Library Services Grant (IMLS), is working on scanning and digitizing tribal and historic documents and is seeking to build the archival collection through the donation of tribal material from tribal members. The Coquille Indian Tribe Library (Oregon) "places an emphasis on providing information from the perspective of Tribes and Native Americans on subjects including culture, history, health, education and law" and contains "30,000+ pages of archival documents from the combined collections of the Southwestern Oregon Research Project and the Melville Jacobs Collection."

In addition to archives large and small, public libraries are also launching their own oral history projects. The Nashville (Tennessee) Public Library, in an effort to document that city's involvement with the civil rights movement and with a gift from local philanthropists, launched the Civil Rights Oral History Project in 2001. The collection "contains a series of interviews done by library staff members and volunteers with people who were involved in the Nashville and national movement" and includes "discussions about race relations, civil rights, education, economics, social life, and family life." The Diversity Studies Collection at the Plainfield (New Jersey) Public Library includes three small oral history collections developed in collaboration with StoryCorps that contribute to the library's mission to "gather and preserve research materials on the minority groups of Plainfield." The Free Public Library and Cultural Center of Bayonne (New Jersey) holds the Veterans' History Project, which is a series of recordings with veterans of World War II, the Vietnam War, and the Korean Conflict. This collection was recorded in the library and provides "first-hand-accounts of U.S. veterans . . . to preserve their unique experience for future generations."

Each of these collections, from the largest archive to the smallest oral history project to the most local of digital collections, speaks to ways in which libraries are centering themselves within their communities. These projects record, preserve, and make accessible information and resources in an effort to document the people that comprise a community. Whether it is a small tribal library or a metropolitan system, the work that these libraries are doing helps them connect with their communities in new ways. They are meeting community needs, responding to community interests, and inviting community participation. In doing so, they are redefining what they do and highlighting their worth.

BUILDINGS WITH MEANING

Sometimes it isn't just what is in a library that is important to the community—library buildings themselves can be important cultural markers in a community, harking back to the past or looking forward to the future. Julie has written about the significance of the library in symbolizing the higher aspirations of the community (Edwards 2010), and library buildings all over the country serve as gathering places. The buildings themselves, particularly those restored or newly designed, do more than just contribute to environmental capital and community sustainability as we mentioned in the last chapter. They communicate something important about the community and the role of the library within it—as Winston Churchill said, "First we shape our buildings, then they shape us." In 2011 the Whole Building Design Guide, a program of the National Institute of Building Sciences, noted in an article about public libraries that "members of communities are the service population of public libraries and their needs affect the design and planning of public library spaces." Careful consideration of the community is essential in both renovating old and building new libraries.

At the time of this writing the Providence (Rhode Island) Public Library was beginning a restoration process that would update the 115-year-old building while at the same time preserving the historical character of the building. With the goals of preserving the building and ensuring access, the restoration plans included not only behind-the-walls features like improved HVAC and sprinkler systems but also space that will make previously underutilized collections more accessible. The restoration included "plans to create a reference and research room devoted entirely to the PPL's historically significant and unique Rhode Island Collection" as well as a "planned Ship Room, which will showcase the Library's Brownell Collection of Atlantic Coast Ship Models and other seafaring artifacts." In addition to these spaces, the library is purposefully designing meeting space and partnering with a local caterer in order to accommodate "a variety of events—including corporate meetings and conferences, weddings and other personal occasions, [and] community gatherings."

While some communities restore old library buildings to new grandeur, others create their libraries from scratch. In 2000, a group of citizens in North Plains (Oregon) gathered to discuss the need for a public library. A library of their own was so important to this community that they set up their first library in a janitor's closet at the local community center. The popularity of the library grew and it moved into a roughly six-hundred-square-foot space before an individual Oregonian offered to fund a brand new building for the library in partnership with the City of North Plains and the Friends of the Library. In half a year, the Friends group had raised over a quarter of a million dollars, with over $70,000 coming from local businesses and families, and with no money coming at all from public funds. Constructed of wood and filled with local community touches, "the new building became the pride of the town, a unique symbol of what can be accomplished when a community works together."

One of the most recently updated and most talked about library buildings in the world is the Central Library, part of the Seattle (Washington) Public Library System. Designed as a sweeping glass structure by renowned architect Rem Koolhaas, the library opened in 2004 and "gave Seattle both a civic icon and a functional, user-friendly building offering many different services and spaces." The Central Library, designed and built as part of Seattle's "Libraries for All" building program, wasn't universally admired, but it has come to signify the city's library system and is recognizable throughout the world. Like the tiny North Plains Public Library, the Seattle system relied on community partnerships and sees the library as a community treasure, noting that "growth and success could not have been possible without the incredible support of the community, committed staff and Library Board, The Seattle Public Library Foundation, Friends of The Seattle Public Library, hundreds of dedicated volunteers, and the Mayor and City Council" (Seattle Public Library 2008, 4).

No look at library buildings would be complete without mention of the Kansas City (Missouri) Public Library and the New York Public Library. In Kansas City the Central Library features the larger than life "Community Bookshelf" on the outside of its parking garage. The bookshelf, a mural of book spines running the length of the building, features "22 titles reflecting a wide variety of reading interests as suggested by Kansas City readers and then selected by The Kansas City Public Library Board of Trustees" (Kansas City Public Library 2012). In the digital age, this public artwork, created with community input and depicting traditional books, speaks to the power of the written word and to the image of the book. And of course, the most famous feature of the New York Public Library is actually two features—Patience and Fortitude, the library lions, sculpted by Edward Clark Potter and christened with these names by mayor Fiorello LaGuardia, "for the qualities he felt New Yorkers would need to survive the economic depression."

Libraries striving to be community-centered institutions will have to look beyond traditional services to see what they can uniquely contribute to their towns and cities. From funky collections to local archives to interesting buildings and aesthetics, public libraries are making a mark on the culture of their communities in a variety of new and interesting ways. And from the most expensive library renovation project to the smallest-scale digital project, libraries are highlighting their relevance locally in tangible, material ways.

MAKE IT HAPPEN

Are you interested in building a local archive or making your building more culturally significant? Here are some tips to get you started:

- When considering circulating collections, think about what makes your community unique. Is there something that defines your community, or is there a pressing need you notice that could be addressed by an interesting lending collection? Take a look at your patrons and see what you can offer besides books and films.
- Solicit and accept donations for odd, wacky, or weird things. Maybe a local scrapbooker wants to donate a collection of stamps. Perhaps a local gardener has some tools that could be of use for the community. Take a look at what kinds of hobbies your patrons have and think about tapping them to help you build a collection. On the flip side, if you collect a bunch of seemingly random donations, considering putting them together into one larger, eclectic circulating collection.
- Partner with local museums, zoos, art institutes, or other organizations to create a museum pass system. Ask for donated passes or work with your Friends group to purchase passes.
- Consider making some of your unique collections available through digitization. Do you have historic photos that might be of interest to the community? Maybe there is a collection of yearbooks from the local high school that could be scanned and digitized. If you don't have the staff and resources for this kind of project, consider fund-raising and outsourcing the work, or partner with local organizations who might have the volunteers and equipment to make digitization possible.

- Consider an oral history project that focuses on your community. What makes your community special? Is it a local industry? A diverse population? A specific location? Think about what would be most interesting and important to preserve and build your project from there. Not sure where to start? Look online for oral history guides, or consult with other libraries that have launched similar projects.
- Don't forget your building! Is there an interesting architectural feature, meeting room, or other unique aspect to your physical space? Highlight it on your website and consider making it a visual part of your brand. A special or unique physical characteristic helps make the library more recognizable in the community, and can serve as a point of local civic pride and identification.
- When renovating or building, don't forget that the library exists within and for a specific community! Get your patrons involved, listen to what they want and need, and build or redesign with an eye toward what you want your building to *be*, *do*, and *say* to the public. Remember also that place is important—consider your physical environment and geography when you build or renovate, and incorporate design and style elements that speak to your unique location.

BIBLIOGRAPHY

"Archives." 2012. Colorado River Indian Tribes Library/Archives. Accessed June 4. http://www.critlibrary.com/archives.html.

"Archives & Manuscripts Guide to the Collections." 2012. Birmingham Public Library Department of Archives & Manuscripts. Accessed June 4. http://www.birminghamarchives.org/SubjectGuideSuggestedReadin.htm.

"Borrowing Museum Passes." 2012. Hampstead Public Library. Accessed December 19. http://www.hampstead.lib.nh.us/museum-passes.asp.

"Building Facts about the Central Library." 2012. Seattle Public Library. Accessed June 5. http://www.spl.org/locations/central-library/cen-building-facts.

"Cake Pan Collection." 2012. Colo Public Library. Accessed June 4. http://www.colo.lib.ia.us/use-thelibrary/cake.

"Cake Pans." 2012. Keokuk Public Library. Accessed June 4. http://www.keokuk.lib.ia.us/use-ourlibrary/cakepans.

"Collections/Whaling Archives." 2012. City of New Bedford, Massachusetts. Accessed June 4. http://www.newbedford-ma.gov/Library/Whaling/Whaling.html.

"Coquille Indian Tribe Library." 2012. Coquille Indian Tribe. Accessed June 4. http://www.coquilletribe.org/coquille-indian-tribe-library.htm.

"Denver Public Library Digital Collections." 2012. Denver Public Library. Accessed June 4. http://digital.denverlibrary.org/cdm/.

"Diversity Studies Collection." 2012. Plainfield Public Library. Accessed June 4. http://www.plainfieldlibrary.info/Departments/LH/LH_diversity.html.

Edwards, Julie Biando. 2010. "Symbolic Possibilities." In *Beyond Article 19: Libraries and Social and Cultural Rights*, edited by Julie Biando Edwards and Stephan P. Edwards, 7–40. Duluth, Minn.: Library Juice Press.

"Historic Recipe File." 2012. Milwaukee Public Library. Accessed June 4. http://www.mpl.org/file/digital_recipes_index.htm.

"Holdings." 2011. Peabody Institute Library. Accessed April 4, 2013. http://www.peabodylibrary.org/history/holdings.html.

"James C. Hormel Gay & Lesbian Center." 2012. San Francisco Public Library. Accessed June 4. http://sfpl.org/index.php?pg=2000045201.

"John James Audubon and *The Birds of America*." 2011. Peabody Institute Library. Accessed April 14, 2013. http://www.peabodylibrary.org/history/audubon.

Johnson, Cat. 2011. "Libraries Become Centers for Sharing." Shareable. October 3. http://www.shareable.net/blog/libraries-become-centers-for-sharing.

Kansas City Public Library. 2012. "Community Bookshelf." Kansas City Public Library. Accessed June 5. http://www.kclibrary.org/community-bookshelf.

Karp, Gregory. 2011. "You Can Get *That* at the Library?" Spending Smart, *Chicago Tribune*, August 26.

"Kids Museum Passports." 2012. Chicago Public Library. Accessed June 4. http://www.chipublib.org/eventsprog/programs/kids/grkids_museumpass.php#museums.

King, Tina. 2010. "Borrow a Book—and a Cake Pan." *The Good Midwest Life Blog.* October (9:20 am). http://www.thegoodmidwestlife.com/2010/10/borrow-book-and-cake-pan.html.

"Library History." 2012. North Plains Public Library. Accessed June 4. http://nplibrary.org/about-us/library-history/.

"The Library Lions." 2012. New York Public Library. Accessed June 5. http://www.nypl.org/help/about-nypl/library-lions.

"Most Unusual Thing Your Library Loans." 2010. LibraryThing. 2010. Accessed June 4, 2012. http://www.librarything.com.

"Museum Passes." 2011. Peabody Institute Library. Accessed June 4, 2012. http://www.peabodylibrary.org/services/museum.html.

"Museum Passes." 2012. Fairfield Public Library. Accessed June 4. http://www.fairfieldpubliclibrary.org/museum.htm.

"NHAS Library Telescope Program." 2012. New Hampshire Astronomical Society. Accessed June 19. http://nhastro.com/ltp.php.

"NLCL Cake Pan Collection." 2012. North County Public Library. Accessed June 4. http://www.northlibertylibrary.org/services/collections/cakepans.html.

"Oral History." 2012. Archives & Special Collections at Free Public Library and Cultural Center of Bayonne. Accessed December 17. http://www.bayonne library.org/bay_Archives_Veterans.htm#Veterans History Project.

"Oral History: Civil Rights Oral History Project." 2012. Nashville Public Library. Accessed June 4. http://www.library.nashville.org/localhistory/his_sp coll_orhist_crohp.asp.

"Providence Public Library Announces Building Restoration Plan and Space Rental Partnership." 2012. Providence Public Library. February 24, accessed June 5. http://www.provlib.org/news/providence-public-library-announces -building-restoration-plan-and-space-rental-partnership.

"Public Library." 2011. Whole Building Design Guide: A Program of the National Institute of Building Sciences. http://www.wbdg.org/design/public_ library.php.

Seattle Public Library. 2008. "Libraries for All: A Report to the Community." Seattle Public Library. September 12. www.spl.org/Documents/about/libraries _for_all_report.pdf.

"Sun Life Financial Museum + Arts Pass." 2012. Toronto Public Library. Accessed June 4. http://www.torontopubliclibrary.ca/museum-arts-passes/index.jsp.

"Tool Lending Library." 2012. Oakland Public Library. Accessed December 17. http://www.oaklandlibrary.org/locations/tool-lending-library.

"Tribal Archives." 2012. Official Website of the Delaware Tribe of Indians. Accessed June 4. http://delawaretribe.org/tribalsite/services-and-programs/ historic-preservation/museumlibrary/.

"Winter Park History and Archives Collection: Digitized Collections." 2012. Winter Park Public Library. Accessed June 4. http://www.wppl.org/wphistory/ DigitizedCollections.htm.

CHAPTER 12

Libraries as Community Centers
for Diverse Populations

This chapter highlights some ways that libraries build assets with and for non-English speakers, new immigrants, LGBTIQ individuals, and community members with disabilities. While these populations include an astounding degree of diversity internally, and may appear to have little in common with each other, they are groups that have often been neglected (and worse) by society *and* by public libraries. It is vital that a community-centered librarian be conscious of this fact and actively try to reverse this tendency. Some librarians, including those who are working with the ALA's divisions, committees, and roundtables, are already doing this valuable work. ALA's Office for Literacy and Outreach Services, Committee for Diversity, the Ethnic and Multicultural Information Exchange Roundtable, Gay, Lesbian, Bisexual Transgender Roundtable, and Social Responsibilities Roundtable work to help ensure that libraries are culturally competent and inclusive. In the following pages we will showcase some of the work that librarians are doing to engage all residents in the life of their communities. We hope that some of the programs and services highlighted in this chapter will be a great fit for your community, and we certainly hope they inspire you to stretch your concept of what a library can do. But remember—the only way to find out if these programs are truly right for your library is to engage with community members directly, find out what they need and want from the library, and then find out what they can contribute to it.

THE MANY LANGUAGES OF OUR COMMUNITIES

The United States Census Bureau (2010) has reported that the number of people in the United States who speak a language other than English at home has more than doubled in the last three decades. By 2007, census statistics showed that 20 percent of adults and children over the age of five reported speaking a language other than English at home (3). These numbers are expected to continue to rise, making it a sheer necessity that public libraries explore how to best serve non-English speakers.

Something as simple as a library sign in more than one language does more than provide direction; it can serve as an indicator to community members who speak languages other than English that this is *their* library too. Thoughtfully designed, multilingual, physical library collections can serve a similar function. The library's collection should reflect its community. For example, if a community has a majority of Spanish speakers, the collection should reflect that. This rationale extends to designing a library's online presence and collections. Public libraries in communities like San Francisco and Queens (New York) offer their websites in multiple languages. Queens also makes available digital resources for English-language learners through their "English for Your Health" program, which offers listening and vocabulary building exercises designed to assist with medical and dental visits, prescriptions, and emergencies.

Libraries that take serving non-English speakers seriously also offer a wide array of library programs. Turning again to the Queens Library provides a glimpse at the series of programs they offered from 2010 and 2011 called "Financial Literacy in the Community." These classes were presented in both English and a second language. Videos of the presentations are still available on the library's website, making these programs an ongoing service to their diverse community.

English classes are another potential library service, and an offshoot of these classes are library "conversation circles." These groups, which are less formal than a structured class, bring together English-language learners to practice their verbal skills and meet new people. Most public libraries tap into volunteers to lead their conversation circles, which both makes this program workable for libraries of varying sizes and creates a meaningful and rewarding way for residents to engage in the community and library. In a good example of a library partnering with a faith-based group, the Arlington (Texas) Public Library hosts conversation circles with volunteers from the Field Road Baptist Church. It is easy to see how these circles have the potential to be powerful asset builders. With their small size and intimate, casual format, groups can build human capital through the improvement of language skills, but they also strengthen social capital through the interactions among members and leaders.

Simply providing services *to* non-English speakers, however, can cast these patrons in the role of clients instead of valuable community assets. When libraries engage residents in the cultural life of the community, they remedy this problem. The Athens-Clarke County (Georgia) Regional Library hosts "exchange programs" that pair up English- and Spanish-speaking families to learn language skills from each other while completing a fun, hands-on cultural activity. A program like this has many of the benefits of conversation circles, while having the added benefit of emphasizing what the families can offer to each other.

This same library system partnered with other community stakeholders to create a learning center in a mobile home park that houses predominantly Hispanic residents. Among other services (including a Spanish collection and adult education classes), this center offers art classes and frequently hosts community art exhibits. Nurturing cultural capital in their Spanish-speaking population can have rich dividends for all residents, the library, and the community.

Many of the libraries that prioritize service to non-English speakers are in large, urban communities. Of course, this makes a great deal of sense given the sizable non-English-speaking populations that live in large cities. Libraries of all sizes, however, need to consider how to work with these populations. In a 2007 report, the ALA noted that smaller communities (those under one hundred thousand) are increasingly serving a larger proportion of non-English speakers. As diversity continues to filter into suburban and rural areas, all libraries will need to consider how to engage and reflect the cultural, linguistic, and ethnic complexities of their communities.

BRIDGES FOR NEWCOMERS

In the city of Peabody, there are a number of organizations that provide support to new immigrants: several churches, the local Community Action Program, and the library are just a few of them. The same holds true in many communities. Despite having a number of access points, new immigrants still often face what the Institute of Museum and Library Services and U.S. Citizenship and Immigration Services (2007) refer to as a "resource gap" (1). A report issued by these two agencies asserts that libraries can help address this gap by becoming a "bridge" for immigrants to their new community (4), their rationale being that "well-designed bridge programs create opportunities for immigrants to meet and interact with a variety of community members, while also providing valuable information and skills needed by all" (4). In other words, community-centered library programs for immigrants can strengthen social capital and overall human capital in your community.

The public library in Austin (Texas) has chosen to build community assets through their New Immigrant Project. This project fulfills a traditional library role by providing information on resources, like organizations that offer free English or citizenship classes, for the immigrant community. The library also maintains a digital "Newcomers Guide," which covers the topics of cultural groups, job searching, legal and social services, and starting a new business ("New Immigrants Project"). This inclusion of information for immigrant entrepreneurs is especially noteworthy, as it acknowledges, facilitates, and potentially strengthens community members' access to, and the community's overall, financial capital.

The staff at the Memphis (Tennessee) Library have also embraced their library's responsibility to immigrants in their community by developing citizenship workshops. The library's workshops offer test prep for the citizenship exam, as well as assist with filing required paperwork and learning the laws, regulations, rights, and responsibilities pertaining to citizenship (Hanshaw 2012). The library has also hosted naturalization services for over 430 new citizens in the community. By becoming a venue for this meaningful ritual that has both personal and political implications, the Memphis Library is positioning itself as both a community player in the civic life of the community (see chapter 9) and as an asset builder for immigrants.

In an interesting twist on citizenship classes that leverages existing community assets, the King County (Washington) Library System created the "Centered on Citizenship" program, which pairs local teen tutors up with adults who are preparing to take their citizenship exam. What an innovative way to fulfill a community need while simultaneously recognizing teens as valuable community assets! In addition to the wonderful connections (read: social capital) fostered by this program, it's a successful endeavor by more objective standards. According to the district direc-tor of Seattle's Citizenship and Immigration Services Office, immigrants who have been tutored by teens "have a marvelous success rate" on the citizenship exams (Horowitz 2004).

One of the themes that will run through this chapter is how some libraries are moving beyond the simple provision of services to provide connections to community assets. The Boulder (Colorado) Public Li-brary partnered with the Center for Humanities and the Arts at the Uni-versity of Colorado, and the Arts and Humanities Assembly of Boulder County to present "Communities of Exile." This program combined a panel discussion of the experience of being an exile from one's home-land with an open discussion of how to overcome some of the challenges that exist within the community for exiled individuals. The day wrapped up with an inspiring lineup of cultural exhibitions from this population: community members from the Sioux/Assiniboine tribe told stories, Afghans sang folk songs, West Africans performed traditional music, and Japanese, Latin American, and Caribbean dancers displayed their talents. Boulder's collaboration is a truly inspiring example of a library building community assets, and increasing social, political, and cultural capital, by working with immigrants.

COMING OUT IN SUPPORT OF LGBTIQ PATRONS

Moving on to a very different community, we arrive at another population that may need some coaxing to see their public libraries as a resource and community center for them: lesbian, gay, bisexual, transgender, intersex, and queer community members. Libraries serve LGBTIQ residents every day and are often completely unaware of it, which is as it should be. Still, a community-centered library should consider the role that it plays in the lives of all minority community members, not just the visible majority, which means considering how to work with LGBTIQ residents.

LGBTIQ individuals all come to grips with their sexuality at different points in their lives. Increasingly, youth as young as middle school are coming out, which means that YA librarians need to be aware that patrons at the lower end of their service population's age group may be seeking resources and support. Since most young adult resources and literature that address LGBTIQ issues are aimed at high schoolers, librarians need to specifically seek out materials with a younger target audience. On the other end of the spectrum, there are as many adults and seniors who come to terms with their sexual orientation or identity later in life. These patrons have much different things to offer to, and services they need from, a public library. It will take significant thought for libraries to purposefully plan to meet the needs of such a diverse population, but this is true of all the diverse populations discussed in this chapter. Community-centered libraries need to be prepared and willing to put in the necessary forethought when considering how to serve, and also how to work with, LGBTIQ individuals in a manner that benefits the entire community.

The West Hollywood (California) Library Park ran an ambitious fundraising campaign to design a new public library that can serve the needs of their diverse, twenty-first-century community. To that end, the library was designed specifically to be "a place to celebrate the LGBT community." How often is that a stated goal of a public library? The West Hollywood community has a vibrant gay community and recognizes the importance of intentionally including this population in the library. To fulfill this mission they have an extensive LGBT collection and an LGBT book discussion run by the executive director of the Lambda Literary Foundation.

Like West Hollywood, the New York Public Library recognizes that their community has a sizable LGBTIQ population, so they maintain a blog dedicated to "connecting you with the LGBT collections, programs, and expertise that The New York Public Library has to offer." The NYPL also runs an annual "Anti-Prom" event for twelve- to eighteen-year-olds in order to provide "an alternative, safe space for all teens who may not feel welcome at official school programs or dances because of their sexual orientation, the way they dress, or any other reason." It's noteworthy that the NYPL positions its blog and its programming as being for community members regardless of their sexual orientation. Library events and services may have a gay and lesbian theme, but they can enrich the broader community as well.

Libraries that have tapped into LGBTIQ residents' skills and strengths to offer programs are listed in the Programming Librarian's Gay and Lesbian Pride Month website and include the San Antonio (Texas) Public Library, which had community members discuss their personal experiences at their Come OUT event. In Oakland, California, the library put on an exhibit of the Lavender Scrolls, which highlights the lives of eight older adults in the LGBTIQ community. Oakland paired this exhibit with an event that allowed teens to meet the subjects of the exhibit. Several libraries have done something similar with programs that offer guidance and perspective from an older generation to a younger one. These programs provide a way to connect LGBTIQ adults to youth in a way that simply didn't happen for earlier generations. This can be hugely important to sexual minority youth who often feel isolated. Dan Savage (2011), who started the It Gets Better project, writes that the message society has sent gay adults is, "You can't talk to the kids . . . the LBGT teenagers being assaulted emotionally, physically, spiritually. . . . And if you do attempt to talk to the kids . . . we'll impugn your motives, we'll accuse you of being a pedophile or a pederast, we'll claim you're trying to recruit children into 'the gay lifestyle'" (6). Savage's video project, which was turned into a book as well, attempts to change this mind-set. Libraries that offer intergenerational LGBTIQ programming are doing the same thing.

Other library programs for LGBTIQ patrons include movie screenings, legal advice, children's story times, parenting concerns, and author visits. The Queens (New York) Library hit on two of the topics addressed in this chapter when they offered a program on gender and sexual orientation discrimination in Spanish. Queens deserves a lot of credit for acknowledging that people are never part of just one community. When serving diverse populations, in fact when serving *all* populations, librarians should keep this in mind so as to avoid stereotyping. All of these programs are not so different from those offered by most public libraries for their general population, but by adding an element to make it relevant for a section of the community that faces unique challenges and has a unique cultural perspective, libraries of every size can position themselves as relevant to everyone in their cities and towns. In some cases this may mean just being consciously inclusive in our programs. For example, your library's regular book group (teen or adult) can read a Lambda Award–winning book; when you offer reader's advisory, you can include titles with gay themes; or when offering a workshop on college financial aid, you can ask your presenter to talk about how financial aid is different for a teen whose same-sex parents' marriage isn't recognized by the federal government.

As we are all aware, efforts to serve gays and lesbians in your library may not be without controversy. We believe that librarians have a professional obligation to do so anyway. If you need more practical advice on where to begin, librarians from the Ocean County (New Jersey) Library System created a slide show that can help you make the case, train staff, form partnerships, and brainstorm programming ideas (Condello et al. 2009).

ENGAGING PATRONS WITH DISABILITIES

Serving patrons with disabilities is similar to serving non-English speakers, immigrants, and LGBTIQ patrons in two ways. First, it is virtually impossible to generalize about a population that is so diverse: patrons with disabilities may be young or old, have a variety of disabilities and needs, and may belong to one (or more) of the other diverse populations we've discussed here. Second, community-centered libraries should be on the lookout for ways to leverage the skills and talents of patrons with disabilities to strengthen individuals, the library, and the local community.

This is an area of library services where librarians would be wise to consult with their colleagues in youth services, where many of the innovative projects and programs for patrons with disabilities get their start. Libraries may also need to provide training to staff members who may not be familiar with the best methods to serve patrons with disabilities. Of course, when considering professional development in this area, libraries should tap both professionals within their community who serve those with special needs and the individuals with disabilities themselves.

The Centers for Disease Control estimates that one in eighty-eight children is now autistic. To respond to this, many public libraries are looking for ways to better serve these children and their caregivers. Two popular programs that can meet the needs of autistic children are opportunities for children to read to service dogs and "sensory story times." The Deerfield Public Library in Chicago has instituted both sensory story times and Read to Rover for kids with autism, featured in an article called "Story Time Star" in *Library Journal*. Chicago Public Libraries have also created accessibility kits that can be downloaded at home before a library visit. These kits introduce the library and will help it feel more familiar, and therefore manageable, for children with autism (Winson and Adams 2010). The Temecula (California) Public Library has its own versions of these programs, and librarians have also created a "Play and Learn" (PAL) activity center in their children's room. PAL includes magnets, blocks, and shapes that will appeal to autistic children. Taking it a step further, the library is also working to connect residents through a series of workshops on parenting children with autism. Next on their agenda? Recent research suggests that using tablets, like the iPad, will help autistic children's reading ability (Russell 2012). Sensory story times are in such demand in communities that the ALA offered a program on them at their annual conference (Nguyen 2011).

Carrie Banks from the Brooklyn Public Library was honored as a 2012 "Movers and Shakers" in *Library Journal* for the innovative approach she has pioneered in library services for children with special needs. Banks created the Child's Place for Children with Special Needs in five Brooklyn library branches. The goal of these spaces and the programs they offer there is to provide an environment where "children with and without special needs play and learn together in an inclusive setting." Features of the Child's Place include fully accessible facilities, story times and events that incorporate multiple intelligences, sensory gardens, adaptive toys and craft supplies, interpreters, and communication boards (Brooklyn Public Library, 2). Importantly, the staff at these libraries have educational backgrounds in special needs. Hiring staff members who have nonlibrary training is a smart move for community-centered libraries that decide to expand into areas well outside those covered in most library science degree programs. Another key feature of Brooklyn's services for children with disabilities is the "Kidsmobile" that brings services to clinics, daycare centers, homeless shelters, and other locations. According to one coworker, Carrie Banks sees the Kidsmobile as a crucial component of her library: "It is closer to an imperative of the public library to ensure that people receive services no matter where they happen to be" ("Movers and Shakers" 2012). While library buildings are an extremely important asset for local communities, a community-centered library should consider the entire community as "their" space.

In an example of how libraries can learn about offering services to individuals with disabilities from their youth services counterparts, the Peabody Institute Library's South Branch offered a story time for adults with disabilities. This program was instituted at the request of an organization that served adults with special needs. A group from this organization regularly visited the library and children's books were extremely popular with these patrons, so the request made sense. Library staff ran the program like a traditional story time and it was very well received by its intended audience. By being receptive to a suggestion made by a group that served adults with special needs, the library was able to meet a community need in a fairly simple manner.

The Contra Costa (California) County Library was also inspired to start a program for adults with disabilities when a community group began bringing a large group of its members into the library. Staff wanted to engage these patrons, so they started off by giving the group a very extensive tour of the library and showed them how to perform certain tasks that librarians take for granted, like getting the key to the restroom. This simple tour was such a success that the library, in conjunction with the adults with disabilities, moved their efforts to the next level and created the Wednesday Club, which provides a variety of weekly programs. A 2008 grant allowed the library to purchase video game equipment to offer fitness-focused programs in the Wednesday Club. Most importantly, these programs have created "new community relationships with special speakers, musicians, educators, performers, and donors."

An initiative that the Peabody Library implemented after being approached by a community partner shows how a library can build assets for and engage patrons with disabilities in the library and the community. For years, we librarians discussed our desire to have a café or coffee service available to patrons and staff in the library. The director put feelers out in the community, but it quickly became evident that the library could not garner enough business to make a traditional coffee shop economically feasible. The solution presented itself when the Life Skills program from our high school received a grant to do a job readiness program for its students with special needs. With the support of the library director, they set up a coffee cart five mornings a week in the young adult room. Staffed by one or two students and a job coach from the school, and offering baked goods prepared by the high school's culinary arts department, the "Bookworm Café" has been operating in the library for several years now and is a tremendous success. Library patrons and staff love to have the coffee and baked goods available, and the students gain important job skills. Melissa's desk sits just a few feet away from the cart, and she finds it inspiring to see the connections and social capital that the Bookworm students build with librarians and community members, and to watch them grow in confidence and skill in their jobs.

Community-centered librarians will often have to reach outside their comfort zone or area of expertise to create a library that is welcoming to diverse populations. The process may not be easy and librarians might need to rethink some of the fundamental orientations of our profession. As with many new projects, libraries may also need to persevere in their efforts to serve diverse populations until word spreads and community members begin to see that the library is a place for "their kind." Ultimately, librarians should take the long view regarding the success of their projects. As the Working Together outreach librarians concluded, "Sometimes, the most important outcome of community-led service planning is not the actual products or services, but the change in socially excluded community members' sense of their importance to the library, their right to be involved, and their ability and confidence to engage" (Working Together 2008). Once diverse populations are ready to engage in their community, through their libraries, they will help us all reach our professional obligation to serve *everyone* within our communities.

MAKE IT HAPPEN

- If community members from diverse populations are not using your library yet, reach out to places where they currently feel welcome and accepted. This may be churches, social clubs, support groups, or social services agencies.
- Take a look at your collection. Does it fairly and accurately represent the linguistic, ethnic, racial, and sexual diversity of your community? If not, begin to take steps to rectify that.
- Look at your signage and website. Do your community demographics indicate a need to translate signs, marketing materials, and online resources into another language?
- Sit down and talk to individuals who belong to minority groups. Consider doing an asset map for immigrants, non-English speakers, people with disabilities, or LGBTIQ residents. Develop a plan that leverages their talents and skills for the good of the community.
- Consider how you can add to your current programs to serve a wider section of the population. Alter your story times to make them valuable to children with disabilities. Pick a book with LGBTIQ characters for your next book group. Have a translator available at your health lecture. No step is too small for a start.
- Above all, respect and embrace the diversity of your community. You're not an expert on their lives, but you can be an important community facilitator for them. In return, they will add great value to your library.

BIBLIOGRAPHY

"Anti-Prom: Monster Prom." 2012. LGBT@NYPL. June 8. http://www.nypl.org/events/programs/2012/06/08/anti-prom-monster-prom-0.

"Bridging the Gap for Hispanic Newcomers Case Overview." Shaping Outcomes: Making a Difference in Libraries and Museums. http://www.shapingoutcomes .org/course/cases/bridging.pdf.

Brooklyn Public Library. "Universal Design: Programs That Meet the Needs of All Children." Brooklyn Public Library. http://www.brooklynpubliclibrary .org/sites/default/files/files/pdf/childsplace/3965_FL_UniversalDesign_BR_ Final.pdf.

Centers for Disease Control and Prevention. 2012. "Autism Spectrum Disorders: Data and Statistics." Last Modified March 29. http://www.cdc.gov/ncbddd/ autism/data.html.

"Committees." 2012. American Library Association. Accessed December 9. http://www.ala.org/groups/committees.

"Communities of Exile: A Community Symposium on Exile & Cultural Celebration." 2006. Center for Humanities and the Arts at the University of Colorado. www.colorado.edu/ArtsSciences/CHA/downloads/exile.pdf.

Condello, Pham, Karla Ivarson, and Julie Tozer. 2009. "GLBT Programming in the Ocean County Library System: Programming, Partnerships, Promotion and Pitfalls." SlideShare. October 17. http://www.slideshare.net/kivarson/serving -glbt-library-customers-partnerships-program.

"English Conversation Circles @ East." 2012. Arlington Public Library. Accessed October 31. http://www.arlingtonlibrary.org/calendar/english-conver sation-circle-east.

"English for Your Health." 2012. Queens Library. Accessed August 7. http:// www.queenslibrary.org/services/health-info/english-for-your-health.

"Features." 2012. West Hollywood Library Fund. Accessed August 19. http:// weholibraryfund.org/The-New-Library/plan/features.

"Financial Literacy in the Community." 2012. Queens Library. Accessed December 17. http://www.queenslibrary.org/services/multilingual-services/financial -literacy.

"Gay and Lesbian Pride Month." 2012. Programming Librarian. Accessed August 19. http://www.programminglibrarian.org/library/events-and-celebrations/gay -and-lesbian-pride-month.html.

Hanshaw, Angela. 2012. "Featured Library: Memphis Public Library." *Programming Librarian* (blog). May 1. http://www.programminglibrarian.org/ blog/2012/may-2012/featured-library-memphis-public-library.html.

Horowitz, Joanna. 2004. "Young Immigrants Help Their Elders Prepare for Citizenship." *Seattle Times*, July 21.

Institute of Museum and Library Services and U.S. Citizenship and Immigration Services. 2007. "Library Services for Immigrants: A Report on Current Practices." http://www.uscis.gov/USCIS/Office%20of%20Citizenship/ Citizenship%20Resource%20Center%20Site/Publications/PDFs/G-1112.pdf.

"LGBT@NYPL." 2012. New York Public Library, *LGBT@NYPL* (blog). Accessed July 23. http://www.nypl.org/voices/blogs/blog-channels/lgbt.

"Member Innovations 2010: Insiders Contra Costa County Library, CA." 2010. Urban Libraries Council. Accessed August 21, 2012. http://www.urbanlibraries .org/wednesday-club-innovation-424.php?page_id=90.

"Movers and Shakers 2012: Carrie Banks; Services for All." 2012. *Library Journal* 137 (5): 30.

"New Immigrants Project." Austin Public Library. Accessed April 4, 2013. http:// www.austinlibrary.com/newip.

Nguyen, Erin. 2011. "Sensory Storytime Handouts." ALA Connect. July 8. http:// connect.ala.org/node/150986.

Russell, Brian. 2012. "Featured Library: Temecula Public Library." *Programming Librarian* (blog). July 31. http://www.programminglibrarian.org/ blog/2012/july-2012/featured-library-temecula-public-library.html.

Savage, Dan. 2011. Introduction to *It Gets Better: Coming Out, Overcoming Bullying, and Creating a Life Worth Living*, edited by Dan Savage and Terry Miller. New York: Dutton.

"Serving Non-English Speakers in U.S. Public Libraries." 2007. American Library Association. Accessed August 12, 2012. https://www.ala.org/ala/ aboutala/offices/olos/nonenglishspeakers/index.cfm.

"Story Time Star." 2012. *Library Journal* 137 (5): 34–35.

United States Census Bureau. 2010. "Language Use in the United States: 2007." U.S. Department of Commerce. April. http://www.census.gov/prod/2010pubs/ acs-12.pdf.

"West Hollywood Library." 2012. County of Los Angeles Public Library. Accessed August 19. http://www.colapublib.org/libs/whollywood/index.php.

Winson, G., and C. Adams. 2010. "Collaboration at Its Best: Library and Autism Programs Combine to Serve Special Audience." *Children & Libraries* 8 (2): 15–17.

Working Together. 2008. "Community-Led Libraries Toolkit." Working Together. http://www.librariesincommunities.ca/resources/Community-Led_Libraries_ Toolkit.pdf.

CHAPTER 13

Libraries as Centers for the Arts

Baroque music wraps a beautiful historic room in the sounds of harpsi-chord, violin, and cello. A gala-style art show opens, complete with live music and a welcoming reception. Children participate in a drum circle led by a professional drummer. These events sound like those found in big-city symphony halls or museums, but each happened in a public library, and each was offered free and open to the public. "A recent survey of public participation in the arts found that approximately 40% of the population participates in some form of the arts and cultural ac-tivities (National Endowment for the Arts 2003). Unfortunately, cultural resources are often viewed as something consumed by the rich and not related to middle-class and working-class residents" (Green and Haines 2012, 255). This is where libraries come in.

No discussion about libraries' changing roles as community asset builders and cultural centers would be complete without addressing ac-cess to the arts. In a recent edition of the *Boston Globe*, a reporter stated that "libraries are no longer hushed places where librarians stamp books and dole out the dreaded 'hush.'. . . They're morphing into the cultural centers of the 21st century" (Plumb 2011). There is evidence of this meta-morphosis in libraries all over the world, and this chapter will highlight success stories to inspire and give direction to arts events you might want to host at your own library.

MUSIC IN THE STACKS

Throughout history, libraries have been regarded as quiet places of study, places where conversations are hushed and the turning of the page is the loudest sound. While libraries still offer quiet places to read, study, and reflect, they also provide opportunities to socialize, recreate, and, as is important to this chapter, listen. More and more libraries offer music programming in the form of concerts as well as educational lectures. According to Scott Simon (2008), "While music performances in libraries support the universal human rights of free expression and participation in cultural life, they also connect local musicians with their communities; expose new, ethnic, or historical forms of music to an appreciative audience; and provide opportunities for music education as well" (44). What Simon is pointing out is that music programs not only build cultural capital, but also strengthen social and human assets. As libraries embrace their roles as cultural centers, access to live music and music education becomes a very important component to their missions. The following are examples of library programs that bring this musical mission to life.

Self-described as "Bringing Literature, Music, Art, Science & the Humanities to the Community," the Pequot (Connecticut) Library does just that with a wide variety of programming including an annual series of concerts and related educational events. Known for a long-standing commitment to music, when the library initially opened in 1893, its first event was a Yale Glee Club concert. Currently, Pequot collaborates with the New Haven Symphony Orchestra, the Greater Bridgeport Symphony Orchestra, and the Westport Arts Center to present classical and jazz concerts throughout the year.

While Pequot's music calendar is impressive, what makes the library's musical commitment unique is their dedicated Friends of Music at Pequot Library Group. The Friends of Music group is new to the Pequot Library and, according to information available on the Pequot Library's website, "This group will organize and produce an annual series of music programs, reach out to new audiences, seek financial support for programs, and present related educational events to augment the musical experience." Shortly after forming this group in 2011, the Friends of Music presented two fall concerts of early classical music performed by the Sebastian Ensemble and the vocal group TENET. When a library has a volunteer fund-raising group dedicated not to books, not to computers, and not to facilities, but to music, it's very clear that cultural events are becoming a fundamental service in public libraries. The Friends of Music at Pequot Library Group is a sure sign of the growing importance of cultural events in libraries and a model for other libraries to emulate as they reposition themselves in their communities.

They may not have a Friends group dedicated to music, but the Morecambe Library in Lancashire, England, offers a program that generated county council funding and earned the library's 2007 Love Libraries Award, an honor awarded by the public. Get It Loud in Libraries literally brings rock music right into the stacks. After hours, service desks are pushed aside in favor of a stage and space for hundreds of fans. According to Tom Holman (2009), "Dozens have played there, including several, like Adele, The Wombats, Bat for Lashes and Florence and the Machine, who have gone on to major chart success" (22). Because Lancashire is not a popular area for touring bands, Get It Loud in Libraries brings rock music to an underserved population, bringing many community members not only into the library for the first time, but sometimes to their first concert as well.

In addition to rock and classical music, there is also a vibrant jazz scene in libraries. In partnership with the Jazz Arts Foundation, the Lexington (Kentucky) Public Library presents Jazz: Live at the Library! This monthly concert series began in 2007 and offers performances by both regional and international jazz musicians. All performances are offered free to the public and each concert is recorded and subsequently aired on the Library Channel, a local cable television station.

Taking jazz in libraries one step further, from 2008 to 2010 the New York Public Library offered the Duke Jazz Series and Talks. A combination of live performance and oral history, the series included eight live performances and an oral history with each ensemble leader. The series also included the "presentation and documentation of four one-on-one conversations between GRAMMY-nominated and GRAMMY Award-winning jazz artists" and the "production and documentation of ten oral histories with musicians performing in the 2008–2009 and 2009–2010 Jazz at Lincoln Center seasons." This series is a fine example of not just music in libraries, but music education in libraries.

Like the New York Public Library, in addition to musical performances, many libraries also provide access to music education programs. The Dundee Township (Illinois) Public Library offers a Lyric Opera Lecture Series (Danhey 2011). A member of the Lyric Opera of Chicago's Education Corps presents each lecture, enlightening audiences about the story, composer, and musical highlights of the selected operas. The Lyric

Opera gears the lecture to those who might plan to see the opera but would like some background information prior to the performance. A number of venues throughout the Chicago area offer these lectures, including a number of public libraries.

Another example of music education programming is the Peabody Institute Library's Approaches to Listening. A lecture and performance series that offers insights on listening to classical music, Approaches to Listening is a partnership between the library and local chamber music ensemble Music at Eden's Edge. At each program, a pair of performers shares insight into how to listen to their program, from historical points of interest as well as instrumental perspectives. Music at Eden's Edge developed this series especially for the library and provides presenters and curriculum while the library provides publicity, an appreciative audience, and a popular performance venue.

These examples barely touch on the ways that libraries invite their communities into the world of music, or the ways in which musicians invite the library into the community. In addition to the programs discussed, there are libraries that use local music festivals as opportunities to market themselves to new audiences, those that have dedicated performance spaces, and those that offer annual concert series. All of these events boil down to a huge cultural win for libraries and, most importantly, their communities.

ART ACCESSED

Libraries in communities both large and small find unique ways to bring visual arts to wide audiences. From exhibitions to classes to circulating art collections, libraries offer multiple opportunities for free access to the world of visual art. Although gallery space may not be something people commonly associate with libraries, some communities find that combining these services and resources allows them to offer greater numbers of opportunities to enjoy the visual arts. The following examples explore how this support of visual arts allows libraries to further reposition themselves as community cultural centers.

An excellent example of a library that combines services to better serve its small community is the Frankfurt (Indiana) Community Public Library. This library not only offers an art gallery, but also has a theater, music studio, and coffee bar. The library's gallery displays works from the library's permanent art collection as well as work by local artists. In addition to an art gallery, the FCPL also provides a circulating art collection and art classes offered through the Anna and Harlan Hubbard School of Living. According to an article in *Indiana Libraries*, "The FCPL fulfills the traditional role of the public library well, but by expanding its programs and goals, the library better serves its small community" (Bodnar 2007, 1).

In Chicago, the Percent for Art Program is a city ordinance that has "been putting art in libraries and other public places since 1978" (Watkins 2011, 12). This ordinance requires that 1.33 percent of construction and renovation budgets go toward the installation of original artwork at the project site. Thanks to this impressive municipal commitment to cultural capital, at least forty of Chicago's library branches have works from the Chicago Public Art Collection. In his article about Chicago's Public Art Program, Chris Watkins (2011) states that "adding art to libraries can strengthen, inspire, and mobilize . . . support in ways that go beyond resources on a shelf or a hard drive or on the internet" (12). In other words, art in libraries strengthens communities, but it also strengthens libraries too.

Before the passing of Nashville, Tennessee's, own public art ordinance, the Nashville Public Library allocated $600,000 of its construction budget to public art, resulting in "six integrated public artworks, five posters created by local artists, and photographs by five local photographers." In addition to these works, the main library has two galleries, the Art Gallery and Courtyard Gallery, which display works that explore "a wide variety of ideas." Exhibitions often have a local history focus, but the broad range of topics have included "Shaped Poetry: A Suite of 30 Typographic Prints by Arion Press," "Tradition—Tennessee Lives and Legacies," and "The Zen of Seeing: Selections from the Albert Hadley Interior Design Collection." The galleries are open to the public during regular library hours and, in the spirit of access to the arts for all, admission is free.

Offering more than five thousand programs annually, the San Diego Public Library is "San Diego's largest provider of free cultural programming," so it's no surprise that the library's Visual Arts Program is nationally recognized and helps to make the library a true cultural center for the San Diego community. Boasting a curator, "museum-quality art exhibitions," artists' lectures, and televised interviews with exhibiting artists, this visual arts program is truly comprehensive and brings the arts to a broad audience with its free to the public programming. According to their brochure, San Diego's Visual Arts Program "is solely dependent on a modest commission from art sales, augmented by grass-roots donations from the community" (Friends of the Central Library 2012). Due to the program's great success, San Diego's new main library will have a 3,500-square-foot gallery and all future branches of the SDPL will be built with gallery or exhibit spaces.

Although San Diego's gallery initiative is impressive, bringing art exhibits to your library need not be an overwhelming, large-scale endeavor. Begun in 2001 in an effort to promote the community's local visual arts, the Peabody Institute Library, in partnership with the local high school, offers a rotating display of student art in the young adult room. Twice a year, a teacher from the Visual Arts Department brings new artwork to refresh the exhibit, providing the library with an attractive gallery display and the students with an opportunity to share their work with the community. Easily put in place, a program like this one is a great opportunity to create a partnership with another local organization and a chance for libraries to attract new users with each new set of artists represented.

While gallery and exhibit spaces are gaining popularity, many libraries also offer visual arts lecture opportunities. At the New Canaan (Connecticut) Library, visual arts come alive in the form of the Stoddard Art Lectures, an endowed series begun in 2011 in honor of Pat and Hud Stoddard. The mission of the Stoddard Art Lecture Series is to "enrich and broaden the community's understanding and enjoyment of the arts in its various forms." In another example of arts lecture series, the Pima County (Arizona) Public Library in partnership with the Tucson Museum of Art offers the Focus on Art Lecture Series. Each week, museum docents present lecture and slide-show presentations about art and artists. Both the Tucson and New Canaan programs provide opportunities for lifelong learning, community enrichment, and arts education for all.

Another example of not only an arts lecture, but a great partnership between the library and other community organizations, is Chelmsford (Massachusetts) Public Library's Cultural Road Show. Cosponsored by the Cultural Organization of Lowell (COOL) in an effort to "raise awareness of the museums and other cultural organizations in the community" (Herzog 2011), the library organized a monthly lecture series that invites a different local group or museum to present at each program. Lectures have included the New England Quilt Museum, Lowell Celebrates

Kerouac!, The Whistler House Museum of Art, and the Lowell Parks and Conservation Trust. The Cultural Road Show is a great opportunity to draw new patrons to the library, attract new patrons to area museums, and promote the library's museum pass collection. Talk about a great way to build the community's cultural capital! This partnership between the library and other community cultural organizations is a wonderful example of a public library that is truly community centered.

Visual arts programs and exhibitions add value to public libraries, but most importantly provide unique cultural opportunities that are easily accessible to library communities. At the heart of every library's mission is the exploration of ideas, and visual arts have the potential to take this exploration beyond the realm of books and computers and into an immediate, eye-catching, and, most importantly, thought-provoking place. In addition, these programs provide opportunities for collaboration that help reposition libraries as community asset builders.

COMMUNITY ARTS

As libraries move to reposition themselves as centers of their communities, a wonderful opportunity to connect with local artists, musicians, and writers arises. These connections provide promotional opportunities for local artists and also bring high-quality programs, events, and services to libraries as we mentioned in chapter 1. When libraries raise awareness of talented artists in their own neighborhoods, the library's position in the community's cultural life becomes all the more valued.

"Think libraries, think live, local music" is the slogan for Christchurch City Libraries' New Zealand Music Month program. Every May since 2001 the country celebrates New Zealand Music Month, a series of concerts designed to promote homegrown music. After five years of New Zealand Music Month, music sales for local acts jumped from just 6 percent to 29 percent. Christchurch City Libraries supports this powerful series with its own annual calendar of events, a series of free performances by New Zealand musicians with local libraries as concert venues. The libraries' New Zealand Music Month programming is a great way to promote the libraries, their music resources, and, perhaps most importantly, the local bands.

Novello Festival Press (NFP), "the nation's only public-library sponsored literary publisher," is another fine example of a library that reaches out to and provides opportunities for local artists. Sponsored by the Public Library of Charlotte and Mecklenburg County (North Carolina), which also receives all proceeds from the press, NFP's mission is "to enhance awareness of the literary arts and expand opportunities for readers and writers from within our community and beyond it." With over three hundred writers in print and books reviewed by recognized sources like *Publisher's Weekly* and the *New York Times*, NFP not only puts local writers into print but provides writing workshops to help further the community's literary arts.

In New York City, the Creative Aging Libraries Project is another wonderful program that not only provides hands-on fine arts education, but also offers opportunities for participants to build social capital by sharing their talents with others. A partnership between Lifetime Arts Inc. and the New York Public Library, Creative Aging offers professionally taught arts programs to seniors. With Creative Aging, seniors have learned memoir-writing skills, storytelling, and watercolor painting and even participated in a choral group. "The free programs promote creativity and provide opportunities for meaningful social engagement. In each library, the workshops conclude with a public culminating exhibition, reading, or performance."

Sometimes we need look no further than our own backyards to find just the things we seek. Libraries can only thrive as cultural centers when they become directly involved in the cultural lives of their communities. Offering opportunities for local musicians, writers, and artists benefits both local talent and the libraries themselves.

As libraries reposition themselves for future success, establishing their importance as cultural centers is critical. Examples of successful cultural programming in libraries abound, and getting started in this area need not be difficult and can be a lot of fun, too. Our hope is that the examples in this chapter inspire libraries to bring the arts to the hearts of their own communities, providing abundant opportunities for creative expression and enjoyment for all who wish to participate and attend.

MAKE IT HAPPEN

Do you want to bring exciting arts programs to your library's community? Here are some tips to get you started:

- Find out what cultural organizations exist in your library's community, learn about what they're doing, and then figure out how you can work together.

- Take advantage of your community's assets. Reach out to library patrons with careers in the arts. These connections can lead to events that feature local artists, and provide your community with opportunities previously unavailable. Who knows? A specialized Friends' group, like the Friends of Music, might grow out of the connections you build.
- Join local committees focused on cultural organizations and opportunities. The library should be represented here, and the connections made will directly benefit library services and programming.
- Look for program ideas in unlikely places. Skip the library websites, and go straight to colleges, theaters, coffeehouses, art galleries, and so forth to see what they're doing. Just about anything can become a library program.
- Give strong support to your library's fund-raising group(s). Whether this means filling out grant applications or just promoting their mission at library events, the majority of the library's funding for cultural events generally comes from these sources, so your support is essential.
- Think small. You don't have to have a gorgeous gallery space to host art exhibits and displays in your building. Look for local artists, find some blank wall space, and collaborate!
- Say yes! If local artists or musicians approach your library for exhibit or performance space, try to accommodate them within your library's mission. One of our mantras with programming is "Say yes and figure out the details later."

BIBLIOGRAPHY

"Art and Artwork at the Main Library." 2012. Nashville Public Library. Accessed December 13. http://www.library.nashville.org/artgallery/art_libraryartarchitecture.asp.

Bodnar, E. 2007. "Incorporating Art into Indiana Public Libraries." *Indiana Libraries* 26 (2): 1.

"Concert Series." 2012. Pequot Library. Last modified 2010. http://www.pequotlibrary.org/index.php/calendar-events/annual-events-series/concert-series.

"Cultural Programming." 2012. San Diego Public Library Foundation. Accessed December 13. http://supportmylibrary.org/projects/culturalprogramming.

Danhey, M. 2011. "Lyric Learning Lectures at the Library." *Courier News* (Chicago), December 11.

"Duke Jazz Series." Last modified 2012. New York Public Library, *Duke Jazz Series* (blog). http://www.nypl.org/voices/blogs/blog-channels/duke-jazz-series.

"Focus on Art Lecture Series." 2012. Pima County Public Library. Accessed December 13. http://www.library.pima.gov/about/news/?id=3117.

Friends of the Central Library. 2012. "You Can Help Support the San Diego Public Library's Visual Arts Program!" San Diego Public Library. June 29. http://www.sandiego.gov/public-library/pdf/visualartsprogramfacts.pdf.

Green, Gary, and Anna Haines. 2012. *Asset Building and Community Development.* Thousand Oaks, Calif.: Sage.

Herzog, Brian. 2011. "Reference Question of the Week—11/27/11." Swiss Army Librarian. November 27. http://www.swissarmylibrarian.net/2011/12/03/reference-question-of-the-week-112711/.

Holman, Tom. 2009. "Bring It On, Turn It Up: The Public Library Service in Lancashire Is Trying to Widen Its Appeal by Putting On Live Music in Branches." *Bookseller* 5397: 22.

"Jazz: Live at the Library!" 2012. Jazz Arts Foundation. Accessed December 13. http://www.jazzartsfoundation.org.

"The New York City Creative Aging Libraries Project 2011–2012." 2012. Lifetime Arts. Accessed October 30. http://lifetimearts.org/programs_2011_New_York_City_Libraries.shtml.

"New Zealand Music Month." 2012. Christchurch City Libraries. Accessed December 13. http://christchurchcitylibraries.com/events/nzmusicmonth/.

"Novello Festival Press." 2012. Charlotte Mecklenburg Library. Accessed December 13. http://www.cmlibrary.org/Novello_Press/aboutus.asp.

Plumb, T. 2011. "Branching Out: No Longer Just a Place for Reading and Whispering, Libraries Are Now Vibrant Cultural and Community Centers." *Boston Globe*, December 4.

Simon, Scott. 2008. "Jamming in the Stacks: Music as a Progressive Librarian Ideal." *Progressive Librarian* 31: 37–45.

"Stoddard Art Lecture." 2012. New Canaan Library. Accessed December 13. http://newcanaanlibrary.org/articles/stoddard-art-lecture.

Watkins, C. 2011. "Art in Public Places: Chicago's Public Art Program." *Illinois Library Association Reporter* 29 (2): 12–15.

CHAPTER 14

Libraries as Universities

As librarians, we've all heard that the library is the people's university, and there is no denying the truth of this description. According to Daniel Akst (2012), writing for the *Carnegie Reporter*, the reason that "libraries persist is the notion of *improvement*. . . . Americans were early proponents of universal education and individual initiative, and we long ago recognized the importance of giving people a chance to make their lives better by gaining knowledge and cultivating their minds." Providing opportunities to learn and grow is what libraries do best. For years, libraries have offered access to books and information on everything from the Civil War to learning to play the ukulele. Just about everyone knows that if you have a question, you're sure to find an answer at the library. And not just an answer, but the assistance of a librarian who will help you find the best answer.

Whether providing books and information, informative lectures, or hands-on skill-building classes, libraries strengthen human capital by providing equal access to learning and knowledge every day to everyone. As libraries move into more community-centered roles, this won't change, but the way they go about it will and should. In an interview with *Public Libraries*, Nina Simon (2012) states:

> What people are catching on to is the reality that we live in a world that now is heavily focused on a participatory culture. . . . There have been all kinds of studies that show that people are more likely to take up an instrument than they are to go to the symphony; more likely to garden or cook at home than they are to go to a play or a museum. . . . [Libraries and museums] need to be places that invite people not just to read or see things, but really invite them to make and share and do things. (9)

The community-centered library provides people with opportunities to learn and explore that go beyond the traditional realms of reading and researching by offering programs and classes where people share and engage in learning with each other. In addition, the community-centered library offers patrons the ability to take their new knowledge, and their personal creativity, to the next level by offering spaces for them to create and bring their ideas to life. In this chapter, we will provide examples of ways that libraries serve as the "people's university"; illustrate how libraries offer opportunities for remote access, making it possible for those who can't get to the library to still access the library's cultural and educational offerings; and show how libraries go beyond providing content to enabling patrons to create their own content.

THE PEOPLE'S UNIVERSITY

Lifelong learning is a term used frequently in the library community, and with book groups, lectures, classes, and discussions, public libraries offer numerous opportunities for their patrons to engage in learning at every age. According to Reed and Nawalinski (2004), "Hosting special programs at the library . . . can bring in new patrons and show that the library is a central place for lifelong learning" (53). A "central place" is exactly what public libraries should be and, as libraries increase the number of educational programs that they offer, they begin to become just that.

In some libraries, scholar-led lectures provide much-needed opportunities for patrons to challenge themselves in thought-provoking courses on a broad range of topics. One very successful example is the American Library Association's Let's Talk about It (LTAI) reading and discussion series. LTAI programs are grant funded, usually through the ALA and another partnering agency, and gather patrons for a series of discussions on books of a common theme. A requirement of the grant is that applicant libraries have a commitment from a certified scholar who will facilitate all discussions. Past themes included "Exploring the West," "What America Reads," "Women's Autobiography," "Family," "Contemporary Japanese Literature," and more. "In the past 25 years, the model has been adopted—and adapted—by hundreds of libraries across the country. *'Let's Talk about It'* has reached more than four million people around the United States."

In Peabody, LTAI programs generated so much enthusiasm from the community that the library developed an annual scholar-led summer reading program for adults. Each summer, the library offers a series of lectures and discussions that focus on a great work of literature. Past programs included James Joyce's *Ulysses*, a series on gothic novels, *Moby Dick*, and Walt Whitman's *Leaves of Grass*. A patron who attended the Whitman series said, "It's one thing to sit alone in your house or on vacation and read a book, but there's also something to having a community around a common series of ideas. . . . I think there's a sense of community that even with blogs and Twitter and all of that stuff, technology just can't replace" (DiDomizio 2012). In other words, this patron appreciates the way the library is strengthening social capital. This sentiment gets directly to the heart of programs like these. As we mentioned earlier, library patrons don't want to just learn, they want to participate and interact. Scholar-led discussion series are perfect examples of programs that provide opportunities for both learning and engagement.

The Lunch and Learn program at the Halifax Public Library (Nova Scotia) is another fine example of a scholar-led program that provides opportunities for both learning and community connection. Begun in 1977, as a partnership between Halifax Public Libraries and Saint Mary's University, the university uses the library "as an off-campus extension centre with professors teaching lectures in several branches . . . what is unique about this partnership is that members of the public are invited to attend and, at no cost to them, to sit in on lectures alongside students who are taking the course for university credit" (Gillis and Totten 2006, 244). Many public participants are seniors, and these attendees not only value interacting with each other, but with the young university students as well. The result is an intergenerational program that generates lively discussions and valuable social opportunities for all who participate.

Some educational programs send patrons home not just with new knowledge and new friends, but with new skills too. In Iowa, in partnership with the Iowa State University and Iowa Insurance Division, the Ames Public Library offered Smart Investing @ Your Library®. A combination of face-to-face classes and online courses, the series provided different tracks for patrons at different places in their lives: "'Starting Out' for Generation X participants, 'Building Up' for Baby Boomers, and 'Making It Last' for retirees" (Monsour 2012, 37). The program was such a success that the State Library of Iowa "expanded the initiative to twenty-five libraries and small towns across the state" (37).

Not just for the academically or financially inclined, libraries also offer many opportunities to learn more about, and build skills for use in, recreational activities. In Connecticut, the Darien Library offered Homebrew 101, a class that turned the library "Conference Room into a brewery" (Shea 2012). At the New York Public Library, which "offers more than 25,000 free public programs at its 89 locations," patrons can sign up for everything from adult yoga to poetry workshops. And, in Peabody, kids recently learned how to make their own Claymation movies at the library's "Imagine It. Create It. Animate It." program.

TAKING IT TO THE STREETS

In order to reach the entire community, it is important that public libraries recognize that not all patrons can get to the library. From books to programs to technology, the following community-centered libraries have found ways to reach out to patrons who are unable to reach out to them.

At the most basic level, public libraries do their best to get books to patrons who can't make it to the library themselves. At the Reading (Massachusetts) Public Library, Library Takeout provides the "delivery of books and other materials to Reading residents of any age who cannot visit the Library because of physical difficulties, including temporary disabilities." The library also offers monthly deliveries to local senior communities, and maintains the "Book Nook," a rotating large-print collection at the local senior center. These services ensure that patrons of all physical abilities have access to the information and materials that the library offers.

For some communities, their remote location is their barrier to access to the library's books. In Finland, the Public Library of Pargas's Bookboat has operated for thirty-five years, bringing books "out to islands that don't have road connections" (Tana 2012). With a hired boat staffed by library volunteers, the Bookboat makes deliveries approximately five times each year. With the Bookboat, the Public Library of Pargas ensures that the entire community has access to library materials.

While it is important to recognize barriers of physical difficulty and location, it is also important to recognize the time constraints of busy patrons. No matter how hard we try, the library's standard operating hours just don't always work for everyone. In Australia, when circulation statistics at the Gosford City Library (GCL) fell, the library knew it needed to address the needs of the city's high number of commuters. These commuters were potential library patrons, but work schedules prevented their use of the library. The library decided that the best solution was to meet these potential patrons, and provide library services, where they already were: the train station. With the support of City Rail, Australian Posters, the Central Coast Commuters Association, and a grant from the Library Council of New South Wales, the library started Book Express, an open-air trolley library that operates out of Gosford and Woy Woy Stations. Patrons can check out and return books and even register for library cards, right at the Book Express branch of the GCL. The service began in 2001 and still operates today.

Like GCL, many libraries make an effort to serve patrons at times that the library would not normally be open. In some cases, robolibraries, self-service kiosks that allow libraries to "reach customers during off hours without adding work for employees" (Mannion 2012), are the solution. Similar to the Redbox DVD rental units that you see in the grocery store, robolibraries are like vending machines that accept library cards instead of dollar bills. "Eva Poole, . . . of the Public Library Association, said she sees robolibraries as part of what people expect today from their libraries. 'People don't want to be limited by time or location'" (Mannion 2012). Robolibraries certainly don't have the personal touch of an actual visit to the library, and may even seem anathema to the community-centered library approach, but they provide access to the library's collections to those who might not be able to take advantage of these offerings otherwise. Being community centered doesn't mean only that the library creates social opportunities for patrons, but that the library recognizes and meets the needs of all its patrons whatever, wherever, and whenever those needs may be.

On the flip side, some libraries go so far as to provide remote access to interactive library programs, not just collection resources. Bartlett (Illinois) Public Library offers Pages across the Ages (Russell 2012), a pen pal book group that matches senior citizens and young children who read a common book each month and discuss the book through handwritten letters. A valuable opportunity for the kids to practice reading and writing, and for seniors to connect with young people in a meaningful way, this program culminated in a "field trip" where the children visited their pen pals at the senior community. If libraries are, in the words of Keith Richards, to be the "great equalizer," that means that librarians should make an effort to have all services reach the entire community. For seniors in particular, attending events at the library is not always an option, and the Bartlett Public Library found a wonderful way to build social capital by bringing a library event to them where they already are.

In some cases, technology is the library service that community members are not able to get to the library to access. In Zimbabwe, a donkey cart library service brings "Information Communications Technology (ICT) to rural communities" (Misa 2011). According to a representative from the Rural Libraries and Resources Development Programme (RLRDP), the goal of the program is "an informed rural society where every person is guaranteed adequate access to relevant information and a sustainable socio-economic and political environment" (Misa 2011). Similarly, in Columbus, Ohio, a high-tech mobile library brings "free broadband technology to residents of three rural communities." According to Beverly Blake, program director for the Knight Foundation, "Digital access is essential to first class citizenship in our society. Without digital, you lack full access to information; you are second class economically and even socially." The high-tech mobile library's services include Internet-accessible computers, books, DVDs, programs, and even voter registration. Talk about a nice way to bridge the digital divide.

Although online resources are not the focus of this book, in a discussion about remote access, we would be remiss not to mention remote access to databases, remote access to library catalogs, and M-libraries. With remote catalog and database access, patrons can do research anytime, anywhere—not just during library hours. For a college student trying to put together a paper at the last minute, services like these can be real lifesavers, or at least grade savers. M-libraries, although not a completely satisfactory replacement for full Internet access via a computer, are extremely useful for some patrons:

> Groups that have traditionally been on the other side of the digital divide in basic internet access are using wireless connections to go online. Among smartphone owners, young adults, minorities, those with no college experience, and those with lower household income levels are more likely than other groups to say that their phone is their main source of internet access. (Zickuhr and Smith 2012)

Given this fact, libraries with mobile-friendly websites are in a better position to provide remote access to community members who rely on their phones for Internet service.

THE COMMUNITY CREATION STATION

In addition to providing remote access to reach patrons unable to take advantage of library resources during library hours, libraries also offer unique services and programs to enable people to bring their knowledge and creativity to life. Whether providing software and hardware not available in the average patron's home, or offering hands-on classes where community members create something with learned skills, libraries are places where patrons young and old can come to make, build, perform, and create.

Encouraging children to learn "through all five senses and from the page to the stage," ImaginOn is a combination children's library and children's theater. A partnership between Children's Theater of Charlotte and the Public Library of Charlotte and Mecklenburg County, their shared mission is "bringing stories to life" (Holt 2008, 188). In addition to children's theater production and classes, ImaginOn offers opportunities for creation through animation and video production equipment in the teen area's Studio i, a space open to teens and families who wish to create movies and music.

In the spirit of ImaginOn's Studio i, some public libraries now offer learning labs. These labs provide "hardware and software that most people wouldn't have at home. By providing these creative tools to their patrons, libraries fill a valuable niche in the community, a niche consistent with their historical commitment to bridging gaps in technology access" (Farkas 2012). Opened in 2009, the Skokie (Illinois) Public Library's (SPL) Digital Media Lab (DML) was "used more than 1200 times in the last fiscal year" (Jacobsen and Anthony 2011, 37). While iLife and iSuite are the lab's most popular programs, the DML is most commonly used for video production. Inspired by the success of libraries like the SPL, the Lawrence (Washington) Public Library has made "Creation Zones" a priority in its plans for expansion (Lawhorn 2012). The zones will house sound equipment, video equipment, and computer tools. In addition to encouraging art production, the library director hopes the Creation Zones will strengthen local businesses with access to web and graphic design software.

An offshoot of media lab success, with the advent of 3-D printing, public libraries have begun to explore the idea of fab labs, or makerspaces, designed to make this technology available for public use. In an effort to be "the first library in the United States to build a free, public access Fab Lab," the Fayetteville (Illinois) Free Library hired a transliteracy development director to coordinate the project. Fayetteville believes the library's role is to "provide a safe and accessible space where anyone in the community can interact, understand and develop through use of this technology." Given the expense of and current lack of public access to 3-D printers, public library fab labs will be a welcome addition to their current technology offerings. In addition, some libraries go beyond 3-D printing to offer less technical creation tools such as soldering irons or sewing machines. Whether the tools offered are high or low tech, the point of these spaces is to provide opportunities for community members to graduate from the roles of content consumers to content creators.

David Gauntlett's (2011) book, *Making Is Connecting*, describes at length how the opportunities provided by learning labs and makerspaces build social capital. He says, "Making is connecting because through making things and sharing them, in the world, we increase our engagement and connection with our social and physical environments" (2). As libraries talk more about digital media labs and makerspaces, they will continue to discover new ways that libraries can provide spaces and programs that strengthen assets for individuals by teaching them new skills, and build social capital and increase innovation at the community level.

Libraries will always be the "people's university," but as they move into the future it will be important to expand and redefine that role. The growing interest in "participatory culture" (Simon 2012) is at the crux of this transition. As demonstrated by the examples in this chapter, public libraries should explore ways to encourage interactive lifelong learning; provide access to seemingly out-of-reach populations in their communities; and offer opportunities for creative, hands-on content creation. When community-centered libraries offer services like these, they guarantee the creation of diverse, enthusiastic, and engaged patron bases that will grow and learn with each other and with the library.

MAKE IT HAPPEN

Do you want to bring exciting programs like the ones mentioned in this chapter to your library's community? Here are some tips to get you started:

- Look for grants to support educational programs in your library.
- Partner with local colleges and universities to offer scholar-led lectures and discussions.
- Identify potential patrons who are unable to access the library due to physical disabilities or time constraints, and find ways to bring library materials and services to them where they already are.
- Partner with local senior communities to offer rewarding intergenerational programs.
- Think of ways that your library can bridge the digital divide in the community. Consider a digital bookmobile to bring technology to underserved areas.
- If your library doesn't have one already, create a mobile-friendly version of the library website.
- Support content creation in your library. Start small by offering iLife or graphic design software for public use, and expand as demand grows.
- Talk with your city and county governments, and your other sources of funding, about the importance of the library as a learning place. Assess your programs, gather statistics and personal stories, and use them to advocate for more funding for technology, outreach materials, or positions like Fayetteville's transliteracy development director.

BIBLIOGRAPHY

"About ImaginOn." 2012. ImaginOn: The Joe and Joan Martin Center. Accessed September 19. http://www.imaginon.org/About_ImaginOn/default.asp.

Akst, Daniel. 2012. "Today's Public Libraries: Public Places of Excellence, Education and Innovation." *Carnegie Reporter* 6 (4). http://carnegie.org/publications/carnegie-reporter/single/view/article/item/309/.

"Book Express." 2012. Gosford City Council. Accessed September 18. http://www.gosford.nsw.gov.au/library/branches/express.html.

"Classes @ NYPL." 2012. New York Public Library. Accessed September 20. http://www.nypl.org/events/classes.

"Delivery Services." 2012. Reading Public Library. Accessed September 29. http://www.readingpl.org/adult-services/older-adults/delivery-services/.

DiDomizio, Milva. 2012. "Walt Whitman (via a Popular Prof) Still Packing Them In." *Boston Globe*, August 12.

"A Fabulous Laboratory at the FFL." 2012. Fayetteville Free Library. Accessed September 19. http://www.fayettevillefreelibrary.org/about-us/services/fablab.

Farkas, Meredith. 2012. "Technology in Practice: Providing the Tools." *American Libraries*. January 31. http://americanlibrariesmagazine.org/columns/practice/providing-tools.

Gauntlett, David. 2011. *Making Is Connecting: The Social Meaning of Creativity, from DIY and Knitting to YouTube and Web 2.0*. Malden, Mass.: Polity Press.

Gillis, Sara, and Julie Totten. 2006. "Creating Lifelong Learning Opportunities through Partnership: A 30-Year Success Story." *Feliciter* 52 (6): 244–46.

"High-Tech Mobile Library Will Bring Free Broadband Access to the Valley." 2012. Knight Foundation: Informed and Engaged Communities. Accessed September 18. http://www.knightfoundation.org/press-room/press-release/high-tech-mobile-library-will-bring-free-broadband/.

Holt, Glen E. 2008. "ImaginOn, the First Twenty-First Century Public Library Building in the U.S." *Public Library Quarterly* 27 (2): 174–91.

"Imagine It. Create It. Animate It." 2012. Peabody Institute Library. Accessed September 20. http://www.peabodylibrary.org/children/claymation.html.

Jacobsen, Mikael, and Carolyn Anthony. 2011. "Build Your Own Digital Media Lab." *Library Journal*, no. 1: 36–40.

Lawhorn, Chad. 2012. "Director Sees Library's Role as Creation Hub." LJWorld. com. Accessed September 19. http://www2.ljworld.com/news/2012/jul/29/director-sees-librarys-role-creation-hub/.

"Let's Talk about It!" 2012. American Library Association. Accessed September 20. http://publicprograms.ala.org/ltai/index.html.

Mannion, Annemarie. 2012. "Robolibraries Rolling Out in Suburbs: More Self-Service Options Eyed as Way around Shortfalls at Public Facilities." *Chicago Tribune*, March 7.

Misa. 2011."Donkey-Drawn Carts Take ICT News to Rural Areas." *Zimbabwean*, November 5. Accessed September 18, 2012. http://www.thezimbabwean. co.uk/news/39513/donkey-drawn-carts-take-ict-news-to-rural-areas.html.

Monsour, Margaret. 2012. "Libraries Innovate with New Financial Education Programs." *Public Libraries* 51 (2): 36–43.

Reed, Sally Gardner, and Beth Nawalinski. 2004. *101 Great Ideas for Libraries and Friends*. New York: Friends of Libraries, U.S.A.

Russell, Brian. 2012. "Featured Library: Bartlett Public Library District." *Programming Librarian (blog)*. September 4. http://www.programminglibrarian

.org/blog/2012/september-2012/featured-library-bartlett-public-library
-district.html.

Shea, Erin. 2012. "Hoppy Hour at the Library: A Homebrew 101 Workshop."
Programming Librarian (blog). July 26. http://www.programminglibrarian.
org/blog/2012/july-2012/hoppy-hour-at-the-library-a-homebrew-101-work
shop.html.

Simon, Nina. 2012. "Participation 2.0: An Interview with Nina Simon." *Public
Libraries* 51 (2): 8–10.

Tana, Jonas. 2012. "All Aboard the Bookboat!" Finnish Libraries Now! Accessed
December 13. http://now.libraries.fi/bookboat.html.

Zickuhr, Kathryn, and Aaron Smith. 2012. "Digital Differences." Pew Research
Center's Internet & American Life Project. Last modified April 13. http://pew
internet.org/~/media//Files/Reports/2012/PIP_Digital_differences_041312.pdf.

CHAPTER 15

Libraries as Champions of Youth

Kelley and Melissa have over fifteen years combined experience leading children's and young adult departments in a public library, so it's safe to assume we wouldn't forget to include a youth services perspective in this book. That's why we've included examples of creative ways that libraries are serving youth in chapters discussing digital media creation, diversity, the arts, and more. Still, because youth are an important of a community's human capital, a book on how libraries are, and should continue to be, deeply embedded in their communities wouldn't be complete without devoting a chapter specifically to how libraries contribute to the positive development of our communities' children and young adults (libraries have different definitions, but we consider "youth" to be anyone under eighteen). Library services to youth are a core part of the mission of public libraries. Even small libraries usually have staff members who work specifically with children and offer story times and other programs for young patrons. This solid foundation gives libraries a great position from which to expand their youth services into new and exciting territory. It is important for a community-centered library to strive to engage all residents in the life of the library and the community. This engagement must include youth because a community (and a library) that does not engage its community's young members impoverishes itself.

In this chapter, we want to share some ways that libraries act as youth advocates when they claim roles for themselves as partners in youth development, act as equalizers to ensure that all of the community's young people have the chance to succeed academically, and act as encouragers of civic engagement as they help teens gain the necessary skills to thrive as involved and valued community members.

PARTNERS IN CHILD AND YOUTH DEVELOPMENT

Youth service librarians, like most librarians, tend to undersell what they do, and in the process they miss the opportunity to position themselves as crucial community players. As a group, librarians are often just too humble! We need to tell our communities how valuable libraries are to youth. Libraries that offer story times encourage early literacy, a library's LEGO club encourages creativity and design skills, and a family sing-along introduces children to music and strengthens family bonds. But how often do we frame our work in these terms? Not nearly often enough.

Part of the problem is that most librarians aren't trained in education, youth development, or community development, so they aren't familiar with the way these disciplines successfully communicate their importance. However, some libraries have begun to frame their youth services work in terms that really stress their value to the community. The Boston Public Library, for example, has adopted language used in education policy to describe their services. They refer to their events for school-aged children as "out-of-school time" activities and programs. Their website reads, "The Boston Public Library's out-of-school time programming is focused on enrichment, opportunities, partnerships, and youth development." There is an increasing recognition in education that what children and teens do during their out-of-school time has a strong correlation to their academic success. The Boston Public Library clearly intends to position itself as an educational ally. By doing so, they frame their services as essential. Certainly, libraries have options for what language they choose to adopt, but if they stress their dedication to positive youth development, libraries can better convey their importance to their communities.

One major benefit that libraries provide for their young patrons is their physical space. Libraries have served as safe havens for countless youth. By creating the best possible spaces for youth, libraries support several of the Search Institute's developmental assets that we discussed in chapter 1. These include safety, a caring neighborhood, and engagement in learning. YOUmedia in Chicago and other digital media and fabrication labs, like those described in the last chapter, are on the cutting edge of physical places that support the needs of twenty-first-century teens. For both teens and younger children ImagineOn's facility, which we also discussed in the last chapter, encourages creativity, exploration, literacy, and just plain fun. The Middle County (New York) Public Library has turned their outdoor library space into the hands-on Nature Explorium for children and families. This outdoor learning place includes areas for a climbing: playing with messy materials; building; creating nature art, music, and performances; planting; gathering; talking; and reading (Delgado-LaStella and Feinberg 2011). The library now also dedicates its programming to the development of environmental literacy skills in its youth. Some of their programs include a Green Teens Club that provides opportunities for teens to do environmental community service projects and take field trips, book clubs that read books like *Seedfolks* by Paul Fleishman and do related community gardening activities, family story times under the stars, outdoor water explorations, nature sketching, letterboxing, building birdhouses, and a vast array of others. Not all libraries will have the resources to replicate these types of spaces, but all libraries can take a fresh look at their buildings and outdoor areas to determine how they can be used to better support youth development.

Programs that bring together patrons of various ages are another way libraries routinely support youth development. Intergenerational activities and events can help strengthen both family bonds and social capital for the community at large. The Northland (Pennsylvania) Public Library hosts an annual Storytelling Festival that reaches out to children, teens, adults, and elders using professional storytellers and workshops. Other cross-generational programming provides youth with the chance to develop important relationships with adults. When it comes to the creation of positive relationships between youth and adults, libraries can really do some important work. Program presenters, volunteers, and other community members brought in to run or participate in programs can build important connections with youth. In Peabody, a local community member volunteered to come to the library's Summer Food Service program and teach kids and teens how to knit. During these knitting lessons, one teen bonded with the volunteer, who invited the teen to stop by her office any time she needed help with her knitting. This mentoring relationship flourished and was extremely valuable for the teen. This young woman is now an adult, and she still uses the library and has a knitting project with her at all times.

BRIDGING THE ECONOMIC AND ACADEMIC DIVIDE

Libraries offer such a wide array of programs and services that support educational goals that it would be impossible to discuss even a representative sample of them here. Still, a few specific services geared toward building important assets for youth and for the community are worth a mention. Free homework help programs are popping up in libraries across the country. These programs encompass a wide array of services. Some provide one-on-one tutors in the library for children and teens who need help with their homework. Libraries tap adult or senior volunteers, students from local colleges, local business people, high-achieving high school students, and even paid tutors to meet the homework needs of their students. Both the Boston Public Library and the Chicago Public Library have started Teachers in the Library programs. Teachers from within the public school districts are paid to provide after-school tutoring to youth at library branches. Chicago's program is paid for by the Chicago Public Library Foundation, but in Boston it's the city's teacher's union that funds this library program.

When considering homework assistance services, the issue of access to library locations rears its head again, but creative librarians are finding ways around this obstacle. Chicago provides access to remote service through their homework help phone line. If finances allow, many libraries are investing in online homework help services, like those provided by Tutor.com. All children, teen, and adult learners in Alabama now have access to the live online tutors provided by this service. Rather than burden individual library budgets, in this case, the state picked up the tab (Rogers 2005, 32). Convincing your state to fund a statewide homework help program accessible for free with a library card—now there's a project for an ambitious youth advocate!

Librarians have long touted the benefits of childhood engagement in books and literacy before they even begin school. Now, though, librarians have some important ammunition to back up their claims. The Urban Libraries Council's (2007) report, "Making Cities Stronger: Public Library Contributions to Local Economic Development," identified early literacy programs as one of the five most critical ways that libraries strengthen the local economy (7). Their study cites a growing body of research that ties investment in early childhood literacy to improvements in the long-term economic success of a community. Investing in children's literacy skills when they are young makes good financial sense, according to economists, because these efforts are "creating a solid foundation for later human capital investments, such as education, youth development and job skills training" (7). In other words, by supporting positive youth development, libraries are also building important community capital.

These compelling arguments are encouraging libraries to create valuable programming for children. The Peabody Institute Library worked with Mass Humanities to offer a Family Adventures in Reading (FAIR) program. The FAIR program connects libraries with storytellers who present high-quality picture books and lead discussions and activities with children and their parents/caregivers. The goal is to provide literacy programs for children and to encourage families to engage in literacy activities at home. By creating a structure to discuss children's literature, the program allows parents and children to learn and share different perspectives. Mass Humanities reports that FAIR "provides a rich experience of reading and sharing of ideas that brings families together." In terms of youth development, FAIR strengthens families, provides creative activities for children, and encourages reading for pleasure. From a community development viewpoint, FAIR will also build human and financial capital for the community at large.

The Urban Libraries Council's (2007) report highlights the work of some other libraries around the country who are "expanding traditional story-time activities, retooling children's literacy programming to meet developmentally appropriate standards, and creating more comprehensive child literacy support services for parents and child care providers" (7). One example comes from Tennessee, where the Memphis Training Wheels Program brings an early-literacy bus to child-care centers so that librarians can present story times to children and simultaneously train center staff on how to incorporate literacy into their program (10). Training Wheels, like FAIR, extends the influence of library work by coaching adults to continue literacy work beyond the thirty- to ninety-minute library program.

Another staple of library youth services can help bridge the academic divide: the summer reading program. Students of all socioeconomic backgrounds need to keep their skills sharp during the summer months, and carefully designed library programs are helping to meet this need. The Multnomah County (Oregon) Public Library has created a summer reading program that is so popular that 73 percent of their county's youth take part in the preschool, kids, and teens programs. To achieve such amazing participation, Multnomah cleverly turned summer reading into a "game," with prizes like a trip for four to a water park, a party for ten at a children's museum, a $250 shopping spree, and a bike. The Charlotte Mecklenburg (North Carolina) Library also saw a 26 percent leap in participation in their 2012 summer program, which they credit to moving their program online and aligning it with their schools' curriculum. Like Multnomah, Charlotte Mecklenburg also enticed readers with impressive prizes: iPads, Kindles, and gift cards.

As an alternative to expensive prizes, the Portland (Maine) Library firmly centered their 2011 "I Heart Reading in Portland" program in their local community. The main prize for readers who completed the program was tickets to a Portland Sea Dogs baseball game and, in a unique partnership, the library and the METRO Bus and South Portland Bus Service teamed up to give any youth (under eighteen) who checked out a library book a free ticket to ride the bus and a bookmark highlighting cultural and recreational destinations to check out on the bus route. This innovative idea helps youth access community assets, encourages the use of the city's bus lines, and promotes reading.

In a yet another approach, some libraries are rethinking the concept of using prizes or incentives to encourage children and teens to read over the summer. The Nashua (New Hampshire) Public Library designed their program to appeal to the natural altruistic tendencies of young people. Their summer reading program for teens allowed participants to "Read for Charity." Every book they read earned a $0.25 donation to Kiva (an online network that allows individuals to give microcredit loans to people around the world). The library's goal with this program is to encourage teens to "act locally but think globally." The Indianapolis (Indiana) Public Library allows young readers to trade in their summer reading points for school supplies for children in need. Many libraries offer children and teens some combination of incentives, charity opportunities, and other perks. In fact, both Nashua and Indianapolis include a component in their programs that allow children and teens to "read" off overdue fines. With late fines being a major barrier to library use for some youth, this is a creative way to restore access and promote reading.

Free tutoring, early literacy, summer reading, and other educational enrichment opportunities are needed by our community's youth. Public libraries must continue to offer these programs in their communities to ensure that lower-income youth have access to services similar to those available to wealthier children and teens. In 2005–2006, families in the top 20 percent of national incomes spent $7,500 more per year for *each* of their children to participate in out-of-school time enrichment programs and activities than did families in the bottom 20 percent (Duncan and

Murnane 2011, 4). That number is no doubt discouraging for families who cannot afford to bridge such a gap. Here, though, is one important place the community-centered library's youth services can make an impact.

LIFE SKILLS FOR TEENS

Librarians should never lose sight of the fact that while libraries can help strengthen assets for youth, all youth are themselves important. They are an undertapped source of human capital. To put it another way, teens are talented! Libraries that have recognized and leveraged this are reaping great rewards.

When talking about teen services, it is imperative to remember the mantra, "Nothing for us without us." The "best" library services to teens cannot reach their full potential if they fail to empower teens in the process. The Search Institute includes empowerment as a necessary developmental asset for all youth. Their research has found that children as young as three to five need to be valued by the community, be seen as resources, and be given opportunities to serve others. In this way, youth developmental assets are fully in line with the values of a community-centered library. By the time youth reach the age of eleven or twelve and become young adults in the eyes of most libraries, they are at an exciting and pivotal age. Through teen advisory boards, teen programs, and employment opportunities for teens, libraries can strengthen any number of individual assets for youth. At the same time, libraries will find that youth are capable of strengthening their libraries and communities.

Teen advisory groups have become a staple for libraries seeking to reach teen patrons. Done well, these groups can be effective vehicles for enriching communities and youth. Over the years, the Peabody Library's teen advisory board, the Youth Advisory Klatsch (YAK), has undertaken a vast array of projects. They have made podcasts and public service announcements featuring book reviews and commercials about the library's summer reading program. They have designed creative library programs and engaged in service projects with outside groups to benefit seniors and homeless children. But, in the end, it is not YAK's list of accomplishments that is most important to its members. Rather, it is the skills they gain from participating in a group that values them as full community members and pushes them to engage in their community. YAK alumna

Lejla Huskic is now a college student, and she recently wrote a note to Melissa telling her that she had successfully landed an internship: "I want to thank you so much for teaching me dedication, commitment, and vision for projects and goals. Being in YAK has totally shaped me regarding how I act at work." The experiences that teens have as library volunteers can arm them with confidence and skills that will enrich their lives and their communities well past their last teen advisory board meeting.

The input and leadership of a teen advisory board is a foundation upon which libraries can build programs and services that strengthen assets for youth and utilize youth assets to benefit other community members. Teens in San Antonio, Texas, for example, identified barriers they face in regard to eating healthy and then helped librarians build a nutrition program that addressed these barriers. The program included hands-on cooking demonstrations and nutrition discussions for teens. At the Milwaukee (Wisconsin) Public Library, teens worked with a media company and local actors to create videos introducing important financial literacy information to six thousand high school students in the community (Monsour 2012, 38). In a third community, bilingual teens produced a Dial-A-Story service in Spanish. The project was a great success and averaged an impressive seven hundred calls a month (Spielberger et al. 2004, 8). Teens involved in these projects as planners, participants, or both, come away from the experiences with concrete skills and knowledge and oftentimes a new sense of self-efficacy.

In addition to teen advisory boards and teen-focused programming, many libraries also hire teen employees. Often these employees perform simple, routine tasks like shelving books, dusting shelves, or cutting out construction paper pieces for children's story times. All library jobs can be valuable for teens, if they stress foundational job skills like responsibility, communication, and punctuality. Still, teens have more to offer libraries than the performance of rote tasks. Libraries that are willing to place extra trust and responsibility in their teens are often amazed at the results. The coordinator of one teen employee program examined by the Wallace Foundation reports, "We've come to trust them with tasks and job responsibilities that are far beyond what we had traditionally allowed them to perform. Staff are learning that youth can accept those roles, perform them very well, and can be real contributors" (Spielberger et al. 2004, 7). A good example of this is the Benicia (California) Public Library, which has taken the teen advisory board to a new level by turning over the running of the group to paid teen employees, who are appointed to their positions. These teen coordinators are responsible for ensuring that teen services in their library maintain their "cool and nifty demeanor" ("Teen Advisory Board" 2012).

Like all employees, teens need to be paid. Finding the money in the budget for such employees can be a challenge for libraries that are striving just to maintain their current staffing levels. Other community agencies can sometimes be of assistance. For several summers now, the Peabody Library has applied for funding from their local workforce development board to pay teen summer workers. The teens' primary responsibilities are to run the day-to-day operations of the library's Summer Lunch Program. They set up, accept food deliveries, follow food safety requirements, complete paperwork, serve and clean up lunches, and also run a variety of activities for children after lunch. The lunch activities range from coloring contests to arts and crafts projects to games to hip-hop dance classes.

In addition to these primary jobs, the library works with the teens to identify projects that match their individual skills and interests. In the summer of 2011, teen employees painted beautiful murals in the library's teen room. This project was completely teen driven, with the young artists selecting color schemes and a theme, and planning and painting murals that depict the Taj Mahal and the Sydney Opera House. Library staff were struck by the thought the Youth Artists in Residence put into their project. These teens chose an international theme both to celebrate the diversity of the Peabody community, and also to encourage other community youth to "dream big" and to ask themselves "How far will you go?" In the summer of 2012, the teen summer workers decided to organize a Back to School Beauty Day. They found a makeup company that donated samples, researched and put together "Beauty Tips on a Budget," and ran a successful event. Even more importantly, they learned how to write businesses letters, talk on the phone in a professional manner, and design promotional materials. In both cases, the library benefited from their teen employees' efforts, and the experience empowered teens by allowing them to utilize their interests and gifts while also building new skills.

The Brooklyn (New York) Public Library's Multicultural Internship Program (MIP) was another program that engaged teen workers in projects beneficial both to the teens and to the library. The year 2012 was the last summer of MIP, but for its three-year duration, Brooklyn's program sought to engage a diverse group of teens in an "innovative, hands-on" stipend-funded internship. The library benefited from the diversity that these teens brought to the library staff. The teens, meanwhile, gained skills from performing a range of library-related jobs, such as answering reference questions, providing public service, and running children's programs. They also provided technology assistance, and interpretation and translation help for library patrons. Alumni of MIP took with them an appreciation of libraries and brought their new skills to future jobs.

Supervising teen employees and volunteers is not easy. To do it well, library supervisors need to devote significant time to their young employees, go over policies carefully, encourage questions, clearly lay out expectations, and, above all, communicate in a simple and straightforward manner. Despite these responsibilities, the significant time and resources it takes to manage a successful teen employment program is worth it for the community-centered library. Librarians surveyed by the Wallace Foundation believe that having teen employees increased both teen and adult patronage of the library (Spielberger et al. 2004, 8).

Despite the endless benefits youth can gain from library services, librarians—especially youth services librarians and directors—have a lot of work to do to convince community stakeholders and funders that libraries are central figures in a community's youth development. Youth services librarians are well versed in storytelling. We need to start using those skills to tell the many, many stories of libraries and youth.

MAKE IT HAPPEN

- Hire a teen librarian. If you don't have the money to immediately create a new position, advocate within your community. This person will be the main contact between teens and the library, and will have as the focus of his or her job the responsibility of building relationships within the library and the community in order to foster the creation of viable and sustainable programs in collaboration with teens.
- Learn about the Search Institute's Developmental Assets. Start talking about them to library administrators, trustees, and community stakeholders in relation to the programs and services you offer for children and teens at your library, and start reframing your youth services in language that goes beyond story time and teen programming.

- Use positive and proactive language. Don't fall into the trap of talking about providing services to teens because "they need someplace to be" or "they need something to do." Even referring to teens as "our future taxpayers" takes away from the fact that they are also *current* patrons, with needs, ideas, and perspectives on the community that are as valid as any other community members'.
- The next time an issue affecting youth comes up in your community's dialogue, consider whether you should get involved as a youth advocate.
- Build relationships with the youth who use your library. It can start as simply as asking children and teens how their day was and showing real interest in their answers.
- Take stock of how your library supports academic success in youth. Consider enriching your early literacy programs or adding a homework help service.
- Explain to parents and teachers the value of the library's summer reading programs, and build partnerships with local schools and businesses to support and grow these programs in new ways.
- Hire teens, and start entrusting more responsibility to your teen employees and volunteers. Don't expect it to save you time or effort; instead, look at it as a way to support youth development and create better services for your community.

BIBLIOGRAPHY

Delgado-LaStella, Tracy, and Sandra Feinberg. 2011. "Discovering the Nature Explorium." *American Libraries.* Last modified February 23. http://american librariesmagazine.org/features/02232011/discovering-nature-explorium.

"Developmental Assets." 2012. The Search Institute. Accessed September 21. http://www.search-institute.org/developmental-assets.

"Developmental Assets and Library Connections." 2012. The Search Institute. Accessed October 3. http://www.search-institute.org/system/files/librari ans8x14.pdf.

Duncan, Greg, and Richard Murnane. 2011. "Executive Summary: Whither Opportunity? Rising Inequality, Schools and Children's Life Chances." Russell Sage Foundation. https://www.russellsage.org/sites/all/files/Whither Oppor tunity_Executive Summary.pdf.

"Family Adventures in Reading." 2012. Mass Humanities. Accessed October 6. http://www.masshumanities.org/family_adventures.

"Gear Up for Good: Summer Reading Program." 2012. Indianapolis Public Library. Accessed October 16. http://www.imcpl.org/events/srp2012/.

"Homework Help." 2012. Chicago Public Library. Accessed October 6. http://www.chipublib.org/forkids/kidspages/homework_help.php.

Monsour, Margaret. 2012. "Libraries Innovate with New Financial Education Programs." *Public Libraries* 51 (2): 36–43.

"Multicultural Internship Program." 2012. Brooklyn Public Library. Accessed October 7. http://bplsite.brooklynpubliclibrary.org/support/volunteer/mip.html.

"Nature Explorium." 2012. Middle County Public Library. Accessed October 4. http://www.natureexplorium.org.

"Out-of-School Time Youth-Focused Programs and Activities." 2012. Boston Public Library. Accessed October 3. http://www.bpl.org/boost/.

"Resources for Libraries." 2012. The Search Institute. Accessed September 21. http://www.search-institute.org/librarians-0.

Rogers, Michael. 2005. "Alabama Signs Tutor.Com." *Library Journal* 130 (6): 32.

Spielberger, Julie, Carol Horton, and Lisa Michels. Last modified 2004. "New on the Shelf: Teens in the Library." Wallace Foundation. http://www.libraryworks.com/INFOcus/0812/New-On-The-Shelf-Teens-in-the-Library.pdf.

"Summer." Last modified 2012. Multnomah County Public Library. Last modified 2012. http://www.multcolib.org/summer/.

"Summer Reading." Last modified 2012. Charlotte Mecklenburg Library. http://www.cmlibrary.org/about_us/info.asp?id=45.

"Summer Reading Program 2011." 2011. Portland Public Library. Accessed October 16, 2012. http://www.portlandlibrary.com/summer/index.htm.

"2012 Top Innovators." 2012. Urban Libraries Council. Accessed October 7. http://www.urbanlibraries.org/associations/9851/files/2012_Top_Innovators_Brochure.pdf.

"Teen Advisory Board." 2012. Benicia Public Library. Last modified February 3. www.benicialibrary.org/teens/tab.

"Three Rivers Storytelling Festival." 2012. Northland Public Library. Accessed October 4. http://home.comcast.net/~3rstf/index.html.

Urban Libraries Council. 2007. "Making Cities Stronger: Public Library Contributions to Local Economic Development." Urban Libraries Council. http://www.urbanlibraries.org/filebin/pdfs/MakingCitiesStronger_Full_Report.pdf.

"You Are Here: Summer Reading." 2012. Nashua Public Library. Accessed October 16. http://www.nashualibrary.org/TSR.htm.

"YOUmedia Chicago." 2012. Accessed December 13. http://youmediachicago.org.

Conclusion: It's Up to You

We're glad you read this book. We're even happier if you found some inspiration within these pages. But what would make us elated is if you put the book down, get out into your community and *do* something!

If you've read this far, you have the language you need to advocate compellingly for your community's public library, you know what you need to do to build valuable connections and make innovative programs and services possible, and perhaps most importantly you've learned about public libraries that are already making community-centered library services a reality. These institutions prove that community-centered public libraries are not just our future; they are our present.

We're calling on you. The librarians, the administrators, the Friends, and the boards. The mayors, the city councils, the government employees. The teachers, the business owners, the artists, and the youth. All of you and everyone else who cares about community. We're calling on you to stand up for your public library, to be a part of shaping its mission, to take advantage of all it has to offer, and to make sure that public libraries always stand firmly at the center of their communities to bring people together and ensure that everyone has a place to learn, to explore, and to grow.

In 1790, the Franklin Public Library was established as the United States' first public library. The original opening day collection, gifted to the town by Dr. Benjamin Franklin for the free use of its citizens, is still housed in the library's Reading Gallery. For over two hundred years, public libraries have served their communities. If we all work together and do it right, they'll be serving their communities for two hundred more.

Index

About the Authors

Julie Biando Edwards is the ethnic studies librarian and multicultural coordinator at the Mansfield Library at the University of Montana in Missoula. A public librarian at heart, she began her career working in public libraries in Wyoming and Massachusetts. She holds an MSLIS from the University of Illinois, Urbana-Champaign, an MA in English literature from the University of Connecticut, and a BA in English literature from the University of Montana. She has authored several articles and coedited with Stephan P. Edwards *Beyond Article 19: Libraries and Social and Cultural Rights*. Her interests are in libraries, community, and human rights.

Melissa S. Robinson is the teen librarian at the Peabody Institute Library in Peabody, Massachusetts. She completed her MLS at Southern Connecticut State University; received a graduate certificate from the Program for Women in Politics and Public Policy at the University of Massachusetts, Boston, where she concentrated on community development policy; and earned a BA in political science from Merrimack College. During her ten years in teen services, she has focused on building community partnerships and increasing teen participation in the library and community. Her newest project is developing a digital media lab/makerspace in the library.

Kelley Rae Unger is the adult services librarian at the Peabody Institute Library in Peabody, Massachusetts. She holds an MS in library and information science from Simmons College; a BFA in writing, literature, and publishing from Emerson College; and an advanced graphic design certificate from Sessions College. Kelley has seventeen years experience in public libraries, including work in youth services, reference, and adult services. Currently, her library work focuses on event planning, marketing, and collection development.